"*5Q* is a five-star masterpiece ... A breathtaking achievement that is life-giving for the church."

—**Leonard Sweet**, best-selling author; professor, George Fox University, Tabor College and Drew University; founder/contributor to preachthestory.com

"Comprehensive, brilliant, revelatory. This exciting new book by Alan Hirsch ushers in not just new information, but a whole new way of thinking about what it means to be the church, what it means to follow Christ and serve others, and what it means to be human. I am so ready to see the church put these ideas into practice."

—**Linda Bergquist**, church planting catalyst and adjunct professor; author of *Church Turned Inside Out* and *The Wholehearted Church Planter*

"My friend and mentor, Alan Hirsch, offers us a new and brilliant understanding of how to unleash the latent capacity within you, the church and every group for the Jesus mission. Hirsch broadens his reputation as a premier thought leader in *5Q* by giving us both a framework and a practical application from Ephesians 4 for how to activate the Body of Christ. *5Q* is a book that needs to be read thoroughly and meticulously by every leader who loves the church, its people and its mission."

—**Dave Ferguson**, lead pastor of Community Christian Church; lead visionary for NewThing; author of *Finding Your Way Back To God* and *Starting Over*

"This must-read book will blow the minds of those who still believe the fivefold functions (APEST) are relegated to the first century and no longer relevant. Hirsch sees APEST mentioned in Ephesians as primordial code embedded into creation and revelation that explains just about everything ... even Jesus. A category-changing book indeed."

—**Bill Easum**, president, The Effective Church Group

"With remarkable passion, and with Scripture as his guide, Alan Hirsch delves ever deeper into the symphony that is God's church. More than practical, *5Q* really informs and inspires. Slowly, as we read, the fivefold gifting unfolds as visible in all creation, a masterpiece of God's marvelous design, magnificent to behold."

—**David Fitch**, B. R. Lindner Chair of Evangelical Theology, Northern Seminary; author of *Faithful Presence*

"This is the book that I have been waiting for. In it, Alan gifts us with a book that has profound theological depth as well as some pretty punchy tools and processes for implementation. I am willing to even say that 5Q is precisely what the church needs to understand in order to move forward and be who Jesus has made us to be. For those wanting to stop circling in the ecclesial wilderness, get this book and take the journey!"

—**Christine Caine**, founder of A21 and Propel Women; author, and speaker

"Alan Hirsch's brilliant and probing mind is on full display in this, his latest work on understanding the implications of APEST, the five-fold ministry of Ephesians 4. In this punchy volume, Alan's call for the recalibration of the church reaches its full crescendo. The signature theme of APEST provides the symphonic whole to his vision of how Jesus has gifted his church for its mission in the world."

—**Reggie McNeal**, author of *Kingdom Come* and *Missional Renaissance*

"5Q is destined to become one of the defining works of our generation. In it, Hirsch dramatically changes and redefines the paradigm through which we understand the church. He masterfully weaves in such depth of biblical insight to this paradigm that his conclusions seem undeniable. He provides not only theological depth, but practical implications. This book should come with a warning: 'Reading will dramatically change the thinking and behavior of your church!'"

—**Dana Allin**, synod executive, ECO: A Covenant Order of Evangelical Presbyterians

"5Q gives the whole church a place to see ourselves in the story of God in a way that invigorates passion and purpose. A must-read!"

—**Tammy Dunahoo**, general supervisor, The Foursquare Church

"This is Alan Hirsch at his very best – brilliant! If only the profound insights and admonitions of this book regarding APEST were embraced and applied, how radical and transformative— and biblical—that would be!"

—**Dr. Sam Metcalf**, president, Church Resource Ministries, US; author of *Beyond the Local Church: How Apostolic Movements Can Change the World*

"I believe that there are few topics more important for the renewal of Christ's people and the subsequent transforming of the world around us than what is addressed here by Alan Hirsch. As is always the case in his writings, Hirsch brings his genius to bear on this essential subject with insight and profound breakthroughs."

—**Neil Cole**, author of *Organic Church*, *Primal Fire*, and *One Thing*

"Alan Hirsch has done it again. A modern-day prophet, offering ancient wisdom wrapped with future hope! This book inspires, provokes and engages. It will be a catalyst for mission in the years to come! Get it."

—**Danielle Strickland**, international social justice advocate; author and speaker

"Alan Hirsch's *5Q* is an erudite and innovative theological analysis of the Ephesians 4 ascension gifts that uniquely explores their nexus to missiology, ecclesiology, biology, creation, and culture. An intellectual adventure."

—**Frank Viola**, author of *God's Favorite Place on Earth, From Eternity to Here,* and *Jesus Speaks* (with Leonard Sweet)

"In Alan Hirsch's new book, he presents a persuasive case that Ephesians 4:1–16 is not only a clear prescriptive biblical text, but it also provides an important hermeneutical key that unlocks a whole way of understanding God's design for life and ministry. He also provides us with a clear model showing us how Jesus is active in and through the church. The fivefold typology (*5Q*) re-establishes the ministry of Christ in the Body of Christ, and in so doing gives the church the biblical foundation and practical handles for a desperately needed recalibration. Wonderful."

—**Brad Brisco**, co-author of *Missional Essentials* and *Next Door as It Is in Heaven*

"In a time when many writers of so-called biblical models of leadership are merely rehashing insights from the fields of management, marketing, psychology and communications, along comes Alan Hirsch with a fresh new approach drawn directly from Scripture. In this book, he distills his previous thinking into a rich, practical, multidimensional understanding of Paul's primary paradigm on ministry, leadership, and organization. Not so much a book of ideas as a pair of glasses through which to see the world differently. As Alan says, it's *5Q*, baby!"

—**Michael Frost**, author of *Surprise the World!* and *To Alter Your World*

"In *5Q*, Alan Hirsch presents us with an opportunity to see anew a horizon filled with the imagination and strategy of APEST design including its power to activate our individual and collective capacities. This is not written for those interested in the status quo. Instead, this book conveys an imperative and urgency, calling strategic leaders to reflectively consider theology and theory in concert with planned assessment and intentional action. This book offers a why, what, and how approach to understanding APEST, assessing an organization, and coaching/mentoring others."

—**Alicia D. Crumpton**, PhD; program director/PhD in Leadership Studies, Johnson University

"In this book, Alan Hirsch takes us on an exhilarating adventure. *5Q* offers profound theological insight and opens up a whole new paradigm for us to understand and engage with God, church, culture, and the world. A must-read for those who want to see the church grow into the fullness and maturity of Christ and who want to be an active part of that process."

—**Rich Robinson**, founder and leader of
Catalyse Change; leader of 5Qcollective

"I wouldn't be shocked if the church history textbooks of the future described our era as 'the age of irrational exuberance' for our unbridled enthusiasm toward ecclesiological constructs that are only leading to the sterility of the church. Alan, in his previous works, has called the church to regain her missional authority by returning to its biblical form. In *5Q*, Alan bolsters this conviction while simultaneously assisting church leaders to practically implement the APEST idea. Hirsch always seems to have insights that are both sobering and encouraging, and *5Q* is no exception to this. I will be recommending this book to many."

—**Jeff Christopherson**, vice president of Send Network (NAMB);
author of *Kingdom Matrix: Designing a Church for the Kingdom of
God*, and *Kingdom First: Starting Churches that Shape Movements*

"Alan Hirsch reminds us that 'the task is not so much to see what no one has seen, but to think what nobody has thought about that which everybody sees.' His genius is not in framing the fivefold gifting in terms of intelligence, helpful though that is. The genius of *5Q* is in exposing what is just outside the frame of our sight—the ongoing adaptive work of God in equipping his church for mission, in ways always new and fresh. Finally, a paradigm for church health that actually requires the active presence of the Spirit among God's people!"

—**Len Hjalmarson**, adjunct professor, Portland
Seminary and Tyndale Seminary

"*5Q* represents a passionate earthquake that will certainly shape innumerable congregations. In fact, it has all the potential to change the core and life of the Western church."

—**Nelus Niemandt**, professor in Missiology,
University of Pretoria; South African church leader

"Equipping and mobilizing every Christian for the missional task is the unfinished business of the Reformation. *5Q* not only highlights this issue but creates pathways to enable it to happen."

—**Alan McWilliam**, minister of Whiteinch Church of
Scotland, Glasgow; director, Forge Europe

"Ta-ta-ta-taa—the start of Beethoven's 5th Symphony captures us as listeners and takes us to new depths and heights. In the same way, Hirsch, with theological precision and depth leads readers to live into 5Q so that the church might be the song, the poem sung to and for the world in order to bring all people into the dance of God. There was EQ, and IQ—now we have 5Q."

—**JR Woodward**, author of *Creating a Missional Culture*;
co-author, *The Church as Movement*; national director, V3 movement

"Despite a growing awareness and appreciation for APEST among present-day leaders and organizations, there is still so much more that we have yet to discover about this central teaching on Ephesians 4:1–16. Alan himself has been a gift to the church in the West by helping us rediscover APEST and its potential to catalyze movemental energies in the body. In 5Q, he gives us another gift that will help us move even closer to realizing that potential. This is a must-read for any practitioner looking to implement a fivefold approach to ministry and leadership."

—**Tim Catchim**, team leader at One Life;
co-author of *The Permanent Revolution*

"Hirsch has shifted the paradigm yet again! Where others have stopped at the back of the wardrobe, thinking they've exhausted the contents of fur coats and mothballs, Alan, the missional Magician's Nephew, has pushed through into another world for us to explore. Instead of a universe, Hirsch has opened a multiverse in Ephesians 4, where the church might again hear the roar of Aslan, and wield again some of the lost magic it once knew. That magic feels a lot like 5Q."

—**Peyton Jones**, author of *Church Zero* and *Reaching the Unreached: Becoming Raiders of the Lost Art;* host of The Church Planter Podcast

"This new book by Alan Hirsch is like drinking from a fire hose. It is so full of insight and power, that we cannot begin to adequately describe it. It is a powerful statement on the importance of restoring fivefold ministry and the analogies in all of culture that show the character of the work of God!"

—**Daniel Juster**, founding president, the Union of
Messianic Jewish Congregations and the Tikkun International

"A provocative and fruitful contribution to the biblical shaping of the missional church."

—**Darrell L. Guder**, Henry Winters Luce Professor of
Missional and Ecumenical Theology, Princeton Theological Seminary

"*5Q* is an imagination-grabbing invitation to reimagine leadership combined with practical guidelines for reconfiguring our church systems and leadership praxis. Digging deep into Scripture, biology, hermeneutics, Christology and more, Hirsch's latest work on APEST is at the top of my missional reading list recommendation for my students and all missional practitioners."

—**Darren Cronshaw**, professor of Missional Leadership, Australian College of Ministries; mission catalyst and pastor, Baptist Union of Victoria; co-author of *Sentness* (with Kim Hammond) and *Dangerous Prayer*

"Alan Hirsch has created a scripturally rich and invaluable resource for leaders who are committed to building and equipping the church. His robust research and thoughtful engagement with Scripture, philosophy, and culture in *5Q* has resulted in a book that has the potential to transform your thinking on how Jesus intended to partner with the church in the spread of his Kingdom. A rich resource."

—**Bruxy Cavey**, teaching pastor, The Meeting House; author of *(Re)Union* and *The End of Religion*

"Alan Hirsch, in his role as a prominent missiologist, has consistently been a leading voice for the church to help shape our future and direction. His writings and teachings have been used to inform, challenge, and guide church leaders, all around the world, to increase our level of effectiveness in expanding the Kingdom of God on earth. In *5Q*, his newest book, Alan has taken some of the most complex, yet crucial, topics in the Scriptures related to the church and the mission entrusted to us, and has brilliantly broken down these principles in a way that is easy to understand and apply. This book is a must-read for anyone who has been placed in a position of leadership or influence in a church, Christian network, or denomination."

—**Jimmy Carroll**, lead pastor, Journey Church, Raleigh North Carolina; president, Liberty Church Network

"What I love about Alan's writings is the way that he is not afraid to tear down our existing paradigms in order to bring us back closer to Jesus and our call to extend God's Kingdom. This book does just that! Packed with fascinating insights, one-line zingers, and lots of practical theology, *5Q* will provoke you to think deeply and lead differently. You will love reading this!"

—**Alex Absalom**, author of *Discipleship That Fits* and founder of dandelionresourcing.com

"In *5Q*, Alan Hirsch continues to be on the leading edge of calling the church back to a genuinely biblical understanding of ministry that will lead us into a highly impactful future. Read *5Q*! It will challenge you, inspire you, and redefine the way you think about, love, and lead the beautiful body of Christ."

—**Gregg Nettle**, president of Stadia Global Church Planting

"Alan's book *The Forgotten Ways* had a tremendous impact on those who are wrestling with the larger questions of mission and the church. This new volume, *5Q*, takes those earlier insights and adds additional depth and color. Those who long for our world to be impacted deeply by the gospel will enjoy Alan's new contribution. I commend it to all those on the journey of mission, especially in the unfamiliar and rapidly changing context for mission in the western world."

—**Martin Robinson**, founder of ForMission; missiologist; writer

"For years, Alan has helped us understand God's abiding DNA in the church, the APEST functionality that's irrevocably present—indeed, the true marks of the church. Turns out these marks were deeper than we realized, present across cultures, embedded within archetypes, synthesized and fulfilled in Jesus—and finally given back to the church in and through this APEST functionality. I gladly offer my highest recommendation for this book."

—**Dr. John D. Lee**, doctor of Executive Leadership, University of Charleston, West Virginia

"In his own unique style, Alan Hirsch dives into a subject that might very well be the key to see new movements released in the Western church. A must-read!!"

—**Martin Cave**, founder of IMI-Kirken, Stavanger, Norway

"Alan's latest book, *5Q*, continues his creative call to recover the adventure of discipleship through recalibrating the church with APEST. By rooting APEST in the doctrine of God, Alan invites us into a beautiful journey with far-reaching potential. I highly recommend it."

—**Tom Smith**, pastor; co-founder of Rhythm of Life; author of *Raw Spirituality*

"In a world of many echoes, Alan Hirsch represents something very different: Creativity, insight and practical wisdom. A true gift to everyone in and beyond the church."

—**Egil Elling Ellingsen**, senior leader of IMI-Kirken, Stavanger, Norway

ALAN HIRSCH

REACTIVATING THE ORIGINAL INTELLIGENCE
AND CAPACITY OF THE BODY OF CHRIST

MOVEMENTS

Copyright © 2017 by Alan Hirsch

First published in 2017 by 100M
100movements.com

The publisher has no responsibility for the persistence or accuracy of URLs for external or third-party internet websites referred to in this book, and does not guarantee that any content on such websites is, or will remain, accurate or appropriate.

All Scripture quotations, unless otherwise indicated, are taken from the Holy Bible, New International Version®, NIV®. Copyright ©1973, 1978, 1984, 2011 by Biblica, Inc.™ Used by permission of Zondervan. All rights reserved worldwide. www.zondervan.com The "NIV" and "New International Version" are trademarks registered in the United States Patent and Trademark Office by Biblica, Inc.™

Scripture quotations marked THE MESSAGE. Copyright © 1993, 1994, 1995, 1996, 2000, 2001, 2002 by Eugene H. Peterson. Used by permission of NavPress. All rights reserved. Represented by Tyndale House Publishers, Inc.

Scripture quotations marked NASB taken from the New American Standard Bible® Copyright © 1960, 1962, 1963, 1968, 1971, 1972, 1973, 1975, 1977, 1995 by The Lockman Foundation
Used by permission. www.Lockman.org

Scripture quotations marked (ESV) are from ESV® Bible (The Holy Bible, English Standard Version®), copyright © 2001 by Crossway, a publishing ministry of Good News Publishers. Used by permission. All rights reserved.

ISBN 978-0-9986393-0-7

Printed in Colombia

Cover design, interior design and typesetting by Ben Connolly
www.AngelandAnchor.com

DEDICATION

My enduring thanks to God for the ministry and teachings of Hans Urs von Balthasar, who has so deeply enriched me and has helped me to recognize the truly beautiful form of Christ in new and genuinely life-changing ways. His influence on me will be felt in this book.

SPECIAL THANKS

To Anna and Rich Robinson, who have become dear friends and colleagues in and through the writing of this book. Anna proved to be a devoted editor, and Rich, a brilliant practitioner of APEST, generously contributed to the chapter on tools and processes.

To Dave Zimmerman for providing something of a first round of edits that helped the book take its current shape.

To Jessica Cruickshank, for being a great friend and partner in helping me develop the 5Q Systems Tests and in co-leading the 100Movements team.

To those who read the manuscript and offered me necessary feedback. Thanks Neil Cole, Mimika Garesch, Tom Smith, and Alicia Crumpton.

•

You grace humanity with knowledge
and teach mortals understanding.
Grace us with the knowledge, understanding
and discernment that come from You.
Blessed are You, LORD,
who graciously grants knowledge.

The Siddur

•

· Contents ·

Preface

In Praise of Soft Eyes

To look at something as though we had never seen it before requires great courage.

—Henri Matisse

One of the reasons, I believe, that knowledge is in a state of useless overproduction is that it is strewn all over the place, spoken in a thousand competitive voices. Its insignificant fragments are magnified all out of proportion, while its major and world-historical insights lie around begging for attention. There is no throbbing, vital center.

—Ernest Becker

You've got to think about big things while you're doing small things, so that all the small things go in the right direction.

—Alvin Toffer

"You know what you need at a crime scene? ... Soft eyes ... If you got soft eyes, you can see the whole thing. If you got hard eyes—you staring at the same tree missing the forest ... Soft eyes, grasshopper" (Detective Bunk, *The Wire*).[1] No one is actually sure of the exact origin of the phrase "soft eyes," but it is likely that it was used by Native Americans when tracking and hunting animals. Having soft eyes is essential to hunters, detectives, and to all new discoveries and learning. You have to defer judgment and remain open.

If you're looking at a crime scene, for example, with hard, cynical eyes, you're going to miss the details necessary to solve the crime. "Hard eyes" often reflect an unconscious prejudice due to some internalized bias or external pressure to prejudge outcomes: *hard eyes have already reached a conclusion before really seeing the scene.*

Most of us aren't homicide detectives, of course, but we all require soft eyes at numerous critical junctures of life. A doctor needs soft eyes in diagnosing a complex medical syndrome; a mechanic when repairing the electrics of a motor vehicle; a political analyst in anticipating global trends; the economist tracking the invisible hand of the market; the scientist doing breakthrough research; a scriptwriter in a successful TV series; a computer programmer in developing the killer app; the business entrepreneur in seeking to exploit unanticipated gaps in the market; and so on. In fact, hard eyes—the unwillingness to look deeper in order to accurately diagnose the real situation—in any of these situations would likely prove to be disastrous.

The difference between soft and hard eyes can be compared to the difference between *analytic* and *synthetic* (or systems) thinking.

Seeing the Trees

Analytic thinking attempts to explain the behavior of a complex system by reducing it down into the constituent parts. The key word here is "reducing" because in order to really scrutinize something, and to be able to make the resultant knowledge useful, ideas need to be simplified into working formulas that can be commonly shared. We pry apart the primal phenomenon in order to analyze its constituent elements. We become accustomed to reading things by starting from the bottom and working our way up, rather than by working from the whole to the parts.

Analytic thinking is a good and necessary thing and is especially effective when the context is stable and when conventional formulas seem to work and make sense; the continuity and stability of the whole affords the opportunity to delve deeper and to examine each of the component parts.

However, in times of disruptive change, reduced formulas are at best patchwork; at worst, they can prove to be dangerous traps for the collective mind. If we no longer have a sense of the holistic, systemic-level vision, then it stands to reason that the partial, which can only be understood correctly as belonging to the whole, will undoubtedly be misinterpreted.

And so, too much fine-toothed analysis inevitably leads to what is called "reductionism," and this can be very problematic indeed. Reductionism occurs when in an eagerness to understand the parts, and with an overreliance on routinized habits, the insiders fail to consider, or even see, the governing idea. People get lost in the details, losing the sense of overall direction and so end up unable to see the forest for the trees. Or to use another metaphor, we become like the proverbial blind men trying to describe an elephant by describing one of its parts.

In a situation of rapid paradigmatic change, our traditional analytic skills can't help us; in fact they blind us to the real problem.[2] When people or organizations are stuck in a rut of acquired habitual knowledge, as well as facing a crisis, they need to think *differently* ... or risk becoming obsolete.

Figure P.1 Reductionist Descriptions of an Elephant

Mark the word "reductionism," dear reader, because in this book we are going to have to address many *theological reductionisms* all along the way. Whether we have willingly chosen them or not, the contemporary church is heir to many theological reductions that are now blocking our capacities to see the "whole" and to respond to the challenges of our times. Alvin Toffler, one of the leading futurists of our times, could well be speaking of the church when he says that:

> Lacking a systematic framework for understanding the clash of forces in today's world, we are like a ship's crew, trapped in a storm and trying to navigate between dangerous reefs without compass or chart. In a culture of warring specialisms, drowned in fragmented data and fine-toothed analysis, synthesis is not merely useful—it is crucial.[3]

Seeing the Forest

As opposed to analysis, which studies discreet parts, synthesis tends to explain reality more ecologically, understanding that the whole is greater than the sum of its parts.

Social psychologist Daniel Pink prefers to call synthetic thinking *symphony*.[4] Symphony happens when we combine and blend disparate pieces in the light of an imaginative new whole. Symphony, like all forms of true art, requires imagination, holism, play and divergent thinking. This renewing of imagination and vision, in turn, leads directly to innovation and other various forms of creative experimentation. Theologically, we can even say that because God's truth is living and dynamic and continues to unfold itself in new and fresh ways, it too is "symphonic."[5] Renewal—spiritual, social, or organizational—in some sense means always returning to the originating whole and rediscovering hidden new meaning there.[6]

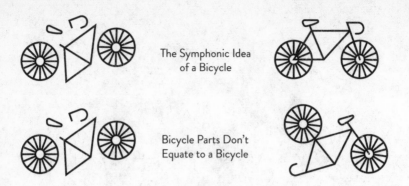

The Symphonic Idea
of a Bicycle

Bicycle Parts Don't
Equate to a Bicycle

Figure P.2 Wholeness Gives Context and Meaning to the Individual Parts

The art of symphony is very much needed when it comes to grappling with big biblical or theological themes. My favorite theologian, Hans Urs von Balthasar, says that in trying to make sense of the big ideas in Scripture, we need to recognize that all the various concepts,

> depend on the perception of the whole form and on the interrelatedness of its various aspects. If any single aspect is taken in isolation from the others the total form has already disappeared.[7]

He goes on to note that while the analysis of a singular theme or aspect might in fact grant a real clarity that makes it more apt for "scientific" elaboration, it nevertheless breaks the spiritual bond that arises from its relation to the other parts.

In order to see that each individual aspect receives its full meaning only by its overall relationship to the whole, he suggests that an "art of total vision" is required. So, for instance, by having a picture of "the whole" in mind, the archaeologist can reconstruct the statue from just one arm, and the paleontologist can reconstruct the whole animal from a single tooth. A trained musicologist, knowing the whole architecture of music, should be able to tell from a single fugue motif whether it was intended as a part of a double or a triple fugue, etc.[8]

Something similar to this "art of total vision" occurs in understanding theology. So, for instance, eschatology, taken on its own, is incomprehensible without the cadence of Christ's life and suffering. Likewise, we can't understand the Father, Son, and Holy Spirit as isolated aspects of the godhead, but only as part of the whole Trinity. Seeming antinomies can only be resolved through the lens of synthesis.

In fact, the problem of heresy itself has its roots in theological reductionism because it involves

> the selective disjoining of parts. By doing this, heresy is thus able to analyze individual parts more exactly in themselves, and, in certain

cases, where the wholeness of vision is lacking, heresy can call attention to what is missing or has been omitted ... But heresy can never make a whole with the parts that have been stolen.[9]

An architecture of wholeness (symphony) is necessary to give context and meaning to the individual parts.

I think that all readers of this book would basically agree that the church could do with replacing reductionist heresy with some serious symphony. We sense the need for symphony in order to renew our outworn theological paradigm, to invigorate our tired mission of the church, and to revitalize the significantly outmoded ministry of the church. We long for a new sense of wholeness that only an imaginative vision born of symphony can provide. I believe that what I call 5Q is one of the surest ways to experience a renewed sense of symphony in our lives, ministries, and organizations. In its simplest form, 5Q is the synergy of a holistic recombination of the apostolic, prophetic, evangelistic, shepherding, and teaching (APEST) capacities referred to in Ephesians 4.

• Eyes to Discover Truth, Goodness, and Beauty

Christian leaders will need soft eyes if they are to negotiate the increasing complexities of the world in which they are responsible to lead. Our human craving for easy answers, ready-made formulas, quick fixes, stability and order have made our eyes hard and have predisposed us to simply repeating what we already know. But as a result, we have been blinded to the deeper patterns, concepts, and potentialities that God has built into human life, the church, and in his cosmos. Soft eyes are therefore necessary to see beyond what has become overfamiliar and habitual with regard to church and ministry.

I exhort the reader to approach this book attuned to the symphony that it offers. In order to experience new symphony, try to lay aside the many conventional formulations of church and ministry that have been handed down to you. Be a detective of divinity: pursue the truth, keep your eyes unfocused, take the whole into account. Look with the soft eyes of the true seeker. Try not to overfocus on constituent parts; avoid the temptation to burrow down into any particular rabbit hole. Rather, attempt to discern an overarching framework, sense the big idea. Look for the threads that weave their way through. And, importantly, do not prejudge the outcome before you have assessed all the evidence. I suggest that if you do this, like a stereogram breaking out in 3D, you will see ministry and church as you have never seen it before.

As for me, I found the sheer symphony I encountered in discovering 5Q astonishing. In the lifetime of study on APEST dynamics that led up to this writing, but especially in the research that went into this particular book, I have come to appreciate an elegance, beauty, and significance in the symphony of fivefold-thinking that for some reason I had not fully recognized before. In this book I have given that symphony a name ... I call it 5Q.

I will provide comprehensive descriptions of what I mean by this in chapter two, but for now think of 5Q as the capacity to see APEST synthetically, as a whole and in the largest way possible. It can also be viewed as a fractal, an intrinsic and irreplaceable part of the very coding of a system that God has designed and embedded into the whole world and then most especially into the Body of Christ through the redemptive work of his Son, Jesus. In other words, 5Q fits the definition of what we have here already referred to as *symphony*—seeing the various APEST parts in light of the greater purpose and built into the whole system. It will become clear that 5Q is not some fancy new idea. Rather, it is the rediscovery of something that was already there, a latent potential in the very being and structure of the church. It is a kind of deep cultural genome, an overarching map of the genetic system that was always there but left unarticulated.

Hopefully this will become clearer as we become more familiar with it, but understand that for me it has become a breakthrough concept that has system-wide implications for the way we understand and experience our identity, purpose, calling, and function. It therefore has huge implications for organizations as well as for leadership. Following Kafka's unforgettable assertion that we must allow a good book to be "an axe for the frozen sea inside us," consider this offering as an opportunity to open up the vast potential, frozen inside you and the church or organization that you lead.

It is not coincidental that this breakthrough has come at a time in my life when my spiritual life has never been better—I am experiencing God in a whole new dimension. I find myself spending whole days in prayer and meditation. My prayer life is rich to the point of overflow. In a real way, I believe that 5Q has played a significant role in this sense of overflow. 5Q feels both personal to me, but I also feel its universal significance.

I don't want to be misunderstood as claiming "special revelation" from God here; ideas that are to be slavishly adopted by those who hear it … not at all. It has more to do with how God has simply attuned me to be able to see what was already present throughout. But now I have seen the elegant fractal pattern, I cannot unsee it—nor do I want to. Rather, I want you to see it as well, and so I present it here for your discernment.

I now feel an intense sense of personal responsibility under God to bear witness to what I have seen. As a steward, I feel compelled to pass it on to you in a way that liberates you to be everything God has intended—and has already equipped—you to be. If you will allow me, my role in this book will be something of a guide, a mentor, to you the person on the quest. I will therefore play the Yoda to your Luke Skywalker, Gandalf to your Frodo, or a Morpheus to your Neo. You shall be my *Padawan*, and teach you I will.

Despite the seemingly frivolous nature of this illustration, I do intend to engage with you as if you, my reader, are indeed the Jedi Knight-in-training. Skywalker didn't really even know that "the force was with him" when he began his quest—it was somehow *latent* in him—and similarly, my task will be to call forth aspects of yourself, and the Jesus movement, that is waiting to be born in and through you.

Perhaps it will be clearer to simply say that I am going to adopt a rabbinical approach here. As a rabbi, I will be your guide, coach, and teacher. But to be a good rabbi, I have to be more active in pointing out key ideas and lean toward being more prescriptive than being merely descriptive.

In my assumed role as rabbi Yoda, I am going to provoke, cheer, encourage, challenge, instruct, and guide. I'll be with you in this role throughout the book. Feel free to step away at any part of the process, but if you decide to stick with me, we are going to go deep. Every now and again I will directly address you as a disciple of Jesus (a learner), a Padawan, because the Christian movement we call church really does need you to be a Jedi leader at this time, and that requires not just information, but formation. Whereas information can be merely intellectual, remaining on the bookshelf or in our head, formation is transformative and is worked into our heart and life as well as our minds.

Rest assured that I take this role seriously and consider it holy ground. And so, as a *responsible* guide, I have determined to always connect what I am proposing with the logic that I find in the Scriptures. The reader will find a strong commitment to ground just about everything I say in terms of (biblical and systematic) theology—the sacred language by which the church seeks to understand God; by which we articulate our knowledge; and with which we pray and are subsequently guided by him. This will also allow you to test what is said in the light of our common heritage in the Word of God. Hopefully this connection with the Scriptures will convey to the reader a renewed sense of the enduring authority, the sheer logic, as well as the redemptive logic of 5Q as revealed to us in Holy Scripture.

• Repentance: The Price of Admission to the Symphony

But the desire, as well as the ability, to see things in their original whole-ness exacts a price on those who find themselves captive to reductionisms of various sorts and varieties. The price of admission to the symphony is first and foremost, repentance. Actually, repentance is the price required for any new learning in any domain—it's just that outside the church it's called unlearning, whereas inside the church it's called repentance. No one can learn, who is not first prepared to unlearn. Likewise, no one can grow in God unless they are willing to repent regularly.

To be able to learn something new, whether it is related to God or to other forms of learning, we need to be willing to let go of obsolete ideas and open our eyes and our hearts to being willing to grow, mature, and get back on the road of discipleship and learn again. The learner needs to venture out of fixed paths into the unknown, and not allow their heart and head to be stunted by mere routine—this is especially true of religious routine. In fact, I would suggest that new breakthroughs are only gained by those who break out of the arbitrary boundaries that have been set by mere convention—that's why they are called breakthroughs.

So, the first key lesson, my dear Padawan, is that only by what we can unlearn do we show whether, and to what extent, we are capable of actually learning.[10] The second lesson is actually implied in the first: to be willing "to look at something as though we had never seen it before requires great courage" (Henri Matisse).[11] And so, if you are willing, relinquish the (false) security of hard eyes and adopt soft eyes. If you are able to sense something of the symphony of God's beautiful design along the way, will you have the courage to change? Are you willing to change? Will you pay the price to learn again? Honestly, if you are not able to resolve this, at least in principle at this point, then return the book to the store and get your refund now.

My hope, of course, is that you will indeed continue. Not just because you now find yourself in situations that require transformation through radical change and renewal, but because you love God and his purposes for our world, and are willing to adjust yourself according to his purpose. Adjusting your view to make room for a bigger picture of reality, and repenting of reductionisms, like all true encounters with God, will require change. As Bonhoeffer reputedly said, "to know God is to change."

If you want transformational Gospel movement—*really* want it—then you are going to have to unlearn some very ancient churchly habits and be willing to relearn some new—and yet paradoxically more ancient— more authentically *biblical* ones. You're a leader; I speak to you as a leader responsible for your generation. Take responsibility for your current reality, for the part you've played in creating that reality, as well as the part that involves you changing it as necessary. And quite frankly, if you are not willing to take responsibility, you should not be in leadership in the church—or any organization that requires moral leadership for that matter. Don't let the drag of the inherited Christendom system set the primary definitions. Rather, as a faithful leader you must take charge of redefining it *according to the Word of God.*

We live in a century that is rightly characterized as VUCA: volatile, uncertain, complex, and ambiguous. This radically changed and changing context demands a corresponding change in imagination and competencies in the church. The problem is that the reductionist formulations of church and organization that we have inherited are derived from, and are inseparably indexed to, another significantly different and less challenging context than that of the twenty-first century. After 1700 years of entrenched European formulations of church, we have to acknowledge that much of it simply no longer works; the maps don't fit the territories, and more importantly it does not fully square with the New Testament. But mainly Christendom is just plain old obsolete because it was formulated for an entirely different set of conditions. Apple trees don't produce oranges!

Without wanting to claim too much, I want to declare upfront that I am nonetheless convinced that 5Q (the substance of this book) is an absolutely crucial key to lasting systemic change. But if we are going to be able to reactivate it, we are going to have to first do some decoding (unlearning) and then some subsequent theological recoding (relearning) along the lines prescribed in one of the most important and primordial genetic codes of the church, the APEST typology of Ephesians 4:1–16.

   Godly reflection or conviction should lead us to godly repentance—to the paradigm shift needed to recalibrate our operating system. When leaders refuse to take responsibility for realigning the system, in effect it means handing over the organization to the patterns of thinking and behavior that got us to the disaster point of systemic decline in the first place. Repentance—both individual and corporate—is a gift from God.[12]

   For this reason, I pray that God will use this book to guide the reader, at least in some small measure, into an ever-greater fullness of truth in Christ Jesus, and beyond that to be a more faithful and authentic witness for his cause. I pray for soft eyes necessary to see past the mesmerizing power of obsolete forms to the sheer beauty of the fivefold system viewed in its wholeness; for a heart willing to follow where God leads; and for power to actually apply the insights gained along the way.[13]

   And so, put your helmets on! Let us begin the journey into the future waiting for you, your church, organization, or denomination.

Introduction

Briefing for the Journey

After a time of decay comes the turning point. The powerful light that has been banished returns. There is movement, but it is not brought about by force. The movement is natural, arising spontaneously. The old is discarded and the new is introduced. Both measures accord with the time; therefore no harm results.

—ancient Chinese saying

The composition of this book has been for the author a long struggle of escape, and so must reading of it be for most readers if the author's assault upon them is to be successful,—a struggle of escape from habitual modes of thought and expression. The ideas which are here expressed so laboriously are extremely simple and should be obvious. The difficulty lies, not in the new ideas, but in escaping from the old ones, which ramify ... into every corner of our minds.

—John Maynard Keynes

When we suffer from [theological] amnesia, every form of serious authority for faith is in question, and we live unauthorized lives of faith and practice unauthorized ministries.

—Walter Brueggemann

The church in the West celebrates the 500th anniversary of the Reformation this year (2017). Beyond that, Europe has had 20 centuries of the Gospel in that context. The Americas, in turn, have had up to five centuries of Christianity with a history in Western forms of Christianity. There has been some incredible Kingdom breakthrough in this long history in these various contexts. However, I have to admit that I always find myself shocked that after 20 centuries of Christian faith and practice in Western contexts, that still the average Christian in the average church in the West is profoundly unformed and immature in Christ. This is the gospel of the resurrected King Jesus Christ we are talking about—world-transforming power! Twenty centuries of the Holy Spirit, of Christian thinking and acting, and this is what we have ended up with? There has been so much by way of church and theology and yet so little transformational impact. How do we account for this? How can we possibly justify this to ourselves, let alone to the God who has commissioned us and to whom we are ultimately accountable?

What is more, this rather inadequate (can we say "deformed"?) Western Christianity now finds itself in a moment of unprecedented strategic signifi-cance, a moment for which we are alarmingly ill-prepared. As I mentioned in the preface, we are now inextricably entwined in a radical paradigm-shifting sea change, in which the old maps, largely formatted for Christendom Europe, no longer make sense of the new territories. Who does not know this to be true? Who does not feel it at the level of instinct?

This is most certainly at the root of many of the problems we now face. The rise of the secular state has seen a corresponding "de-churchifying" of culture. The social contract that the church had with culture has been almost completely severed, or at least thoroughly renegotiated in a way that has rele-gated Christianity to the realm of private opinion and personal values. The problem is that *the church still largely operates with the intrinsic rationality of this Christendom paradigm.* The net result: We are trying to negotiate the post-Christian, postmodern, late capitalist challenges of the twenty-first century with a pre-modern, pre-Enlightenment, European template of the church. It's like we are trying to negotiate New York City using a map of Los Angeles.

An illustration from history might help here: The Romans were legendary at building roads, aqueducts, and other feats of civil engineering. In fact many of the roads they built still exist today. When Rome fell, around AD410, the center of the empire was destroyed, and Rome abruptly ceased to operate as the global world power. But as Britain, or more particularly Ireland, was on the far, inconsequential, reaches of the empire, no one bothered to inform the regional governor and the road building teams. As a result they carried on building the roads as if Rome was still the imperial power. Everything had changed, but they carried on as if nothing had happened. This is not dissimi-lar to the legacy processes operative in most local churches.[1]

And just so that we are absolutely clear-minded about the urgency of the situation, some have predicted that based on the current patterns of decline, 2067 will be the effective end of Christianity in Britain, and it is even worse for the Church of Scotland.[2] It is sobering to consider that, as far as we can tell, Christianity is on the decline in *every* Western setting—including that of North America where the "nones" and the "dones" are now the rapidly increasing aspect of the religious landscape.[3]

Like it or not, as leaders responsible for our times, we simply have to be willing to submit the inherited *ecclesial system* to a thoroughgoing audit. We have to accept that what has got us to this point in history—which is now long-term trended decline in every setting in the West—will simply not get us to a viable future. We can no longer allow ourselves to act as if more of the same thinking and doing is going to bring about fundamentally different results. As the ever-insightful Albert Einstein noted, the problems of the world cannot be resolved by the same kind of thinking that created those problems in the first place.

Nowhere, perhaps, is the church's lack of formation along New Testament lines more evident than in its mishandling of the APEST typology. Most Christian leaders, let alone the average church attender, can give you more than two sentences to describe the apostolic or the prophetic function even though these are laced throughout the Scriptures. In fact, the Scriptures were largely birthed from within apostolic/prophetic consciousness. This glaring blind spot exposes our lack of self-awareness when it comes to the ministry and the purposes of the church and exposes fatal flaws in our discipleship, and by extension, our leadership.

The church has often been guilty of looking at reality through the wrong end of the telescope. It's time to change our perspective. The good news here is that by recovering the lost APEST perspectives that are inherent in the theology, as well as the constitution, of the church, we can experience the possibility of system-wide change. Reconnecting with 5Q allows the church to recalibrate at the level of its operating system and restore long exiled capacities and intelligences into the church. Soft eyes, grasshopper!

• The Great Recalibration

If nothing else, the 500th anniversary of the Great Reformation calls to mind the potent slogan that drove the whole agenda of the Reformation in the first place. It's called *"semper reformanda": that the church reformed, ought always to be reforming, according to the Word of God.* Actually, I think that nothing less will do for the church in our time. So while we thank God for the Great Reformation of the sixteenth century, we also ask our Lord to bring on the Great Recalibration of the twenty-first century.[4]

In the end, all renewal in the church comes down to a question of biblical and theological legitimacy. We are authentically "church" when we are most aligned with the original and originating understandings of the church, namely that of a transformational movement.[5] For the church in any age, the New Testament form (movement) remains the primordial template of the church which tests all others. In negotiating a way forward, we must first and foremost be sure that we are properly aligned with God's original intent and design. Our primary, authoritative text—the Bible, chiefly through the lens of the New Testament—will help us to realign, reassess, and redirect our efforts. All our greatest truths are not new—they are remembered, recovered ... retrievals. And so we don't need to invent a ministry that fits our culture; we simply need to recover the ministry that has already been given.

Or as H. Richard Niebuhr once noted:

> The great Christian revolutions came not by the discovery of
> something that was not known before. They happen when someone
> takes radically something that was always there.[6]

Similarly, in making a case for recovering truths that we have always
possessed, G.K. Chesterton tells a story of a farmer who aspired to know
whether giants once existed or not. So off he went on a search. At some more
distant point on his journey, he happened to look back at his beloved farm
with its all-too-familiar cottage, only to realize that these were but simply
parts of a fossilized carcass of a giant on which he had always lived, but
which was too large and too close to be seen.[7]

Recalibrating the Church

As for the church's ministry, the historical church has largely opted to exclude
apostolic, prophetic and evangelistic frameworks and has viewed ministry through the now severely reduced categories of the pastor (shepherd)
and the teacher (theologian). As a result, we have viewed the entire church,
our purposes and our functions through a profoundly reduced (APE)ST
perspective. The image below says it all.

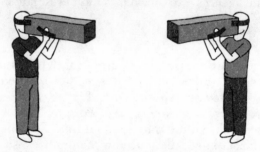

Figure I.1 Paradigm Blinders

When the church *has* sought change, it has largely been through structural
and organizational fixes. Reconceived in terms of a more static hierarchy, the
church has opted for the episcopal Bishop Priest and Deacon (BPD) model of
the high church; the Eldership model of the Reformed; the Deacon-Pastor role
of the Low Church; the contemporary church growth churches have opted
for the models derived from the business corporation with its CEOs, COOs,
Execs, and department portfolios. And yes, all these have had some benefit,
but they have seldom, if ever, been able to reactivate the dynamic ministry we
see demonstrated in the life of Jesus, in the pages of the New Testament, and
that of the various movements that have shifted the tracks of history.

The answer, as always, is embedded somewhere in "the system" itself ...
something we never seem to be able to really see, even though it is always

there. We need correction at the level of the primary mindset or rationale of the organization. Consider this from Robert Pirsig:

> To speak of certain government and establishment institutions as "the system" is to speak correctly ... But to tear down a factory or to revolt against a [particular expression of] government is to attack the effects rather than the causes; and as long as the attack is upon effects only, no change is possible. The true system, the real system, is the prevailing construction of systematic thought itself, rationality itself. If a factory is torn down but the rationality which produced it is left standing, then that rationality will simply produce another factory. If a revolution destroys a systematic government, but the systematic patterns of thought that produced that government are left intact, then those patterns will repeat themselves in the succeeding government.[8]

He's right, you know; applying various reductionist structural solutions to patch a systemic theological problem only exacerbates the problem by hiding it beneath layers of ecclesiological patchwork. Structural solutions can never repair an already cracked church system; more often than not, such solutions end up hindering the agency and ministry of the whole people of God by professionalizing the ministry and creating dependencies that ensure that the people of God remain immature and unformed. Why have we not learned that by now? Why do we keep going back to tired and outworn solutions expecting that they will deliver something radically different?

Ponder in what way your church, denomination, or organization has become captive to reduced ways of thinking? Do you think ministry is just preaching, pastoral care, and teaching? How does that square with what you understand of the New Testament church or other Jesus movements that changed the world (e.g., The Celtic Movement, Early Methodism, or the Chinese underground church)? And what other self-limiting ideas about the church, ministry, leadership and calling have you personally collected along the way. So much for rebooting the church's operating system; we must also go on to recalibrate the theological system.

Recalibrating Theology

The reader will soon see that I am a little bit more "theological" in this book than usual. This is a very deliberate strategy, partly because theological language allows you, the reader, to test what is being presented against the authoritative teachings of the church, but also because I want the padawan-reader to experience just how deeply embedded the fivefold system is in the very fabric of Scripture itself.

I have always believed the APEST typology to be a profoundly important scriptural concept, but as I have indicated, in writing this book I have to say that I found it somewhat mind-blowing as to how deep it really goes. I actually do think that a fully fledged fivefold system offers us a truly elegant solution—a beautiful solution in which the maximum impact is achieved with the smallest or simplest effort. In focusing on the biblical material, I hope to offer the church in our time the necessary confidence to embrace the fivefold typologies with joy and without fear. In fact, as I hope to show, fivefold-thinking (5Q) reaches into our deepest instincts for ministry by reconnecting the ministry of Christ with the Body of Christ.

To ensure that APEST thinking isn't merely considered a fad, we have to recalibrate the church's theological system and realign it to more perfectly reflect Jesus' original intention for the ministry of his people. While such work must employ useful lenses from social sciences and organizational leadership studies, theology remains the primary way in which we understand ourselves in relation to God and the world. There ought to be an instinctive sense of "rightness" about the proposal inherent in this book.

To all the good ole pragmatists reading this, all this theology might appear to be an unnecessary cluttering of an important transformational idea. But in order to have heart resonance and long-term impact in the church, I believe we must substantiate the various paradigm shifts involved in fivefold-thinking by grounding them in Scripture and articulating them in terms of theology. Robert Quinn calls the rediscovery of our primal founding scripts "discerning the inner voice of the organization" and argues that every organization has an inner voice that constitutes its moral center.[9] Theology is the love language of the church that will help you to both hear the inner voice of the church as well as comprehend the sheer transformational power of 5Q in your community. Please try to stay with me on the theological journey preceding the practical section of the book; it will enable you to experience the biblical resonance that is needed as a basis for change.

Before we get into an overview of the book and its distinctive language, I want the reader to be aware that I can actually claim long-term experience in APEST thinking: While I do regularly teach at various seminaries and universities, and I am currently doing a PhD, I cannot claim to be an academic. However, I do think that I can be considered something of an active, translocal, thought leader in the missional movement in the West. My work has included being a local church leader, a church planter, and a leader of a denomination in a profoundly secular country (Australia). Beyond that, I have been part of the founding of missional movements and leadership training systems in Australia, Europe, and North America. I have been involved in training and consulting across the whole spectrum of church—from grassroots movements through to mainline denominational systems, and from there to many of the most successful megachurches in America. So when I say that I believe fivefold-thinking is a pivotal key to unlocking the potential in any of the above settings, I am not kidding! I really do believe this. I have found that it actually does unlock the potentials of the church in all of the above settings.

I have also written extensively on the topic. It appeared in my first book, co-written with Michael Frost, *The Shaping of Things to Come;* it was significantly highlighted in *The Forgotten Ways*; and it has been elaborated on in a very focused way in the hefty *The Permanent Revolution* and the associated group process book, *The Permanent Revolution Playbook*. I mention these here because they (along with very important contributions by Neil Cole, JR Woodward, and Sam Metcalf) are resources that will only enhance the reader's grasp on this important topic.[10] And while this book is a stand-alone text that does not require any pre-reading on APEST, it nonetheless builds on and develops the work I have done so far. I strongly encourage further reading in this regard.

Distinctive Terminology

It is entirely appropriate at this point to provide working descriptions of each of the fivefold functions/callings themselves. These will be thoroughly developed throughout this book, so here only rudimentary descriptions are offered. Because of the active historic suppression of the fivefold language and functions in our churches, and the subsequent lack of any mature self-awareness in all matters APEST, the padawan-reader will need to return to these definitions in order to be able to grasp the paradigmatic significance of the whole 5Q system. So **mark the page.**

Broadly defined, APEST is as follows:

- The *apostle/apostolic*: In Greek, the term apostle literally means "sent one." As the name itself suggests, it is the quintessentially missional (from *missio*, the Latin equivalent) ministry. Interestingly the French translation of the term apostle (envoy) picks up this sense of commission much better than the English transliteration—an apostle is an envoy. It is very much a pioneering function of the church, the capacity to extend Christianity as a healthy, integrated, innovative, reproducing movement, ever-expanding into new cultures. It is also a custodial ministry ... a guardianship. This ministry is therefore also profoundly interested in the ongoing integrity of the core ideas (DNA, organizational principles, or meta-ideas) that generate and maintain systemic health across the organization.

- The *prophet/prophetic* is the function tasked with maintaining an abiding loyalty and faithfulness to God above all. Essentially, prophets are guardians of the covenant relationship that God has with his people. The prophetic is also passionately concerned with living a life morally consistent with the covenant—a simple and authentic life of justice, holiness, and righteousness. The prophet proclaims God's holiness and calls for a corresponding holiness in his covenanted people (1 Peter 1:16).

- The *evangelist/evangelistic* involves the proclamation of the good news that is at the core of the church's message. Evangelism is therefore all about the core message and its reception in the hearts of people and cultures. As such, the evangelist is the storyteller, the all-important recruiter to the cause, the naturally infectious person who is able to enlist people into what God is doing in and through the church.

- The *shepherd/shepherding* is the function and calling responsible for maintaining and developing healthy community and enriching relationships. This involves a commitment to form a saintly people, nurture spiritual maturity, maintain communal health, defend the community against breakdown, and engender loving community among the redeemed family of God.

- The *teacher/teaching* is concerned with the mediation and appropriation of wisdom and understanding. This is the naturally philosophical type that brings comprehensive understanding of the revelation bequeathed to the church. It is a guiding and discerning function. In the biblical tradition, emphasis falls on wisdom and not simply on speculative philosophy. Teaching, of course, also involves integrating the intellectual and spiritual treasure of the community and encoding it, in order to pass it on to others and to the next generations (*paradosis*, or tradition).

Figure I.2 The Five APEST Ministries

The fivefold typology provides us a lexicon of words/ideas that help us better understand the Bible, the church, and the disciple's purpose in this world. Most importantly, as we shall see, it helps us to speak more meaningfully about the work of Christ by bringing the Body into greater conformity with its Head. I will sometimes refer to the distinctly Jesus-shaped version of APEST as J-APEST to distinguish it from the creational and the ecclesial expressions.

An important distinction that will be used throughout this book is the difference between the whole church's corporate APEST *functions* or *purposes* with that of the individual believer's APEST *callings, ministry and vocation*. I now believe we first have to see that the distinctive callings/vocations of any individual disciple in the church are actually derived from the purposes and functions *first* given to the whole Body of Christ as an entirety. The callings of individual disciples are simply expressions of the purposes coded into the whole church by Jesus when he bequeathed APEST to the church in his ascension. In other words, 5Q is coded into the whole Body of Christ, and we are but the living expressions of that Body in our given time and place. Functions are therefore what I call *implicit* APEST, and callings are *explicit* APEST. Both are vital and both are inextricably interconnected—we are a functional body after all. Try keeping this distinction clear in your mind as it is a very important aspect of 5Q.

Another point regarding language and terminology; in order not to overuse the singular term *APEST*, as well as to provide for some nuance, I will use the terms *APEST, fivefold, ascension gifting,* and *Ephesians 4 typology* somewhat interchangeably throughout. Similarly, I will sometimes substitute *purposes, culture, capacities, roles* or *dimensions* for the more technical base-term *function*. Likewise, while I prefer the term callings, I will sometimes replace it with *vocations, identities,* or *personal giftings*. In relation to what I call "5Q"—I will sometimes use the terms *fivefold-thinking* or *APEST system*.

Hopefully all this will become clearer as the reader becomes more familiar with the purposes of this book. Certainly it will be clear what is being referred to in each particular context.

The Five Marks and the 5Q Systems Tests

I started writing this book as a simple explanation of the logic behind the organizational test instruments that I have developed called the 5Q System Test (www.5Qtests.com). I am convinced, and hope to convince you, that approaching the church and its organization through the lens of 5Q presents you with one of the best, theologically grounded and missiologically potent, diagnostic tools by which you can assess the relative function or dysfunction of the church or organization that you lead. The 5Q Systems Test takes all the theology and organizational theory loaded into this book, and shapes it into a very powerful metric/tool for both diagnosis and the development of strategy.

As I have already said, this book goes deep and requires corresponding call to depth in the learner. The result is that because it largely addresses the minds and hearts of *leaders;* this book is likely to be less accessible to non-leaders. However, my colleague Jessie Cruickshank and I have produced a readily accessible version that will summarize much of the ideas here and also provides guidelines about the method and interpretation of the 5Q Systems Tests (the 5Q Diagnostic Test and the 5Q Systems Test). If you decide to do these tests in your church/organization, then you will want to get as many of your staff and cell level leaders reading an inexpensive, accessible, "how-to" book called *Activating 5Q* which can be acquired at www.5Qcentral.com or on Amazon.[11]

Overview of Contents

Before we finish this introduction, something needs to be said about the structure and flow of ideas. You will find that the book you are now reading will start by providing a theoretical reframing (section one) but it moves inexorably toward issues of application and practice (section two).

The preface was just that ... some instruction of how to approach the contents of this book. The introduction that you are now reading provides you with a briefing about the broader contexts within which we will have to function as a faithful people. It also briefs the reader about the core ideas, language, and now the flow of the book.

We now enter section one which lays out the theoretical frameworks of 5Q. By introduction to this, chapter one will provide a basic orientation to a distinctly missional understanding of the fivefold typology developed this far. It will provide the theological foundation upon which the elaboration of the APEST system will be developed. Importantly, this chapter will serve as a primer for those just getting in touch with the whole APEST conversation. Here I will deal with the clear and prescriptive teaching of the text itself. If you are new to this whole conversation, then I suggest you spend a lot of time getting to grips with its foundational and revolutionary content. And beyond that, I strongly urge all readers to engage with these foundational issues more thoroughly laid out in *The Permanent Revolution*.

Chapter two tracks how I actually arrived at the far-reaching, and I believe symphonic, conclusions of this book. This chapter will therefore provide the basic orientation to what I mean by 5Q, as well as introduce the fundamental themes explored throughout the rest of the book. I reveal my hand early to honor you, the learner, by presenting the theoretical model and process—an outline of the symphony up front. But in doing so, I run the real danger of hardening your eyes too early, before you've surveyed the evidence fully. I hope that you, as a disciple-learner, will track with me as we pursue an idea from root to branch in the system articulated throughout the rest of the book. Remember, Padawan, that we need to unlearn before we are able to learn and to do this you need to take in all the evidence at your disposal. So please keep your eyes soft beyond that chapter ... there is so much to see in the glorious elements that together make up 5Q.

Chapter three delves into what I am calling a "prehistory" of APEST. In seeing the fivefold through the lens of creation orders, the gifts of God, archetypes, heroes, and myths, my hope is to show the enduring influence of fivefold archetypes in broader culture, in universal human history, and in the Scriptures *prior* to it being definitively redeemed and reconstituted by the life, person, and work of the Lord Jesus and subsequently bequeathed to the church as its foundational gifting. Chapter four then traces the archetypes back through history and arrives at the being of God. The aim is to show, dare I say, the metaphysical origins/roots of the 5Q system.

As is always the case in my writing, the central and defining role is given to our Founder and to reaffirming the absolute centrality of Jesus in shaping and defining the church and its ministry. Therefore, chapters five and six make the strong case that the church is to manifest APEST in the same way, and for the same reasons, that the Body of Christ is to manifest Christ. We will see how Ephesians affirms that APEST is actually *the way* in which Jesus' presence is actively expressed in and through his Body. These chapters are pivotal in changing the paradigm of how we understand the fivefold ministries.

In section two things take a decidedly more practical turn as the ideas are applied to the local church, organization, and leadership.

Chapter seven explores the various dimensions and aspects of the fivefold *functions* or *purposes* of the Body. This will provide a pretty exhaustive list of the various corporate functions and how they relate to the individual callings expressed in God's people. This will allow leaders to categorize the various tasks involved in being a mature expression of *ecclesia*. This delineation of the functions provides the basis of a chapter on APEST as the five marks of the church. These in turn will be used as a kind of metrics to assess organizational capacities in any church or organization. This is where the power of the 5Q System comes home to roost in the local church. The church activates its God-given agency and reaches for maturity and fullness. The exciting thing is that it is eminently doable.

To help the church recalibrate around the 5Q system, chapter nine will suggest a number of very accessible tools and methods that leaders can use to develop APEST capacities throughout the church. These will help in developing competencies in language, understanding, and in embedding them in the rhythms and practices of organization itself. There is also a super-practical chapter on coaching and process, written by an exceptional APEST practitioner, my friend Rich Robinson, who will be developing and leading out 5Q training and resources alongside me.

But it is not finished there. For those who wish to explore other dimensions of the 5Q system, you can read the various appendices, which will be referenced throughout the book. These, along with the endnotes really bolster the contents without being essential to the flow of the main text. I especially advise the reader to read appendices one and two.

• The Turning of the Tide

This introduction started by acknowledging the extent of the crisis that the exhausted and outmoded church now finds itself in. We are generally not in good shape. But I am overjoyed to be able to affirm that it is by no means all doom and gloom, in relation to the fivefold paradigm at least. I can confirm that we are witnessing some truly *historic* developments in the last decade in terms of widespread adoption of APEST thinking throughout the church at large—from Catholic to Baptist and anything in-between.

As someone deeply involved in the attempt to get broad gospel-oriented Christianity to embrace fivefold-thinking, I can honestly say that I feel like something is shifting on the most primal level. APEST is truly an idea whose time has indeed come—and not a moment too soon.

The increasing adoption of APEST thinking is a sign that we are beginning to adapt, and is a sign of future vitality of Christianity in the West. Not only is there an openness in, for example, Pentecostal circles to be willing to look at the fivefold from a more missional, Christologically[12] defined (and therefore a less hierarchical-power dominated) angle, but there are also real signs of adoption among mainline denominations. Examples abound—for instance, the Evangelical Covenant Order of Presbyterians (ECO) have rewritten their denominational codes and affirmed the fivefold ministry in their constitution. The Mennonite Church USA has now adopted APEST into the official "orders of ministry." Four Square International Church (USA) has invested in the production of the 5Q Systems Test and is committed to applying it across the entire system. The Nazarenes are also engaging this at high level. There is also some very serious uptake on APEST thinking in various Catholic dioceses across the USA. And there are also many others globally, including the Churches of Christ in Australia, New Wine (UK and Europe), Communitas International (Europe and the Americas), C2C Network (Canada). The Hervormde Kerk (Netherdutch Reformed Church of Africa) uses APEST in congregational assessments and ministry training through their seminaries.

Many church planting networks (e.g., NewThing Network, Exponential, Great Commission Churches, Church Resource Ministries, Stadia, etc.) now openly use APEST typology and language. The North American Mission Board's church planting agency (SEND) is now using APEST to assess potential "Church Planting Catalysts" and also use APEST typologies to help train church planters. The Anglican Church in North America is using fivefold to assess all their new church planters and eventually the assessment will be extended to include clergy and bishops.

The same applies to many para-church agencies and organizations (e.g., InterVarsity, Navigators, YWAM, Cru, etc.). But it has to be admitted that, because of the historical deficiencies in fivefold-thinking, while there is a new-found receptivity at the level of imagination, *proficiency in fivefold practices still eludes us.*

While the academic sphere is playing catch-up, nonetheless there are now courses offered at some of our most prestigious institutions (e.g., Wheaton Graduate School, Asbury Theological Seminary, Fuller Graduate Program) and our best missional theologians (e.g., Darrell Guder) are actively in support of re-embracing a fully fledged APEST ministry.

We do well to remind ourselves that language can be a precursor to a more comprehensive change in consciousness. In this respect, this recovery of fivefold phraseology at the heart of the church is nothing short of *historic*. It is historic because, as far as I can tell at least, APEST thinking has been lacking from theological and church discourse for well-nigh 1700 years now! Make no mistake, the language and practice of fivefold typologies has been under strong sanction for almost all of this period—try to find any substantial writing on it in the last 1500 years, and you will be shocked at how little attention it has been given. Almost zero![13] In spite of the fact that it is explicitly stated as constitutionally "given" to the church by Jesus in his ascension (Ephesians 4:1–16), and it is irrefutably an aspect of the practice of the New Testament church (see the book of Acts), the language and practice has been actively suppressed through various historical expressions of what is called "cessationism."[14]

Truth is, the more dynamic APEST system has never suited the more static, hierarchical, fundamentally non-movemental form of the church that has dominated in the West throughout this period. Its reappearance, just as we are emerging from the domination of the European (Christendom) paradigm—at *this* decisive time in history—is extremely significant. I believe this is a work of the Spirit in preparing the church for its challenging mission in the twenty-first century.

SECTION 1

MAPPING THE GENOME OF THE BODY OF CHRIST

The God who made the world and everything in it is the Lord of heaven and earth and does not live in temples built by human hands. And he is not served by human hands, as if he needed anything. Rather, he himself gives everyone life and breath and everything else. From one man he made all the nations, that they should inhabit the whole earth; and he marked out their appointed times in history and the boundaries of their lands. God did this so that they would seek him and perhaps reach out for him and find him, though he is not far from any one of us.

—St. Paul (Acts 17: 24–27)

Neither revolution nor reformation can ultimately change a society, rather you must tell a new powerful tale, one so persuasive that it sweeps away the old myths and becomes the preferred story, one so inclusive that it gathers all the bits of our past and our present into a coherent whole, one that even shines some light … If you want to change a society then you have to tell an alternative story.

—Ivan Illich

Chapter 1

RetroFuture: Biblical Foundations for a 5Q Future

The problem of clericalism that results from that reduction [of ministry to shepherd and teacher] … is certainly one of the major and most daunting challenges that the Western Christian movement faces as it moves out of the protections of established Christendom.

—Darrell Guder

All the forces in the world are not so powerful as an idea whose time has come.

—Victor Hugo

Things are pretty, graceful, rich, elegant, handsome, but until they speak to the imagination, not yet beautiful.

—Ralph Waldo Emerson

As I indicated in the introduction, the purpose of this current chapter is to provide the platform to ensure that we all start the journey on the same page. While I suspect that many of you are "veterans" in the conversation and are looking for further insights in how to apply APEST thinking, some readers might be coming to this conversation unaware of the remarkable recovery of APEST thinking over the last ten years or so. So I will leave the new content until after I have at least provided a summary of the implications of the Ephesians text, as well as a briefing about the new, distinctly missional paradigm of the fivefold which changes our engagement with it.

- ## Ephesians 4:1–16: The Key to Activating the Body of Christ

As the heading suggests, we now have to pay attention to the APEST key that unlocks the powerful 5Q system coded into the core of the church's being. It is time to provide some contours of the text that is undoubtedly the key to all subsequent fivefold-thinking—Ephesians 4:1–16. In doing this, I will also suggest some broad definitions of APEST so that we can understand what is being referred to.[1]

First, I want to restate what Christians have always believed about the authority of the book of Ephesians to define how we are to understand ourselves. We have always treated it as *the* book par excellence on the nature and purposes of the church. It represents best thinking about the church— at least how Paul understood it. Ephesians is the spiritual template for the church in all ages. Certainly, there is a lot of DNA and code written throughout the book.

But like our own genetic code, the book of Ephesians does not so much describe or prescribe a specific cultural form or physical expression of a church. Rather, it presents us with something of the default settings coded in by God on a primordial level. Some have even called this "the invisible church" or, as Eugene Peterson calls it, "the church we cannot see." The invisible church in this sense is the ever-present, but largely unseen, primordial template that seeks to express itself in the life of every church, both now and throughout history. It needs soft eyes for us to perceive its pressure and to break through our theological blind spots and our ingrained ecclesiological habits. But it is always present, secretly exerting its pressure to conform our expressions of church to the one that Jesus intended in the first place. In getting under the hood of this important book, Peterson notes that:

> Ephesians is an inside look at what is beneath and behind and within the church that we do see wherever and whenever it becomes visible. … [It] provides our best access to what is involved in the formation of church, not so much the way the church appears in our towns and cities, but the essence that is behind the appearances: God's will, Christ's presence, the Holy Spirit's work. This … is what we simply must get through our heads if we are going to understand and participate rightly in any church that we are part of. This is the only writing in the New Testament that provides us with such a detailed and lively account of the inside and underground workings of the complex and various profusion of "churches" that we encounter and try to make sense of.[2]

He is absolutely right generally about the whole book, but this must therefore apply equally to Ephesians 4:1–16. This text is weighty precisely because that is exactly how Paul intended it to be read: The language, the grammar, the theme, and the proposed outcomes—all indicate the sheer importance of the text.

Commentators have long-held that Ephesians as a whole is something of the constitutional document of the church.[3] Like all constitutions, it is meant to guide all subsequent thinking and action in the organization so constituted. Read it with this in mind; it is meant to define our understanding of the purpose of God in the church. By extension, constitutional theology ought to define who we are as followers of Christ, how we are to understand ourselves and how we are to direct our affairs in the world.

Here, then, is the text of Ephesians 4:1–16. I have accentuated parts that I think need emphasizing to grasp the significance of the text. I suggest reading it straight through, and then again with a view to the highlights:

> As a prisoner for the Lord, then, I urge you to live a life worthy of the **calling you have received.** [2] Be completely humble and gentle; be patient, bearing with one another in love. [3] Make every effort to keep the **unity of the Spirit** through the bond of peace. [4] **There is one body** and **one Spirit,** just as you were called to **one hope** when you were called; [5] **one Lord, one faith, one baptism;** [6] **one God** and Father of all, who is **over all and through all and in all.**
>
> [7] **But to each one of us grace has been given as Christ apportioned it.** [8] This is why it says: "When he ascended on high, he took many captives and gave gifts to his people." [9] (What does "he **ascended**" mean except that he also descended to the lower, earthly regions? [10] He who descended is the very one who ascended higher than all the heavens, in order to **fill the whole universe.**) [11] So Christ himself gave the **apostles, the prophets, the evangelists, the pastors** [shepherds] and **teachers,**
>
> [12] **to equip his people** for works of service, so that the **body of Christ may be built up** [13] until we all reach **unity in the faith** and in the knowledge of the Son of God and become mature, attaining to the whole measure of the **fullness of Christ.** [14] **Then** we will **no longer be infants,** tossed back and forth by the waves, and blown here and there by every wind of teaching and by the cunning and craftiness of people in their deceitful scheming. [15] Instead, speaking the truth in love, **we will grow to become in every respect the mature body of him who is the head,** that is, Christ. [16] **From him the whole body,** joined and held together by every supporting ligament, **grows and builds itself up in love, as each part does its work.**

We can discern three natural sections within the overall unity of verses 1–16, as follows:

1. Foundations for the Unity of the Church (Ephesians 4:1–6)

The text at the beginning of Ephesians 4 flows out of the famously lofty Pauline prayer for the church in 3:14–21. Here he prays that they might attain to the knowledge of God in Jesus Christ and grow up into being the fullness of Christ (a key theme in the letter) in the world. Immediately after, he goes on to appeal to the Ephesians (and to all Christians everywhere) to live consistently with who God is and what he has done in Jesus ... to "live a life worthy of the calling we have received" (4:1). The elevated speech in these verses reflects both the theological significance, as well as the inescapably foundational nature, of the text.

Ephesians 4 is the pivotal section of the letter where Paul moves from theology to praxis. And like any good preamble to a constitution, Paul first condenses the core theological essentials into seven theological axioms relating to the oneness of God, faith, and church (one body, one Spirit, one hope, one Lord, one faith, one baptism, one God and Father of all). They provide the root beliefs needed to maintain a common identity as well as a deep unity within the burgeoning and increasingly diverse movement described in the book of Acts. Paul knew that these foundational convictions were needed; any movement experiencing spontaneous expansion will inevitably encounter competing systems of meaning and conflicting claims to loyalty and therefore becomes vulnerable to disunity and conflict.

The marvel of the church is that there is within it so many forces held together in dialectical tension. All that previously divided and separated us—race, identity, gender, slavery, etc.—has been resolved and unified in Christ. The tragic truth is that we have seldom been able to live into this calling as is so evidenced in the all too real racial and gender barriers in the church. But when we don't strive for unity in the bond of peace, we eventually break apart; we rend the Body, and opt for more convenient reductions of the total truth. The strong appeal of verses 1–16 is that we are not to separate what God has put together. We are to strive for the unity of the Spirit knowing there is one God, one faith, one baptism, etc. And insofar that 1–6 is organically connected with what follows in 7–11, we are not to break APEST up either. In his ascension, Jesus has "given" APEST to the church as its lasting possession. In other words, the fivefold is a part of the church's inheritance in Jesus. We are to treasure the fivefold precisely because we treasure Jesus and what he is doing through us.

2. The Ascension Gifting of the Church (Ephesians 4:7-11)

Having laid out the basis of ecclesial unity, Paul proceeds directly to affirm the God-given—or, to be more accurate the Christ-apportioned—nature of the ministry of the Body of Christ.

Putting aside for the moment the theological significance of the ascension reference here (I will return to this in a later chapter), Paul clearly states in verses 7 and 11 that Jesus "gave" APEST to the church, distributing it among all the people as he sees fit. It is vital that you, the reader, feel the weight of the grammar that Paul uses to talk about the constitutional *givenness* of the APEST ministries to the church. The verb form used for "given" (Gk. *edothe*, the aorist indicative form of *didomi*) is an aorist indicative, a very resolute verb form perfectly suited for use in constitutions. This is because aorists reflect actions that took place in the past and as such they are once-and-for-all-time events. The effects of the past event are still felt in the present. They are historic in a similar way that the signing of the Declaration of Independence was historic—it will impact America's self-understanding for all time.

The indicative *mood* intensifies the aorist *tense*, transforming it from a significant event into a statement of identity. Aorist indicatives are, in a real sense, *defining words*. They have the ring of constitutionality about them. They are used throughout the New Testament to create a theological basis from which disciples can live authentically in the world, describing the ongoing meaning and significance of the death of Christ on our behalf (e.g., Romans 6:10). In other words, the aorist indicative tense points us to that aspect of an event that possesses authentic and permanent meaning for faith. It presents us with something of a turning point, an anchor in some past event that is still connected to the present. Just so, the aorist indicatives used in Ephesians 4:1,7,11 demonstrate that APEST has, once and for all, been bequeathed to the Body of Christ. It happened; it cannot and will not be revoked. It always means something important. You must integrate it. Must let it define you. *Feel* the strength of it as the Word of God, my Padawan.

And now, factor in that all five APEST functions come as an inseparable unit. In Ephesians 4:7–11, all five APEST ministries come together under the sway of the ruling verb, *edothe* (verses 7, 11). The result is that the one verb attaches to all the APEST functions ... Christ *gave* the apostles, he *gave* the prophets, he *gave* the evangelists, he *gave* the shepherds, he *gave* the teachers. APEST comes as a unit or not at all. We cannot arbitrarily select two and edit the other three out without doing extreme violence to the grammar, as well as the intrinsic logic, of the entire text. Neither the grammar nor the theology allows us to qualify the text to suit our less dynamic, more institutional, preferences.[4] Use of this verb form is the strongest way Paul can say that the fivefold functions/callings are always an intrinsic part of the Body of Christ.

So Jesus constitutionally embeds 5Q into the church via the giving of APEST to his people in every place and time. Based on the text, we can say that APEST is an intrinsic part of the genetic codes of the church in the same kind of way that Jesus himself is. In fact, I will show that APEST is actually an index of Jesus' activity in a church. While aspects might be (and have been) suppressed, the functions themselves (or the possibility of them) are always already given, once and for all, in the ascension commissioning of the church. They are present insofar that Jesus is present! 5Q is at hand: the dormant intelligence and capacity built into the system, and because of this it can always be recovered and reactivated.

And if APEST is part of our foundational theological DNA, as I clearly think it is, then we as faithful leaders are *obliged* to factor it into our thinking, our practices, and the very leadership of the churches we are blessed to lead.

APEST is not only an integrated system; it is derived from the definitive expression of the ministry of Christ himself. It is Jesus' ministry in and through the local *ecclesia*. In fact, one of the major purposes of this book will be to highlight the fact that the Body of Christ exists to extend the logic and impact of the ministry of Christ in the world. As I will show in chapter six, the fivefold ministry is the way, or mode, by which Jesus is actually present in the church, and by which he extends his own ministry through us. The significance of this ought to be very clear to anyone who loves Jesus and wants to serve his cause and the church. We are talking kingdom impact here.

3. Attaining Maturity and Fullness in Christ (Ephesians 4:12–16)

Because each function/calling contributes something to the Body that the others do not, they mutually enrich each other. They are not to be sundered apart, as we have tended to do in church history. In other words, the church *always* needs to experience itself as *sent* (A), the prime agent to God's ongoing mission in the world. The church should always attend to God and his concerns (P), should always share the story and invite people into living relationship (E), should always maintain and develop healthy community (S), should always be rich in knowledge, wisdom, and understanding (T). All are needed in every time and in every place. (This is why I will make the case, toward the end of this book, that they are indeed the marks of a true church.)

In Ephesians 4:12 we discern a shift in Paul's argument from the *prescription* of APEST to the *description* of the expected impact in the church. This section explicitly answers the question, "Why, in his ascension, did Christ bestow the fivefold on the church?"

The ascension gifts are given so that:

- the Body of Christ might be equipped, perfected, or completed (Gk *katartitzo* in v.12)
- the Body of Christ might grow into maturity (vv.13,15)[5]
- we might "attain to the fullness of Christ" (v.13)[6]
- we may in an embodied way live out the unity described in vv.1–6 (v.13)
- we might not be given to theological faddishness or deception (v.14)
- we might grow up into Christ our Head (v.15)
- we will be rightly ordered in our relationship to our Head and therefore to each other as his Body (vv.15–16)

All this so that we might be the empowered and called agents of the Kingdom that Jesus has always intended us to be.[7]

Look again at the list above and at the strength of the grammar. What we are looking at here is the initiating design of the church. The fivefold is part of the church's very constitution, and being divinely originated, can never be made defunct or transcended.

This is no small matter! This is a pretty potent rationale for taking the fivefold very, very, seriously indeed! What Paul is telling us in no uncertain terms is that there is a direct correlation between the extent to which we embrace, and operate, in all five APEST functions, and the extent to which we see the fruit and realization of these purposes. If we mess with the coherence of the APEST functions, then these objectives cannot be attained! We become incoherent ... dysfunctional. We cannot be the Body of Christ as Jesus intended without the fivefold active and present throughout the life of his movement. Said in yet another way, the church's capacity to "attain to the fullness of Christ" is at stake. This alone should make you sit up and pay attention.

This can be represented as follows:[8]

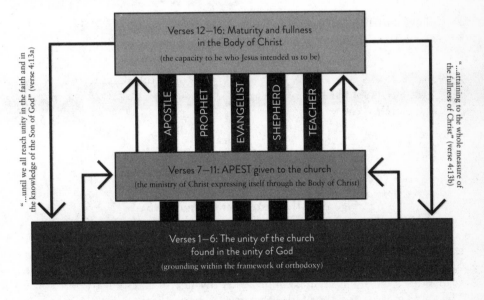

Figure 1.1 Attaining to the Fullness of Christ

This diagram allows us to see the systemic nature of APEST (just note the arrows). A system can be defined as a dynamic of interacting, interrelated, or interdependent elements forming a complex whole. This is why it is a "body." When everything works as it should, we will function according to our true nature.[9] And as in all living bodies, each vital part is inextricably linked to the other. You need your cardiovascular system—try living without it. The same is true for your nervous, digestive, endocrine, muscular-skeletal, systems. You can't function if essential aspects of the system are missing, or if the system itself is sick or dysfunctional.

The sense of system functionality is woven throughout the Ephesians 4 text. Without the fivefold fully active and present in the life of the church, we not only diminish our understanding of the faith, but we introduce significant dysfunction into the system. My friend Brad Sargent rightly notes that all the elements in sick (dysfunctional) systems are just as interconnected as those in healthy ones. If one part goes down, the whole system is degraded.

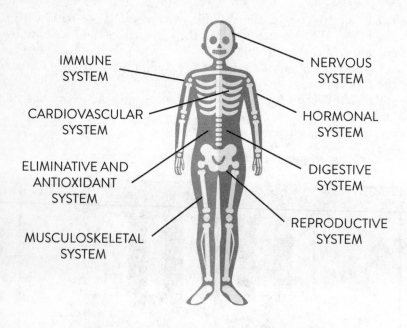

Figure 1.2 The Systems of the Human Body

Because they operate within a system, each individual APEST function enriches, counterbalances, and "corrects" the particular bias of each of the others. In fact, each function actually needs the other to be itself. For instance, your body's cardiovascular system needs the nervous system to even exist. The same is true for the Body of Christ. There is spiritual ambience and dynamic balance when all five APEST systems are operating at peak—this is what Paul called no less than the fullness of Christ. This system synergy and balance results in a more mature expression of church, more grounded in its core truths.[10] If all the parts are present and functional *in the way they were designed to function*, then the system is perfectly primed to do exactly what it was designed to do.

So it stands to reason that if we tamper with the systemic logic of the text and the symmetrical integrity of the fivefold system, we should not expect to produce the outcomes it foresees. This book comes along with an associated test instrument that will indicate dysfunction based on asymmetry in the APEST functions. I will explain it thoroughly in section two, but for now just note that if a church lacks a missional vision or capacities, it's probably because the apostolic (A) function has been degraded or entirely delegitimized; if there is a thoughtlessness and lack of wisdom in the church it is probably because the teaching (T) function is not operating as it should; a lack of concern for prayer, holiness, and justice is very likely due to a dysfunctional prophetic (P) function, and so on.

If the above strengths-deficiencies description actually were true of a particular church, then we might visually represent that church as follows:

A P E S t

If dominated by the ES functions, the symmetry and natural balance of the system is upset and the church will experience imbalance in some form or another—whether due to over-development of one or two functions (what is called "precocious development") or by overt lack of capacity due to significantly underdeveloped or "disabled" functions. Consider again your own body and consider the consequences in terms of your health. Try as it might, the asymmetrical (precocious and/or disabled) church above cannot do what Jesus did or what Jesus intends to do in and through it. How could it? It has limited its capacities to only two of Jesus' ministry-essential APEST functions—it is quite literally *incapacitated*. It is only by activating the others missing from the equation that fullness and maturity of purpose can be attained.

Think of your own body again. If 60 percent of your vital systems went down, you wouldn't live long. And if you managed to live, it would be by means of artificial life support and most certainly you would be severely handicapped.

In the light of this, think about how many of the problems you currently experience in your church/organization can be traced directly to an asymmetry or dysfunction in the APEST system. The 5Q Systems Tests will measure a church's functional asymmetry as I have done briefly above. *More later*.

In relation to the dynamic interconnected and mutuality of the Body, my colleague Tim Catchim says that in order for the APEST giftings to fulfill their Christ-given purpose, we are not only required to *express* our own gifting, we are also required to find a way to *equip* others to do what we have been gifted to do. For example, apostles are to equip the Body to function apostolically; prophets are to equip the Body to function prophetically, and so on down the line.

There is therefore a two-dimensional response required here—that God's people express a calling as well as equip others. Responding to the grace that is given to each one of us in APEST moves us beyond mere self-expression into a dynamic, reciprocal process of training where each one of us becomes both a giver and a receiver, a leader and a follower.[11]

In his comment on Ephesians 4:7–16, Eugene Peterson makes explicit the two-way relationship between the ministry of Christ with that of the Body of Christ: "Each [APEST] gift is an invitation and provides the means to participate in the work of Jesus."[12] APEST is not just the gift-set that Jesus gives to his people. It is also the way his people get to participate in what he himself is doing … what he wants to do through us. Ministry is always a two-way street.

In fact, I think that the perfect metaphor is that of a dance between two partners: In a waltz or the tango, the two dancers correspond perfectly to each other's movements. There must be familiarity and trust between the partners—a knowledge of the other's will, style, body and movements. When done well, it is more art than science. So too, Jesus leads us in a dance that can change the world. We must learn the steps to achieve increasing conformity to Jesus, his way, and his cause. With all five APEST functions operating, the church attains to, or at least has the possibility of attaining to, the fullness of Christ. We are built up, we grow, we mature, and we move ever closer toward the fullness of Christ as we appropriate APEST into our ministries as well as into the organizations we lead.

The Self-Generating Potential in the Body of Christ

In Ephesians 4, the cosmic and eternal purposes in Christ are unfolding so as to include the fivefold typology at the heart of it. According to the text, the whole point of bequeathing APEST to the church is that it might be established with the full possibility for becoming mature and attaining to the "fullness of Christ."

With this in mind, consider the word *katartizō* in 4:12. This word is ordinarily translated as "equip" or "built up," in standard contemporary translations of the Bible. But while these are definitely legitimate translations, they are *only two* legitimate possible translations of the term. But much more is also implied.[13] For instance, *katartizō* can equally be translated as "mend what has been broken or rent" (as in nets and even broken bones), to "perfectly join together," "put in order," "adjust," "strengthen," "perfect or complete," and "make one what one ought to be."

Each of these are legitimate interpretations for the word, and when applied, each one ushers in a completely different dimension to the possible meanings of the text. Using your soft eyes, and with sensitivity to the fractal design, read through the single verse of Ephesians 4:12 *nine times*, but each time using the next possible meaning listed below, and you will see something of the sheer power of 5Q.

Jesus appointed some to be apostles, prophets, evangelists, shepherds, and teachers, for ...

- equipping
- perfecting
- mending
- perfectly joining together
- putting in order
- ethical strengthening
- completing
- fulfilling
- healing

... of the saints, for the work of the ministry.

Having done the multilayered nuanced reading, what do you see?

What I see is that what I call *5Q is absolutely necessary for the health, and vitality of the church and its mission*. Furthermore, all five functions are critical for the church to self-regenerate, develop, and "perfect" itself! In other words, the APEST system, as a whole, is like the self-healing capacity in your body. Your body has inbuilt capacities for self-regeneration, and so if you were wounded in an accident or your body was ravaged by a disease, your body has the innate capacity to heal itself. It has an inbuilt capacity to be restored to functionality.

This body analogy is also perfectly true for the *Body* of Christ! All five functions are needed so that the Body of Christ might be perfected, healed, restored, and that it might self-generate, heal, grow, and develop. The activation and engagement of the fivefold is not just vital for the mission of the church in the West, but signals renewal of the whole life of the church. It offers us a new-found wholeness to our identity, functionality, and ministry. On the other hand, if we exclude APEST from the equation, we will thereby exclude our capacity to be made whole and function as Jesus intended us to in the first place.

And herein, my friends, lies the rub: the historical reduction of ministry down from the fivefold ministry of the New Testament to that of Christendom's twofold function of shepherding and teaching has bequeathed a fatal and degenerative dis-ease into the Body of Christ. The genetic codes have been corrupted. The result is that almost all churches in the West only operate with two of the fivefold functions of Jesus! No wonder we are frustrated, broken, and alienated from each other! We have an autoimmune disease ... we are a body divided against ourselves. The net result is long-term dysfunctionality and self-alienation (autoimmunity) that has led to systemic breakdown ... a diseased body.

This alone should rock your world! The church in the Western/European tradition—just think of your local church or denomination here—has assiduously edited the apostolic, prophetic, and evangelistic functions out of the original fivefold wholeness given by Jesus in his ascension (Ephesians 4:7,11).

By breaking up, or bypassing, or purging the fivefold typology, the church has damaged its God-given capacity to heal and perfect itself! This is why we have never managed to mature or grow up and fulfill all that God has intended for us as mature expressions of his Kingdom on earth. Here is the fatal flaw buried in the heritage of the Christendom form of church.

In pondering the church's Sisyphean history, it is hard not to despair of ever fulfilling the mission that God has given us to do. In Greek mythology, Sisyphus was the guy who somehow angered the gods and was condemned by them to ceaselessly roll a huge rock up a steep hill. After much effort, when he reached the top of the hill, the rock would roll back to the bottom and he would have to retrieve it, only to repeat the whole thing all over again! Wretched Sisyphus, condemned to endlessly repeating the same futile task—one that requires continual effort that never quite pays off. You don't have to be a church historian to discern some real resemblance to Western church history. Just when we think we are getting the job done, it all goes to seed and we have to start again. I have become convinced that much (not all) of this Sisyphean despair is directly related to our bungling of the APEST typology. To break up the APEST typology, and thus undermine the power of 5Q, is a fatal flaw indeed!

The good news is that APEST has been given at the very constitution of the church in Jesus' resurrection and ascension and it cannot be removed, although it can be suppressed. It is there ... latent in the Body of Christ waiting to be activated. No amount of historical suppression can finally remove what Jesus has constitutionally "given" in the very founding of his church when he ascended on high. And suppression can be reversed and latent potentials can be activated. All we have to do to be the church Jesus designed us to be is to remove those factors—what I call movement- killers— that are actively suppressing our innate capacity for health. This can be done, and is *being done*, to great effect. Relegitimize and functionally add APE back into the equation and *voila*, our capacity for maturity and fullness will be restored!

• The Sharp Edge of the APEST Wedge

While I don't believe that there is such a thing as a silver bullet—a single solution that will resolve all our problems—nonetheless I have come to believe that 5Q, properly understood and applied, is *almost* a silver bullet. Because of its sheer elegance, its theological resonance, and its promise of a more dynamic ministry, adopting it will change everything ... for the better.

The metaphor "the sharp edge of the wedge" captures the strategic significance of the whole APEST conversation. Though sometimes used in a foreboding sense, when applied to a revolutionary idea the metaphor of the sharp edge of the wedge refers to something seemingly insignificant that, if adopted, will bring about major changes. Picture a wedge used to split logs. The thin/sharper end breaks through the surface, making it possible to split the log into smaller pieces. The Bedouin Arabs use a similar metaphor: When a camel's nose is in the tent, watch out!—the rest of the camel is coming in after it.

I believe that the fivefold conversation being pursued in this book is likewise the nose of the camel in the tent, ushering in a rush of insights and opening up a whole new way of seeing the church.

In the lifelong study of the nature (phenomenology) of missional movements that deliver societal impact articulated in my book *The Forgotten Ways*, I identify six crucial elements that are all necessary if the church is to achieve transformational impact. Each of these "mDNA" (Jesus Centered, Disciple Making, Risky Engagement, Incarnational Mission, APEST Culture, and an Organic System) must all be present and active in the system for movement to happen. Furthermore, when one of the mDNA is removed or delegitimized, it diminishes the entire system and hinders the emergence of movement. This can be seen in later Methodism which undermined its own initial success by eliminating the APE from its orders of ministry.

The basic theory underlying *The Forgotten Ways* has been accepted as sound by academics and leaders around the world.[14] So when I say what I am about to say, I say it with some authority: As far as I can determine, there has never been a Jesus movement with long-term societal impact that did not also have the fivefold fully operative in its organization and among its members. As far as I can tell, it simply does not happen! Whether the New Testament church, the early church in the first few centuries, the Celtic movement, Early Methodism, or the Chinese underground church, the phenomenon and the explicit language of APEST is demonstrably evident in movements that change the world.

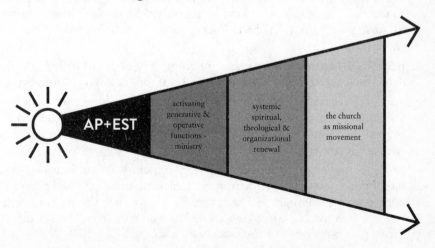

Figure 1.3 The Sharp Edge of the Apest Wedge

It is for this reason that any embrace of the fivefold typology holds out huge promise for the systemic renewal of the Christian movement and its ministry. All I know is that if I were a leader of a large denomination, I'd restructure its ministry and priorities around APEST. I'd do exactly the same in the local church or organization.

At the risk of seeming to claim too much, as a long-term practitioner in APEST thinking, I suggest that fivefold-thinking:

- provides us with a much more biblically legitimate understanding of ministry than the disastrously reduced one we currently have among Western churches, which have almost universally narrowed ministry to suit (APE)ST understandings of the church

- reminds us that ministry is the birthright of the entire Body of Christ—including all of God's people—and not something limited to the roles of the so-called clergy

- invigorates our theology by reframing the doctrine of God to include a theology of APEST, allowing us different perspectives on how we understand God, the world, and the church

- provides us with an inbuilt self-regenerative mechanism for maturity, and the promise of a way to attain fullness in Christ

- gives insight to people's unique callings by creating a distinctive APEST profile that relates personal vocation directly to the ministry of Christ. I believe that APEST profile provides insights into people's spirituality, motivations, aptitudes, and passions. (Do the test at www.apest.org for a multilayered profile of your calling.)

- develops pathways to discipleship and leadership both within and beyond the ecclesial community. In fact Paul directly relates "attaining to the fullness of Christ" to the levels of APEST present in the church. By discipling along APEST lines a church can become "mature" (Ephesians 4:13)

- helps us articulate ministry as something related to all of life and not something limited to the social confines of the ecclesial community

- gives us practical tools for the assessment and development of ministry and mission along APEST lines. (Along with the more sophisticated 5Q System Test and the APEST Vocational Profile, there are a number of such tools presented at the end of this book.)

- provides us with expanded ways in which we can interpret and understand nuances in Scripture (hermeneutics).[15] The prophetic perspective sheds light on Scripture in a way that the pastoral does not.[16] The apostolic approach would be different from the systematic theological approach of the teacher, and so on.

There is so much more that could be said by way of introduction to this hugely important topic, but this "briefing" is going to have to suffice. I will continue to build on this foundation and describe how my own thinking has been blown out, stretched, and deepened. In the following chapters, I will attempt to describe the 5Q system as it reaches back into the Godhead and touches upon aspects relating to the return of the Messiah. From here on in, the APEST system becomes 5Q and takes on a whole new dimension.

Chapter 2

5Q: The Primordial Form

The great Christian revolutions came not by the discovery of something that was not known before. They happen when someone takes radically something that was always there.

—H. Richard Niebuhr

Unfortunately, no one can be told what the Matrix is ... you have to see it for yourself.

—Morpheus, *The Matrix*

A mind that is stretched to a new idea never returns to its original dimension.

—Oliver Wendell Holmes

In the last few years, I have become very interested in what are known as meta-ideas; ideas that determine, frame, and engender other ideas. Some ideas are clearly more important than others, in that they have the power to shape and transform the system. Meta-ideas are in effect the primordial ("of first order," foundational) concepts that everything else builds on, the keystone concepts, the organizing principles that determine the entire system and shape the culture. Discovering, understanding, and unlocking the power of a meta-idea is extremely significant because they offer the power of systemic transformation.[1] I am convinced that the 5Q system that infuses New Testament ecclesiology—and as I will soon argue, the entire Bible from Creation to redemption—is one such primordial-idea. And precisely because it is a *meta*-idea, change at this point will have system-wide impact! We do well to pay attention.

I believe that 5Q promises, as well as delivers, the possibility of fullness in Christ (Ephesians 4:13), and because of this ushers in a mature ecclesial expression. 5Q is thus a truly transformational idea. I dare you to believe it. This chapter will simply provide a narrative as to how I arrived at the symphonic conclusions of this book. It's the executive overview of the ideas loaded into 5Q. I will go on to explore all the key components in more detail in the subsequent chapters. There is much to learn here, so keep your eyes soft, grasshopper.

• The Evolution of a Revolution

As I have already mentioned in the introduction, my initial idea in writing this book was simply to provide a short and accessible introduction to the concept of organizational functionality based on APEST thinking (as opposed to personal APEST callings) and to provide something of a rationale for the 5Q Systems Tests that have been released along with this book. I really thought that, given my extensive writings and research on the fivefold throughout the years, I had an above-average grasp on the subject, and it would therefore not take long to hammer out a small book to suit my purposes. Nothing prepared me for the sheer elegance of what I was about to discover.

The God-Patterned World

As I started writing, I knew that I needed to make a more substantial case for what I had previously called "APEST in the creation order"—the fivefold pattern that can be discerned in and throughout all of God's creation, and not just the church. I had made passing mention of this in prior writings but had never really looked under the hood of what that really meant. I inadvertently relegated it as an interesting but marginal aspect of the fivefold system as I then understood it.

But the deeper I delved into the topic, the more I realized that APEST is a meta-idea that continues to shape, not just the church, but *all human culture* both positively and negatively. It was evidently "there" but it needed to be named and explored. To my knowledge, this had never been done in any extensive way before.[2]

Continuing to approach the issue with soft eyes, I delved deeper. And the more I studied, the more aware I became that APEST can be understood as operating as a type of cultural *template* throughout human personality, society, and culture. In fact it became clearer and clearer that the five patterns are indeed primal *archetypes*—universal patterns of human behavior and thinking, with something akin to the power of instincts in animals. They have universal significance because archetypes exercise enormous influence over human culture and society, directing history in often unseen and yet undeniable ways. Nothing small about that! Here was further evidence, a signature if you will, of the presence of 5Q throughout creation—further evidence that I was tracking a significant meta-idea.

The following chapter will help us better understand the nature of archetypes and orders of creation and their importance for 5Q, but just so that the reader is able to grasp the ongoing influence of archetypal patterns and instincts in culture, ponder, for example, the prevalence of the messianic archetype of leadership in just about every sphere of life. One need only observe a presidential election or watch a movie to see numerous examples of the messianic archetype (positive or negative) at work.[3]

The next step in my attempt to trace the roots of APEST followed naturally: If the fivefold archetypes are indeed laced throughout creation, psyche, and culture, then I was forced to ask, where exactly did they come from in the first place? Surely they didn't just pop out of nowhere. From what or where do they derive their seemingly ubiquitous significance and sway? This question led me to a discovery of something that (again) I had never previously come across in my research: I discovered that the fivefold is, like all of God's creation, grounded and sourced from the Creator-God himself. This is because, as part of creation, they bear what theologians have called "the traces of God" which means they can be traced directly to him. The archetypes still haunt and shape us because God continues to haunt and shape us *through* them.

The significance of this cannot be overestimated: If indeed APEST finds its roots within the very being and purposes of God, then it is unavoidably important for the church's theology (understanding of God) as well as its practice. This adds theological depth, resonance, and beauty to the already evolving elegance of the system.

Prior to realizing the theological roots of APEST in God, I had always simply started with Jesus and would articulate how the fivefold was modeled by him and subsequently bequeathed to his people.[4] Now, having to deal with a much bigger system than I had previously imagined, I had to significantly enlarge my previous "model" of APEST to suit.

J-APEST: The Jesus-Patterned Form

It's vital to recognize at this point that headship of Jesus in his church is absolutely crucial for the church's authenticity and authority: We cannot, for a moment, take our focus off Christ and hope to understand what it means to be his redeemed and empowered people. Jesus remains the living center of the church—we know ourselves and our purposes in relation to him and to God through him alone. Christianity is Christ-focused, Christ-defined, and Christ-led, or it is not Christ-ianity.

Assuming this then, if Jesus is the quintessential embodiment of APEST—or what I will call J-APEST for reasons I will demonstrate in chapters five and six—and if Jesus is the image of the invisible God, as well as the fulfillment of God's redemptive mission (as Colossians 1:15–20 clearly affirms), then APEST must be an intrinsic part of God's unfolding revelation and purpose in and through Jesus. *The fivefold typology is therefore not incidental to Christology but indelibly shapes it and gives it content.* Viewed as such, APEST is not merely five roles that Jesus plays, but also the five identities he assumes, recapitulates, and subsequently fulfills.

Not only does a thorough fivefold categorization of the messianic ministry of Jesus lend new insights into his person and work, Jesus also demonstrates the true holy way of being fivefold in the world. He is the perfected expression of the fivefold.[5] Everything about Jesus marks it indelibly—APEST is thus intrinsic to the church's purpose and function in Christ. In fact, I now believe that the APEST functions and callings are no less than *the modes of Jesus' presence in the church*. It is the way in which Jesus chooses to be present and to operate in and through his people!

The APEST-Patterned Community

The implications of all this for discipleship and church health are immense. And because Jesus defines who we are and sets the agenda of what we are to become, then APEST as modeled by him must also be an intrinsic part of our identity and vocation as God's children. God's people are to be ever-increasingly formed/conformed into the image of Christ (Romans 8:29; 2 Corinthians 3:18)—both as individual disciples and as the Body of Christ. Increasing appropriation of APEST derived from Jesus is therefore not just a pathway to church health, but also a pathway to mature individual discipleship.

And so I came to see how the ascension giftings of Jesus were themselves part of a larger unfolding narrative that reaches into the Godhead, the sending of the Son, Creation, the Fall, the calling of Abraham, the messianic constitution of Israel, the defining life and ministry of our Lord, the unfolding story of the church, and leads ultimately to our final redemption.

Having looked into the prehistory and foundations of APEST, the next step was to explore how Jesus subsequently "gifts/bequeaths" APEST to his people and embeds it at the very core of the *ecclesia* (Ephesians 4:7–11). And here we arrive at a significant moment in the life of Jesus—the Ascension. The Ascension is the actual event through which the ministry of Christ is passed on and is embedded into the very genesis and genetics of his church … *the Body of Christ*. The Body is the primary vessel of Jesus' ministry. Therefore, it is always the means by which Jesus completes his mission. The entity of the church is the primary agency of Jesus' purposes in the world. These purposes are expressed through the fivefold functions given (implicit functions) to the church in all times and places. The individual callings of disciples in any given age (explicit expressions) are derived from what is already given to the whole Body of Christ in the Ascension. APEST is nothing less than the means of Christ's agency in the world through his Body and his people.

If this is true—and I think it is unavoidable—then we can make a case that *the fivefold provides us with the most viable "marks of the church" that we have at our disposal*. The marks must by definition be identifiable in the life, liturgy, and functions of the church; it is here, then, where the fivefold typology really gets to shape church life and culture. This has huge practical consequences because, as we shall see, the marks provide us with a theologically legitimate metric by which we can assess our maturity and viability as a church. 5Q becomes a means of developing a greater compliancy (conformity) of the whole church to the person of Jesus and his work in and through us.

This exploration of APEST as the marks of the church is a unique aspect of this book. I am not aware of this ever being done before—at least not as published material.

I say all this merely to give you, the reader, an overview of the process by which I discovered that 5Q, operating like the DNA at the core of every living organism, was always present, a hidden template influencing the design and culture of the church since its very foundation. In tracing it in this book, I felt I was given a peek into the theological genome (the primary genetic structures) of the Body of Christ.

But having discovered a depth and scope that I had never believed possible, the challenge was to get beyond the veil of familiarity with biblical language and, using the APEST thinking that has been developed over the last few decades as a foundation on which to build, I had to come up with a new concept that contained and communicated the incredible scale of what I was seeing—and here we come to the meaning of the term 5Q.

• 5Q: The Contours of a Primordial Idea

Work with me here, Padawan, as this is important. 5Q is the term I invented to represent this world-transforming concept. I chose the word 5Q to somehow capture the core concept of this book. So, what is it, and how does it clarify and advance the church's understanding and application of APEST?

Firstly, 5Q refers to the **APEST system understood in its largest possible context**—think *symphony* here. For me, the term brings together elements that are derived from the doctrine of God, Creation, Christology, ecclesiology, missiology, and eschatology. It is APEST viewed as a primordial system. In other words, a 5Q paradigm is a master key to understanding much of God's purpose and design for life, ministry, and the church—what Paul calls the "fullness of Christ" (Ephesians 4:13). 5Q is APEST viewed from the angle of its nth degree. And if all this seems like mumbo jumbo to you, then just know at this point that it is pretty darn big and that it is full of Jesus, but it will require soft eyes in order to perceive it.

Secondly, **5Q is the term I invented to name and categorize a latent capacity** that appears to lay dormant in all things but which is especially concentrated in Christ and thereafter in the Body of Christ. Think of it as the élan vital, the active force or impulse of life that resides in the Body. Or, to borrow a metaphor from living systems theory, 5Q is the "distributed intelligence" in the Body of Christ.[6] But the term "quotient" should speak for itself ... a quotient is by definition an index or measurement of a specified quality or characteristic in a given system. It is a gauge of the level of the active presence or relative absence of that characteristic in any given organization or person. Because APEST is derived from and is indissolubly linked to Jesus as Head of the Body, I will go on to conclude that 5Q is in effect a quotient or a measure of Jesus' active presence in a community! While I have yet to show this to you, I hope at the very least you find this idea captivating. In fact, this ought to excite the heck out of you—as it has me.

To get your head around the concept of "quotient" itself, you just have to think about the Intelligence Quotient Index (IQ), the standard test that measures the levels of innate intelligence in a person. To press the metaphor of quotient a little further, we can say that because APEST is absolutely critical to health, effectiveness, and maturity, the fivefold quotient provides an effective measure, or index, of capacity. So then, a high 5Q means a high level of fivefold functionality and is a key indicator of maturity and health. On the other hand, a low 5Q will normally be indicative of dysfunctional organization and immature people or both.

Once APEST is observable and classifiable within the life and mission of the church, we can actively test the degree to which APEST functions are operative within the Body of Christ. We can chart any imbalance or lopsidedness in APEST functionality and thereby diagnose the relative dysfunctions of a church accordingly. It is here where the 5Q System Tests will prove invaluable. The tests will provide church leaders with a profound diagnostic tool that will get to the core of the church's functionality and provide a tool to develop the ministry impact of the church. It will deliver the meta-idea in real terms that can help us "attain to the fullness of Christ!" Just note at this point, 5Q can actually be measured because this forms the basis of the rationale of the test.

Thirdly, **because 5Q is part of the whole system, it has a fractal-like quality and is structured around the APEST typology listed in Ephesians 4.** The metaphor of a fractal is useful because it helps us see how APEST is laced (recurs) throughout culture, is most concentrated in Jesus, and distributed throughout his church and the various and unique people that comprise it. A fractal is a natural phenomenon or a mathematical set that exhibits a repeating pattern that displays at every scale. It is also known as expanding symmetry or evolving symmetry. In other words, a fractal is a detailed pattern that repeats itself throughout a system. Benoit Mandelbrot, the mathematician who discovered them, once said that a fractal is a way of seeing infinity. If the basic thesis of this book is correct, then you can expect fivefold dynamics to be recurring at just about every level of our experience,

Figure 2.1 Example of a Recurring Fractal Pattern

from broader society, to personal identity, to our basic myths and narratives that shape us, to the person and work of Christ as well as to the functions of the Body of Christ. How's your mind doing now, Padawan?

• Synthesis: Seeing the Whole

Hopefully you can now sense why the research and writing of this book has been personally mind-boggling to me. I have been astonished, expanded, stretched, deepened and enriched as I have explored the fivefold as a meta-idea. What I am here proposing is what academics might call a heuristic, a mental-model that unlocks a huge amount of theological and cultural understanding in the organization. I will explore this in more detail at the end of the chapter.

Summarizing the theological and systemic sweep of 5Q, we can say that 5Q is ...

- derived from the nature and purposes of the Creator-God himself
- laced throughout creation in latent forms/archetypes, embodied in historic heroes, expressed in myth, and represented visually in art forms
- recapitulated and reconstituted in Christ's incarnation and atonement
- subsequently given by the resurrected Jesus (ascension gifting) to the Body of Christ

... and thereby ...

- constitutionally embedded/embodied as APEST functions and purposes in his *ecclesia* (implicit)
- expressed through all of Jesus' called and commissioned people (explicit)

... so that the church might attain to the fullness of Christ and that he might be all in all.

Based on the above, APEST thereby provides us with viable marks (defining characteristics) of the church, which once named and defined, APEST can be:

- identified in ecclesial thinking and acting
- measured, tested and corrected
- developed throughout the church's life, structures, discipleship, and leadership

Visually, this can be presented as follows (see Figure 2.2 overleaf):

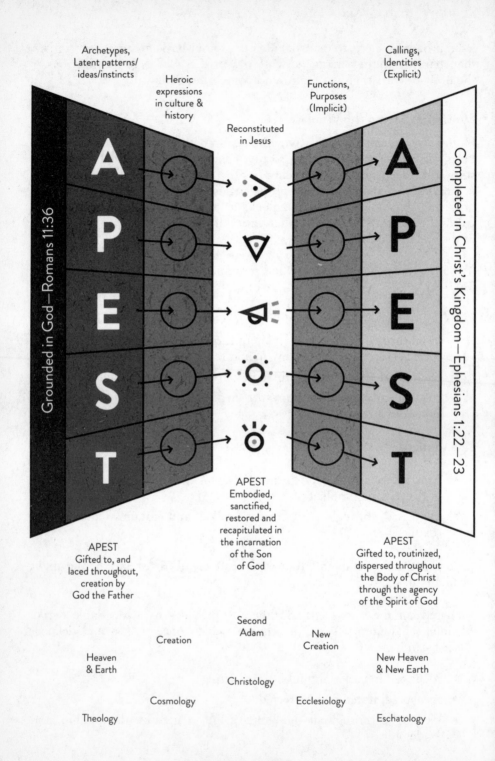

Figure 2.2 The 5Q System

This diagram will be our guiding diagram that will set the structure for the rest of the book. We will return to it often. Please study it and get a sense of its scope and scale.

Having now grasped 5Q as a symphonic system in its widest possible sweep, there is one more category-expanding concept to factor in before we move on to substantiating it in the chapters that follow. This is the idea of using 5Q as an interpretive key that effectively reformats foundational theological categories so that we might perceive and understand the content of revelation afresh.

Attention, Learner, this is another big idea and ought to give the reader a sense of the sheer power of 5Q as a meta-idea.

• Ephesians 4: The Key to Unlocking 5Q

I have already suggested that I gained the glimpse of 5Q as the innate system of distributed intelligence by using the basic Ephesians 4 text as an interpretive key to the rest of Scripture.

When 5Q—understood as a holistic fractal—is applied as an interpretive lens, it presents us with new (and yet deeply primordial) categories by which to understand and appropriate the Word of God in fresh and invigorating ways.[7]

Just so that we know what we are talking about, a hermeneutical key is a defining idea, doctrine, experience, or text that while important in itself, can also be used as a lens, a *portal* if you will, through which to "see" reality with new eyes. It names anew what was always present but largely unrecognized ... *latent*. This new "seeing" in turn opens up new frames of knowing and ushers in a whole understanding of the meaning of Scripture. Using a new hermeneutical key, we can understand what was previously all too familiar in a whole new revelatory light.

Just to get a feel for the power of interpretive keys, consider that Luther's existential tussling (*anfechtungen*) with Romans (esp.1:16–17) and Galatians, in turn led him to unlock previously suppressed insights into the gospel and how it is to be appropriated. Luther's struggle led to the development of a whole new theological model of understanding salvation.[8] Justification by faith became the interpretive key to the rest of Scripture. The rest is history. It is not too much to say that the whole Reformation was initiated on the application of the interpretive principle of justification by faith alone. And this was just one such interpretive key in the history of God's people.[9]

One thing is clear: Christians have always maintained that Christ himself is the key to understanding Scripture and the purposes of God to which it testifies. This is because we believe everything in the Old Testament points toward him and is subsequently fulfilled by him in his life and ministry. Reading the whole of Scripture through the lens of Christ enables us to discern the logic and beauty of God's purposes in Jesus and his people.[10] Precisely because, as we shall soon see, Jesus is the perfect embodiment of APEST types (they are in fact his identities and purposes) we are really only applying a more focused, but still distinctly *Christological*, lens to the idea that Christ himself is the key to Scripture. Remember J-APEST, the definitive (re)formatting of the fivefold archetypes by Jesus, here. Looking at biblical revelation through the lens of Christ's embodiment and reconstitution of APEST, allows us to see 5Q intelligence and capacities active throughout. APEST is the key to understanding the purpose and ministry of the Body of Christ, which by definition is "the earthly-historical form of his [Christ's] existence" (Barth).[11]

To be clear, I am not saying that APEST is the *only* hermeneutical key for understanding Scripture. But what I am saying is it's a very viable, very Jesus-shaped key which opens up the meaning of revelation in new and fruitful ways.

And so, we can graphically present 5Q as a hermeneutical key as follows:

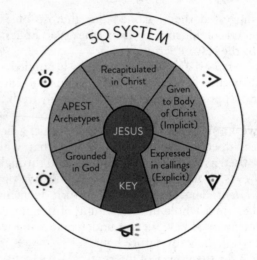

Figure 2.3 5Q as a Hermeneutical Key

Now Let's See How Deep This Really Goes

> After this, there is no turning back. You take the blue pill—the story ends; you wake up in your bed and believe whatever you want to believe. You take the red pill—you stay in Wonderland, and I show you how deep the rabbit hole goes. Remember: all I'm offering is the truth.[12]
>
> Morpheus to Neo, *The Matrix*

OK, now you have at least been brought to the point of being able to recognize the basic proposal of this book. It's big, right? And there can be no denying, that if this is true, it is a world-changing idea. If taken seriously, it will fundamentally alter how you see God's purposes in and through his people—collectively as well as individually. Red pill or blue pill? It's time now to choose to proceed or not. Once you have seen it, there will be no way of unseeing it.

If you have kept your eyes soft, you should now be able to see why I am so excited about the contents of this book. You should be able to sense the size and importance of this idea for the church in our time. As for me, I am now absolutely convinced that with 5Q we are not dealing with something marginal to the design of the church, but rather something absolutely essential—an intrinsic aspect of the genetic coding, anatomy, and architecture of human communities and organizations, but especially the church as the Body of Christ. The 5Q system is a foundational meta-idea that not only provides us with a holistic understanding of the ministry of God's people, but also represents the best biblical lens with which we can assess our participation in the ministry of Christ in the world.

I'll be honest and admit that I've blown my own mind just by writing all this, so don't worry if you don't fully get it at this point. For now, just keep your eyes soft, look for the elegant design, try to sense the system in itself, and let the ever-willing Spirit of truth be your illuminating Guide; stay close as ever to Jesus, discern the Christological shape (the form of Christ revealed), and allow that form of Christ to indelibly imprint your life, as well as shape the church or organization that you lead.

Chapter 3

The Traces of God: A Prehistory of (the Fivefold) Archetypes

For us there is but one God, the Father, from whom all things came and for whom we live; and there is but one Lord, Jesus Christ, through whom all things came and through whom we live.

—St. Paul (1 Corinthians 8:6)

"In our world," said Eustace, "a star is a huge ball of flaming gas." "Even in your world, my son, that is not what a star is but only what it is made of."

—C.S. Lewis, *Voyage of the Dawn Treader*

Lying deep within myself ... I seized a most worthy souvenir, a shard of heaven's kaleidoscope.

—Patti Smith

I have already mentioned that as I began to take seriously the idea that the fivefold typology existed in what theologians call the "created order," the more convinced I became of the world-renewing energy that was somehow contained in the typology. I felt that in delving into this aspect of APEST I was grappling with a meta-idea of the first order. But my view was significantly expanded because I have come to believe that the fivefold typology does not just have significance for the church; it has enduring validity in broader society as well. It appears to me that this was God's original intent all along because as far as I can tell, APEST, in the form of archetypes, myths and hero-expression, was already evident in society long before the earthly ministry of Jesus, and is also evident in current society beyond the church.

I believe this to be very significant to the mission and the effectiveness of all God's people everywhere. APEST is not just found in churches or in Christian organizations. Fivefold functions, intelligences, or capacities are not something limited to the faith community; they don't just pop up only after a person comes to faith. Rather there is a noticeable correlation between APEST as it is expressed in the church with other more generic capacities and functions in broader human culture and history ... a "non-church APEST."

This idea of God shaping our lives before conversion is not at all alien to biblical understandings of calling; Paul and Jeremiah could both say that they were respectively called to be an apostle and prophet from before their birth (Galatians 1:15–16; Jeremiah 1:5). Similarly, looking back over my own life I can discern clear roots of what became a clearly defined calling long before I was aware of its significance in the faith. No doubt you can do likewise. Sure, APEST might bring more enhanced and distinct meanings in Jesus' movement, but there is more continuity than there is difference. The fivefold typology is in some way a category universal to all humankind. To my mind therefore, APEST just got a whole lot bigger and way more important.

Now let me at least try making something of a case.

• The Gifts of God

Any attempt to restrict God's gifts to the so-called "spiritual"[1] gifts imparted following our conversion to Christ ignores the breadth of Scripture's thoughts on the subject of God's gifts to his creation and to his people.[2] When we observe human culture and achievement we cannot but be awestruck at the variety and diversity of God's design, intent, and ongoing work in all people. God's gifts to creation come in every conceivable shape, size, and kind.

Aside from the gifts in and through the natural world, God has specifically endowed humans with a truly amazing variety of physical, artistic and intellectual abilities, intelligences, and possibilities. It was always God's intention, and still is, that every person, together with his or her gifts and abilities, serve as an instrument of blessing for others. In this context, each person has a gift, task, place, and role to use as channels of his or her creative goodness for others (Matthew 7:11; James 1:17).

The fundamental logic behind all creational gifts is that of God's blessing: a blessing to be received, appropriated, and passed on to others. This thought is captured in Genesis, where humans are represented as created in the image of their Creator and subsequently given the mandate to exercise godly stewardship over his creation. This is what theologians refer to as "the cultural mandate." God's image-bearers are literally commissioned and *sent* into the world to cultivate the earth, to engage in productive and creative work, to be fruitful and multiply, and in their own way contribute to human flourishing. Humans were meant to carry out God's will for his creation and to embody his concern for the enhancement of life. In doing so, they were intended to be co-laborers with God in the ongoing work of blessing his creation.

All this creation gifting and mandate applies to all people—to Christian and non-Christian alike.[3] The fact that God's goodness can be experienced "incognito" in all aspects of creation is what Luther rather intriguingly called "the masks of God." He was here referring to what the Latin Fathers call the *vestigia Dei* (the traces of God)—signs of God's existence and being, embedded in creation. The "traces" are evidence of the Creator who reveals himself as the beginning and end of all the world's paths.[4]

These are but masks of God in that God chooses to paradoxically both conceal as well as reveal himself—he does it, to use the words of Luther, "in, with, and under" his Creation. We see this especially in human acts of goodness, and through the various forms of human enterprise—art, science, education, family, politics, rule of law, marriage, recreation, and so on. We can thus say that since everything derives from him and may thus bear his image and trace, all creaturely Being can be experienced as an indicative utterance about God.

The point here is that all these and other various patterns and themes in life and nature are derived from the nature and purposes of God and find their way into the archetypes as strands that come together to form a yarn that in turn is woven into the very fabric of cultural and spiritual life. Therefore, all human intelligences, including 5Q, are originated and derived from the intelligence originating within God. This is also the reason why theologians have always taught that all of life, not just the church, can be viewed as the arena of the sacred ... as incarnational ... as *sacramental*.[5]

Acknowledging God's gifting throughout his human creation means these various human aptitudes, gifts, and capacities can be observed, categorized, and developed. In fact, this is the basis of all education. The assumption of universal gifts and abilities is the basis of all personality or aptitude instruments such as Myers-Briggs and StrengthsFinder. It's not a stretch, therefore, to say that the various APEST types are not simply functions and callings *within* the church; they are dimensions that are woven in and *through all of life*. As strange as it seems at first, once we have the categories to "see" APEST, we can easily recognize these as aptitudes and capacities in all the domains of society.[6]

Of Archetypes, Heroes, and the Orders of Creation

I've been referencing archetypes all along; I think you'll agree that it's high time to define them a bit more. To make this case, we need to understand the nature of archetypes and their relationship to what theologians call the "orders of creation." To do this we have to look into the roots of this somewhat intangible but important idea.

Archetypes R Us

I understand archetypes as those somewhat mysterious, recurrent symbols, values, or motifs that are deeply latent in all story, art, thought, and action. The root word for archetypes is the Greek *arche* which literally means "beginning," "origin" or "source of action" (e.g., in the New Testament, John 1:1–3, "In the *beginning* was the Word ... "). An *arche* is a formative aspect that lies at the very roots of something. Archetypes are therefore the truly *primordial* (of first, and therefore defining, order) ideas that shape our experience of the world.

There are things that all human beings dream about. There are concepts in common that every human has pondered—recurring motifs that often have to do with God, life, death, good and evil, and of course sex. There are experiences that reach beyond language. This is why archetypes exist in the (conscious and subconscious) experiences of every individual and are recreated in literary works or other forms of art.[7] Archetypes influence every aspect of life itself, including human life with its culture, philosophy, art, literature, politics, biology, psychology, etc.

In philosophy, the concept of archetypes as abiding and influential *ideas* is considered the very basis of knowledge itself—the so-called "first principles." For instance, Plato, and the various idealist philosophers that took their cue from him, called these archetypal idea-patterns "forms" and "universals"; the primordial ideas that most fully represent reality, by which all things are determined through interaction with them.

Biologists too have similarly studied those mysterious inbuilt "preprogrammed" responses within all animals that enable them to respond to various stimuli in their environments that produce a stereotyped behavior or fixed action pattern (FAP). Normally called instincts, these produce regular behavior in animals right across their species—for instance, the homing instincts of birds, or the definite mating patterns of an insect species.

The same instinctive patterning behavior can also be observed more broadly in all living systems, including human ones. For instance, in ethology (the study of human behavior and social organization from a biological perspective) what we normally call "instincts" are called innate releasing mechanisms (IRMs). While not exerting quite the same level of purely deterministic influence as instincts do in animals, they are also not all that different. IRMs are an expression of a prior pattern built into the system itself; as archetypes they in some way continue to function as cultural instincts ... memes embedded into life itself. This explains why all societies in some ways have similar social patterns ranging from patterns of small talk, partnering rituals, eating habits, laughter, greeting rituals, parenting behaviors.

As far as psychology and the social sciences are concerned, archetypes are considered absolutely crucial to our understanding of ourselves and of human behavior in general. They continue to determine human thinking and behavior from deep within the vast reservoir of human cultural experience, what psychologists call the collective unconscious, or what social scientists call the social imaginary or the habitus of the culture.[8] It is perhaps because of the pervasive latency of archetypes in the human soul and culture that archetypes always feel so very familiar ... like they are more remembered than learned. They have a strong association with spirituality. So much so, that in a real sense archetypes are not so much in us; rather it is we who are in them. Because archetypal forms are deeply latent in culture, they will be experienced with a deep resonance—and because of this they are the true motivators of action. They have even been called the Culture Code by some commentators and are sought for as a means of unlocking the passions and concerns of a culture.[9]

There are even regular patterns that can be discerned in history itself. In many ways culture and history itself can be viewed as made up of the dynamic interplay of constantly recurring hidden forces and ideas e.g., the idea of a royalty, the democratic impulse, the universality of marriage, the building of cities, the rule of law, etc. They are like cultural memes and are experienced as forces latent in culture.

In literature and art, archetypes are known to exercise a powerful mythical sway over our imagination and practices.[10] Both the superheroes as well as the arch-villains of the various action comics are unambiguously archetypal in content and impact—and they almost all derive from Greek mythology, from various holy books, or other hero narratives, including stories from the Bible. One only has to think about how much biblical language and concepts have shaped history to know that we continue to experience these ideas as archetypal.

And then there are the social-institutional archetypes as well. For instance the biblical cities of Sodom, Babylon, and Rome can be seen as the archetypes of the various decadent cities that appear later in history or literature: Las Vegas, New Orleans, or the "Big Apple" aspect of New York are all prime American examples. Conversely, consider the archetypal power of Jerusalem or Zion as archetypes of God's ideal community.

Organizational archetypes are similarly evident in branding across the spectrum of an organization. For instance, the Explorer/Pioneer archetype pervades Sir Richard Branson's Virgin Group. The Caregiver archetype influences brands like Johnson & Johnson; the Genius archetype continues to shine through Apple Inc.'s brand, etc. Other possible organizational archetypes in society are the commando unit, the family dynasty, frontier settlers, the humanizing force and the arctic expedition.[11]

The Bible and Archetypes

Not only does biblical literature make use of the same archetypes existing throughout creation, but there are actually well-developed ways of both recognizing their influence, and clear language that enables us to name and understand them. I refer here to the biblical teaching on the so-called powers and principalities: For instance, the root word *arche* (the root of the term *arche*-type) is directly used in the New Testament typology of the powers.[12] These "foundational forces" authorities-powers (*exousia*) and elemental spirits/principles (*stoicheaia*), among others, comprise those resilient and ubiquitous spiritual and cultural forces that Paul talks about in Colossians 1:16–17.[13] Just like deterministic instincts (FAPs) and archetypes (IRMs) they continue to influence, direct, and even coerce human behavior. These foundational forces include a wide range of both good and evil influences in religion, society and culture, including both the angelic and the demonic forces, institutions and religions of all varieties, political ideologies, dominant ideas of leadership, theology and dogma, the universality of marriage, the invisible force of the economy, as well as various other controlling metaphors, ideas and ideologies. Even the Torah is included in the list, in that it continues to have determining force in culture! Again, these are broad expressions of what we mean by the term *archetypes*. We interact with these in innumerable ways every day of our lives. In seeking to evangelize the Athenians, Paul assumes the universality of archetypes in pagan history and culture and reinterprets them in light of the Resurrection (Acts 17:24–27).

It is important to note that the Bible depicts these "powers-forces-instincts" as originally created by God and therefore part of the perfect design for life that God instituted in the beginning (e.g., Colossians 1:15–20; Hebrews 1:1–2; Genesis 1–2). The Lutherans actually call these "the orders of creation" in that they all formed part of the perfect order originally instituted by God in creation before the Fall. Archetypes, the powers, the creation order, and the like might well be fallen in this world, but like all orders of creation, they can be traced back to God himself. They are values and symbols in human life because they are sourced from the Creator himself, as Paul writes to the Colossians:

> For in him all things were created: things in heaven and on earth, visible and invisible, whether thrones or powers or rulers or authorities; all things have been created through him and for him. He is before all things, and in him all things hold together.
>
> *Colossians 1:16*

While the Scriptures are also clear that many of the powers are fallen—some in extreme rebellion against God and hence demonic—they nonetheless continue to have some legitimacy derived from creation (e.g., the State in Romans 13). Supremely important is that they have been in *principle* defeated and will be ultimately brought into full realignment with the Kingdom through the work of Jesus (e.g., Colossians 1:19–20, 2:15–23). Taken together, as far as the Scripture is concerned, the archetypes—good and bad, redeemed and unredeemed, powers—are still very much active and continue to shape and influence human behavior (e.g., Ephesians 6:12).

While referring specifically to extra-biblical as well as Old Testament archetypes/forms of spirituality, the great theologian Hans Urs von Balthasar could equally be referring to 5Q when he notes that because all spiritual archetypes converge in Christ, and in him flow into the Body of Christ, this provides the means by which pre-Christian forms of experience are fulfilled in Jesus' people:[14]

> [Archetypes] do not hover over the Body as unattainable ideas, but, rather, each in its own way ... these archetypal experiences are the very foundation of the life-form of believing man.

Far from being inactive ideas, archetypes are an integral dimension of all human life, including that of God's people.

The Hero: The Living Expression of the Archetype

Corresponding to the more impersonal symbol-idea, heroes are those people (and to a lesser degree, organizations) that serve as role models, as standards of action—ideal expressions of the primary archetypes that inform them. These are what we call our heroes.

A hero is a person (or group) that convincingly embodies our aspirations, ideals, beliefs, and cherished collective myths.[15] They reflect our own sense of identity upon which our own heroism is molded. *Heroes enable people to find their own ideals, courage, and wisdom in society*—this is what makes them so important in all cultures and societies. Social philosopher Ernest Becker highlights the fact that in order to pass on its cultural genes, all communities and societies have to find a way to allow for its members or citizens to feel heroic. Without heroes, we are unable to live out the archetypal narratives that communicate the communal vision, aims, and ideals in society.[16] Along with Jesus, God's people have always considered the various saints to be our true heroes (Hebrews 11). They are the ones who have made it easier for the rest of us to believe in God and to remain faithful. Throughout our history, the saint-hero offers us a clear-cut, specifically delineated example of the same archetypes that have come down to us from the biblical world and which point into a future one.

All movies are developed by appeal to archetypal imagery embedded in mythic structure and given living expression in the form of the hero. The resonance and popularity of any given movie/story depends largely on its archetypal strength—its ability to connect with the archetypes resident in the audience. Ponder the archetypal resonance in *The Lord of the Rings*, or *Game of Thrones*, or any of your favorite movies.

Or consider that the extremely popular *Divergent* series actually builds on archetypes that are eerily analogous to the pattern of APEST: The story is set in a future dystopian Chicago where society has been divided into five *factions*. These factions are societal divisions that classify citizens based on their aptitudes and values. They are Abnegation (the selfless), Amity (the peaceful), Candor (the honest), Dauntless (the brave), and Erudite (the intelligent). Problems in this society arise when one faction asserts its dominance and importance to the exclusion of the possible contributions of the other factions. The movie plays itself out in terms of power-relations between the factions. But the whole point of the series is in the name: "divergence" only occurs when the factions actually unite. They need to find each other to resolve the problem. Here we have our own story mirrored to us in secular literature!

Having recognized the nature of archetypes and their ubiquitous presence in history and culture, having traced their unfolding in our primal narratives (myths), and seen how they are embodied in our heroes, we are ready to see how they manifest in the various domains of life in which we all live.

Chapter 4

Scenius:
The Roots and Shoots
of Fivefold Culture

Scenius is like genius, only embedded in a scene rather than in a gene.

—Brian Eno

If we go down into ourselves, we find that we possess exactly what we desire.

—Simone Weil

Divine grace ... is secretly at work in the whole sphere of history, and thus all myths, philosophies, and poetic creations are innately capable of housing within themselves an intimation of divine glory.

—Hans Urs von Balthasar

I love how the brilliant British artist Brian Eno came up with the very fertile term "scenius" to describe the phenomenon of collective creativity as opposed to individual genius. Here's what he said at the Luminous Festival in Sydney in 2009:

> I was an art student and, like all art students, I was encouraged to believe that there were a few great figures like Picasso and Kandinsky, Rembrandt and Giotto and so on sort of appeared out of nowhere and produced an artistic revolution. But as I looked at art more and more, I discovered that that wasn't really a true picture. What really happened was that there were sometimes very fertile scenes involving lots and lots of people—some of them artists, some of them collectors, some of them curators, thinkers,

theorists—all sorts of people who created a kind of ecology of talent. And out of that ecology arose some wonderful work ...

So I thought that originally those few individuals who'd survived in history—in the sort of "Great Man" theory of history— were called "geniuses". But what I thought was interesting was the fact that they all came out of a scene that was very fertile and very intelligent. So I came up with this word "scenius"—and scenius is the intelligence of a whole ... operation or group of people. And I think that's actually a more useful way to think about culture ... Let's forget the idea of "genius" for a little while; let's [rather] think about the whole ecology of ideas that give rise to good new thoughts and good new work.[1]

Here's how Eno summarizes scenius:

Scenius stands for the intelligence and the intuition of a whole cultural scene. It is the communal form of the concept of the genius ... Scenius is like genius, only embedded in a scene rather than in a gene.[2]

Almost identical to the metaphor of a quotient, scenius is useful shorthand to help us see *the matrix out of which culture and values develop within a whole group or society*. APEST archetypes, already existing in and throughout culture, are in fact ideas and patterns seeded into the heart of all culture itself. 5Q is what I chose to call the marvelous scenius laced into the Body of Christ.

Once we have the five APEST categories clear in our own thinking, it is not hard to identify APEST being expressed in and through the many archetypes, heroes, capacities, intelligences, abilities, and even whole domains of human activity.[3] These are not just functions and capacities inside the church; in many ways, they prefigure the church's particularly nuanced application of the fivefold in the New Testament and in subsequent history.

The idea of the pre-existence of the archetypes is further strengthened when we look at the use of language then and now. All the terms used by Paul in Ephesians 4:11 were drawn from extra-biblical sources. So for instance, "apostle" was a secular term drawn from Greco-Roman society; there were "prophets" in all religions; the term "evangelist" likewise has its roots in broader culture; as do the terms "shepherd" and "teacher." The Bible writers just drew from the well of language and ideas in broader culture and gave them a particular *theological* shape, but they did not fundamentally alter their basic meanings.[4]

Recognizing different modes and intelligences and capacities inside and outside the church radically opens up the game and brings significant insight to believers and non-believers alike and across all the domains. For instance, there are individuals *and* organizations that express the apostolic archetype in pioneering and founding new movements, excelling in organizational design, innovation, and entrepreneurship. Similarly, there has always been some form of prophetic organizations and heroes that manifest the prophetic archetype from time to time—Mahatma Gandhi and the suffragettes are cases in point. There are those actors and agencies in history that catalyze decision, communicate and inspire, and mobilize groups into action—a clear manifestation of the evangelist archetype. Reflecting the shepherd archetype, history is likewise peppered with people and organizations committed to creating community, guarding and protecting society, and overcoming conflict. And then of course, there are the forces of learning, understanding, pedagogy and educating that are inspired by the teacher archetypes.

Think of both organizations and/or individuals who embody these. It's not at all hard to recognize once you have the "eyes"—the necessary perceptual categories—by which to "see" it. (Remember the importance of the interpretive lens in helping us categorize, and therefore understand, what we are seeing.) If we don't have the mental model, categories, and the language associated with 5Q, we are blinded to it when we encounter it in real life. In fact once a person or a group has an articulated mental model encompassing the APEST typology, they will be able to recognize that they are archetypally laced throughout all aspects of society. The patterns were there all along; it is we who were linguistically blinded, and we could not recognize what we were always looking at.

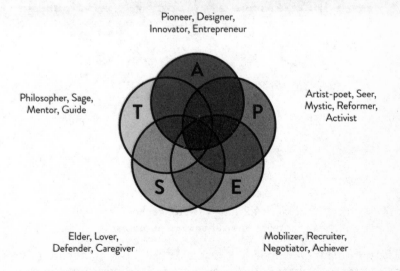

Figure 4.1 APEST Hero Types and Roles throughout Creation

In this diagram, we can readily observe that the fivefold APEST are not *just* functions and callings within a church but existent in so many ways throughout society. (See the table on page 50 at the end of this chapter for full typology and for examples in history.)

• APEST as Aptitudes or Forms of Intelligence

It is my view that APEST, viewed as five key archetypes latent in all creation, gives us a remarkable framework within which to broadly understand and organize many important categories of human thought and endeavor. Of course, there are more archetypes in culture than simply five, but if you consider that Carl Jung, after a lifetime of study, listed only twelve personal archetypes, the fivefold typology actually carries a lot of culture-shaping potency. See if you can find links with Jung's archetypes of personality and 5Q sensibilities. The three layers of the diagram show archetypes (outer level), purposes (middle level) and motivations (center).

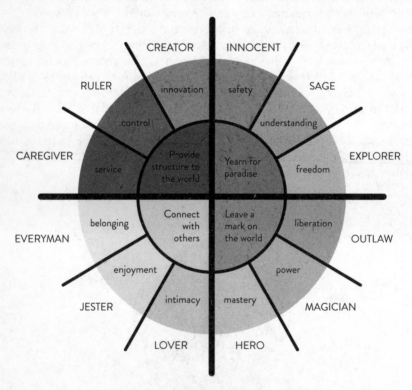

Figure 4.2 Jung's Twelve Archetypes [5]
(with motivations and purposes)

There are many correspondences with APEST. Look at the core motivations (at the center)—then think of the obvious correlations to the fivefold. Then look at the archetypes (the outer ring) themselves; his explorer, creator, and hero are strongly apostolic in nature; the prophetic corresponds to the outlaw, jester, and magician; the shepherd to the caregiver, lover, everyman, etc. Do your soft eyes see the pattern?

But we not only see real traces of APEST in the enigmatic depths of the human unconscious; we only have to look at our pantheon of heroes and villains across culture through the lens of the fivefold to observe the five APEST archetypes in embodied forms (see table on page 50). As we have seen, our heroes reflect back to us what we believe is truly important— that is the very purpose of a hero. Think about your heroes; what do they say about you? It would be a great exercise for the reader to ponder the various super-heroes movies and comics and try to recategorize the heroes and villains using the fivefold types. I actually know a writer who is contracted to write an action hero book series, based on the APEST archetypes.

Perhaps one of the most common ways we experience the use of archetypes in popular culture is in the form of the ubiquitous personality tests available today. Almost all of these (e.g., MBTI, StrengthsFinder, Enneagram) are based on some form of ideal or exemplary personality trait, or archetype. For instance, Isabel Myers (one of the founders of the Myers-Briggs Personality Profile) developed the entire MBTI profile around four temperament and character archetypes each with their own sub-types. David Keirsey went on to refine these to four foundational archetypes which are then subcategorized into the types we know today; they are Artisans (SPs), Guardians (SJs), Idealists (NFs), and Rationals (NTs).[6] Once again, note the glaring similarity to the APEST typology listed in Ephesians 4. The MBTI archetypes have undoubtedly delivered great insights into human motivation, character, traits, strengths, flaws, and so on. They have huge resonance with us because they describe who we are by appealing to the universal traits and patterns already existing in individuals, society and culture.

An approach to the fivefold using Myers-Briggs typology has been developed by people like Jeremie Kubicek and Steve Cockram of GiANT Worldwide. In their model called the Five Voices, they filter MBTI through an APEST lens; the result of this is a typology of five kinds of "voices."[7] They are: the Pioneer, Creative, Connector, Nurturer and Guardian. Another example of a psychometric profile based on the use of archetypes unnervingly similar to the fivefold is found in the writings of Harvard Law professor Erica Ariel Fox.[8] Written to help people learn to navigate high-stakes interactions—from business deals, client calls, and team meetings to family arguments, landlord disputes, and parent-teacher conferences—she talks about the Dreamer, the Thinker, the Lover, the Warrior, the Lookout, and the Voyager. Look at them; these turn out to be but variations of the primal APEST archetypes in a different guise.

One of the most novel applications of the fivefold typology is that being used by a women's magazine called *Tapestry*.[9] The magazine is decidedly Christian in flavor but is dedicated to helping all young women understand their true significance in ways that are relevant in terms of broader culture. The vision is to speak to women through the voices of the fivefold ministry vocations—what they call *the five personas*—these being the Visionary, the Messenger, the Storyteller, the Nurturer and the Teacher. The art, photography and articles are all built around the development of these five personas. Their descriptors of each of the *personas* on their website are in my opinion outstanding.

In many ways, this personality-linked aspect of APEST comes very close to being an identity issue and not just a matter of function and calling. It is quite conceivable that the fivefold could be used as a means to profiling personality and helping people live into their unique sense of identity as a follower of Christ.

From IQ to EQ to 5Q

Likewise, we can see archetypes in action through the lens of different kinds of thought categories, intelligences or aptitudes in society. It stands to reason that each of the fivefold archetypes or heroes perceives, processes, and engages the world in very different and unique ways. For instance, some people can sense the systemic interconnectedness of concepts; others have high degrees of emotional intelligence; some are detailed thinkers; some have an innate capacity to communicate ideas, while others have the ability to get buy-in from members of the broader group.

Over the last four decades we have come to see these various patterns as forms of intelligence. So, for instance, our "intelligence quotient" (IQ) measures our reasoning abilities. Clearly some people have a business intelligence, others "street smarts." More recently educationalists have begun to use the idea of emotional intelligence (EQ) to assess and develop the people skills in people and organizations. The idea has also been extended to include cultural intelligence (CQ) and political intelligence (PQ).[10]

This idea of intelligences (or aptitudes) provides a valuable contemporary metaphor for unlocking the power and functionality of APEST: each particular type has a unique bias, a certain sensibility, and a heightened receptivity to issues that others cannot see. Above all, each brings an enhanced capacity to the multidimensional tasks of the organization. Similarly, we can characterize by a type of intelligence: apostolic intelligence (AQ), prophetic intelligence (PQ), and so on. The combination of the five intelligences creates a synergistic, heightened intelligence in human society in general and the church in particular.

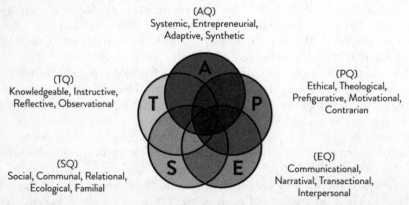

(AQ)
Systemic, Entrepreneurial,
Adaptive, Synthetic

(TQ)
Knowledgeable, Instructive,
Reflective, Observational

(PQ)
Ethical, Theological,
Prefigurative, Motivational,
Contrarian

(SQ)
Social, Communal, Relational,
Ecological, Familial

(EQ)
Communicational,
Narratival, Transactional,
Interpersonal

Figure 4.3 Archetypes of APEST Intelligences and Capacities throughout Creation

Viewing "fivefold intelligence" in such a way helps us see the recurring pattern of the archetypes at work in various personalities and organizations that make up our world. I would further suggest that when these types coalesce in dimensions of society, they constitute what we can call a domain of culture (e.g., education, arts, politics, health, engineering, business).[11]

Five Domains

Having traced some of the theological dimensions of APEST in and through creation, it is time to explore some of the possible implications for life and organization in all the various domains of society. There are a number of these, but most include the arts, recreation-entertainment, architecture-construction, politics, media, industry, economy, education, family, government, media, health, science, and religion.[12] It is even conceivable that universities could structure broad curricula along the lines of the fivefold typology to great effect. So, for instance, apostolic and evangelistic functions correlate to business, innovation and entrepreneurship, marketing, and engineering. Evangelistic and teaching capacities are likely to be expressed in communication and media. The prophetic and pastoral are most likely concentrated in the various social sciences like psychology and human sciences. Philosophy is a correlate of the teaching function as are the hard sciences, and some aspects of engineering. No doubt you get the idea.

I have already tried to categorize the various APEST archetypes, expressions, and modes of thinking in a way that should make it relatively easy for the reader to discern the various latent ideas, cultural forces, and types associated with archetypal APEST working their way through all of culture. I hope at least that readers will recognize the possibilities of APEST thinking in the arena of life beyond the organized church and that this will in turn stimulate renewed missional imagination and practice across the domains of society. (See table 4.1 below for a comparison of archetypes, heroes, domains, and intelligences.)

Fivefold Possibilities in Leadership Theory and Practice

Possibly the easiest way in which to appropriate APEST thinking beyond the church is in the area of general leadership theory and practice. Ephesians 4 speaks directly of fivefold leadership *equipping* followers, building them up, and helping the *entire* Body of Christ come to *unity* and *maturity*.[13] John Lee, a colleague of mine, who wrote his PhD dissertation on this topic, asks if the APEST typology could be a parallel to transformative leadership that elevates maturity and concern for the entire organization, helps transcend self-interest, and motivates followers toward high-level achievement and self-actualization.[14]

There is a vast amount of research and writing describing various types of leaders in all forms of organization. There are numerous leadership typologies each with their own criteria of categorization. Even though they may differ, all rightly assume that leaders usually act in ways which can be observed as discrete types with their own distinctive patterns of process, thought, and behavior. For instance, we can describe entrepreneurial leaders in a way that clearly distinguishes them from less risk-engaging leaders, who, while they might not lead in innovation, nonetheless excel at developing and expanding existing organizational systems. Some leaders are profoundly participative and have great EQ, while others are more autocratic and ideas-based. Leaders have certain observable characteristics and can be categorized.

When considered in the light of the intrinsic balance within the full APEST dynamic, a good case can be made for APEST as an excellent categorization of leadership that will help in the recruiting, developing, and maximizing of leadership teams in every conceivable organization. In my first book, I suggested that the following way of structuring leadership, using APEST typologies, would make for an excellent, well-proportioned, team in any setting.[15]

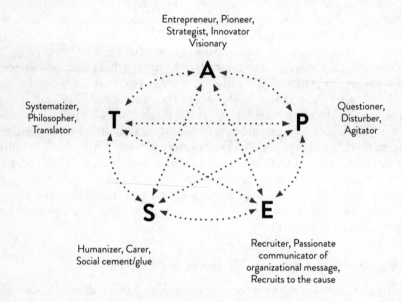

Figure 4.4 Organized for Impact

John Lee likewise notes that,

the Ephesians 4 paradigm genuinely provides a picture of God's view of effective leadership—collaborative, multifaceted, utilizing leadership gifts and mechanisms for extending (A), knowing/creating (P), recruiting (E), nurturing (S), teaching (T), in order to equip and empower the collective for the sake of the overall mission *in any given setting*.[16]

He goes on to make the connection of APEST with the so-called marketplace ministries:

> It is extremely significant ... to note that the context of the Ephesians 4 passage is addressing the equivalent of what would be classified by many as "marketplace ministry" today. When it speaks of "equipping the saints for the work of the ministry" it is not referring to a model that contained professionalized clergy—that did not exist at the time. The implication ... is that these leadership mechanisms seem to be hardwired into the body of Christ in such a way that *they are meant to manifest and operate as the body of Christ expresses itself in any setting ... across the domains of society*. If God has created leadership in his "organization" in such a way that the operation of the APEST mechanisms is necessary to fully empower the collective and carry out the mission, then the possible correlation and/or conjunction of this with leadership in other arenas could prove to be a very fruitful conversation indeed.[17]

Businessman and consultant Walt Pilcher has applied the fivefold to great effect in the corporate world. He uses APEST as the primary grid for understanding and developing the various businesses he manages or consults with. In a somewhat more stylized way, Pilcher sees the following forms of leadership in a business or organization:

- The vision-caster, often the CEO, who faithfully keeps the organization focused on its mission (apostolic).
- People with foresight and a sense of timing to see opportunities, marketplace needs, and potential pitfalls; advise the leadership; analyze situations; call attention to problems; encourage and exhort; create and develop; such as marketing or financial managers and strategic planners (prophetic).
- People who win friends and create the means for growth, such as sales people, recruiters, marketers, and PR people who spread the good news about the company (evangelistic).
- People who have compassion for those struggling to find their place, such as HR people, coaches, ombudsmen, or even outplacement people (pastoral).
- People who understand the vision and can explain and translate it for others into practical action in each functional area, such as managers and trainers (teaching).[18]

In summarizing his "theory of the case" for why the Ephesians 4 model applies to all organizations,[19] he says the following:

1. God provided the fivefold ministry and the gifts to support it for the effective transformational leadership of the church, both the church

at large and the local church. To work best, it requires empowerment by the Holy Spirit.

2. The church and society (marketplace) are inseparable, and so the equipping of the saints (believers) is to better prepare them to serve in church and the marketplace so that their organizations are built up for the glory of God.

3. The Spirit is poured out on all flesh (Acts 2: 17–18) and is manifested in creativity, talents and aptitudes (gifts) of believers and non-believers alike.

4. The result, or fruit, of this pouring out will be more apparent or stronger in believers, who have the Spirit indwelling as well as having an "innate" (from having been born again) and cultivatable understanding of the purposes and power of the Holy Spirit and how to operate in the gifts, than in non-believers, who do not (John 14: 12–14).

5. The fivefold ministry model is therefore as applicable to non-church organizations (e.g., businesses, clubs, homeowners associations, committees), as it is to churches and para-church organizations.

6. Organizations applying the model, even if they are run by non-believers, will be more successful than organizations that do not apply the model, because it is God's model.

7. Organizations populated by believers applying the model will be much more successful than both non-believer organizations and believer organizations not applying the model because of their greater and potentially unlimited ability to operate in the power of the Holy Spirit (again, John 14: 12–14).

Whatever one thinks about the decidedly corporate and hierarchical conceptions of leadership implied in these statements, it's hard not to agree with the overall logic of his approach as well as the legitimacy of his experience. Understanding how each leadership type contributes to the health and productivity of the whole helps leaders to understand how to maximize the impact of the team, to develop each of its members, and to manage creative conflict.

As previously mentioned, the good folks at Five Capitals likewise use a well-articulated APEST typology to coach and mentor people in the business and not-for-profit world.[20] Similarly, GiANT Worldwide use the concept of Five Voices to shape leadership culture and develop organization,[21] and likewise, Lisa Slayton of the Pittsburgh Leadership Foundation uses the fivefold typologies throughout the organization she leads.[22] At the time of this writing, I am in conversation with the postgraduate leadership programs of at least two universities, concerning the translation of 5Q dynamics into the non-ecclesial world.

In regards to other forms of non-ecclesial applications of 5Q, I have had the privilege of working with a number of social activist movements including Momentum, Anyi, and The Center for the Working Poor.[23] Led by

Paul Engler and Carlos Saavedra, these are peak non-religious organizations and all are outstanding practitioners of non-violent movement dynamics.[24] They have a huge resonance with the sheer movemental power of 5Q. To my surprise, they even use the biblical terminology in a secular political activist organization. They have been systematically realigning their organizational systems around fivefold dynamics, from training to strategic development ... to great effect. Carlos, though not a disciple of Jesus, thinks the 5Q System is *the* perfect organizational model for their movement.

While I have limited the examples to the area of business and social movements, I believe that educational institutions like schools and universities, for instance, would benefit hugely from organizing (or developing curriculum) around fivefold domains and functions.

When I first saw the comprehensiveness of fivefold throughout the creation order, I found myself asking, "How did I not see this before?"

So bringing everything together so far, we can create a table and compare the various archetypes with their heroic expressions, the categories of intelligence associated with each, and various examples from life and story.

(See Table 4.1 overleaf)

Table 4.1 APEST in Archetype, Culture and Hero-Expression

APOSTLE

Archetypal APEST	Hero-Expression in General Culture	Categories of Intelligence	Domains of Society	Non-Christian Examples (in life and myth)
Founder, General, Agent-envoy, Visionary, Pioneer, Adventurer	Breakthrough designers, Innovator-entrepreneurs, Embodiments of purpose-mission, Paradigm shifters, Cultural architects, Organizational designers, Movement-makers, Systems thinkers, Business leaders, Problem-solvers, Imagineers, Start-ups	Systemic, Entrepreneurial, Adaptive, Synthetic Other characteristics include: Strategic, Holistic, Future-oriented (Promethean), Pattern-sensitive, Innovative, Adventurous, Ideational, Creative, Design-oriented	Business, Politics, Architecture, Law, Governance, Innovation and Entrepreneurship	Steve Jobs, Catherine Booth, Franklin Delano Roosevelt, Joan of Arc, Theodore Herzl, Angela Merkel, William Clark and Meriwether Lewis, George Washington, Karl Marx, Osama bin Laden, Adam Smith, Thomas Edison, Vladimir Lenin, Genghis Khan, Neo (*The Matrix*), Captain Jean-Luc Picard (*StarTrek*), Aragorn (*LOTR*), Jim Collins

PROPHET

Archetypal APEST	Hero-Expression in General Culture	Categories of Intelligence	Domains of Society	Non-Christian Examples (in life and myth)
Seer, Warrior, Poet, Reformer, Iconoclast, Meaning-maker	Artists, Poets, Shamans, Ethicists, Activists, Futurists, Liberators, Meaning-makers, Iconoclasts, Revolutionaries, Advocates, Existentialists, Anarchists, Hackers, Spiritualists, Mystics, Environmentalists, Whistle-blowers, Aid workers, Psychologists, Politicians, Feminists, Quality controllers	Ethical, Prefigurative, Motivational, Theological

Other characteristics include:

Artistic, Authentic, Loyalist, Spiritual, Future-present-oriented, Principled, Contrarian, Intuitive, Predictive, Aesthetic, Sympathetic, Passionate, Urgent, Synchronic (kairos), Critical | Arts, Psychology, Politics, Aid and development, NGOs, Ethics Environmentalism | Bono, Simone Weil, Malcolm X, Eleanor Roosevelt, Nikola Tesla, Mahatma Gandhi, John Lennon, Friedrich Nietzsche, Bob Dylan, Emmeline Pankhurst, Rumi, Salvador Dali, Pablo Picasso, Leonard Cohen, Aldous Huxley, Søren Kierkegaard, Doctors Without Borders, Gandalf (*LOTR*), Morpheus (*The Matrix*) |

EVANGELIST

Archetypal APEST	Hero-Expression in General Culture	Categories of Intelligence	Domains of Society	Non-Christian Examples (in life and myth)
Messenger, Achiever, Believer, Guerilla leader, Champion, Storyteller	Mobilizers, Recruiters, Negotiators, Preachers, Media workers, Achievers, Sales, Marketers, Organizers, Miracle-workers, Communicators, Raconteurs, Journalists, Motivational speakers, Networkers, Dealers, Buccaneers, Public relations	Communicational, Transactional, Narratival, Interpersonal Other characteristics include: Relational, Communicative, Existential, Emotional, Genuine, Inspirational, Optimistic, Historical	Media and communication, Charismatic leadership, Business, Politics, Advertising, Marketing	Seth Godin, Malcolm Gladwell, Oprah Winfrey, Bill Clinton, Tony Blair, Richard Branson, Tony Robbins, Zig Ziglar, Trinity (*The Matrix*), Zorro (*Zorro*), Katy Perry

SHEPHERD

Archetypal APEST	Hero-Expression in General Culture	Categories of Intelligence	Domains of Society	Non-Christian Examples (in life and myth)
Caregiver, Defender, Peacemaker, Helper, Servant, Selfless, Healer	Elders, Lovers, Police, Guardians, Loyalists, Humanizers, Parents, First responders, Cultivators, Mediators, Military, Counselors, Health workers, Priests, Community workers, Human resources	Social, Communal

Other characteristics include:

Empathetic, Relational, Familial, Sociable, Seek common good, Event-oriented, Engaging, Communal, Personal, Affectional, Protective | Medicine, Family, Psychology, Community development, Police, Defense | Nelson Mandela, Colin Powell, Mother Teresa, J. Edgar Hoover, Florence Nightingale, Dag Hammarskjöld, Aung San Suu Kyi, J.R.R. Tolkien, Malala Yousafzai, Chris Kyle (*American Sniper* is based on his story) |

TEACHER

Archetypal APEST	Hero-Expression in General Culture	Categories of Intelligence	Domains of Society	Non-Christian Examples (in life and myth)
Sage, Thinker, Observer, Philosopher, Guide, Scientist	Philosophers, Sages, Instructors, Ideologists, Investigators, Scientists, Information workers, Educationalists, Mentors, Thinkers, Disciplers, Theoreticians, Debaters, Engineers, Researchers, Theologians, Accountants, Forensics, Legal workers	Knowledgeable, Abstract, Instructive, Reflective **Other characteristics include:** Philosophical, Insightful, Analytical, Socratic, Forensic, Past-oriented, Interpretive, Historicist, Meaning-oriented, Critical, Diachronic	Education, Science, Philosophy, History, Publishing, Engineering	Socrates, Plato, Albert Einstein, Lao Tzu, Hannah Arendt, Julian Huxley, Abraham Heschel, David Attenborough, Helen Keller, Alain de Botton, Stephen Hawking, Yoda (from the *Star Wars* movies)

As has been stated, once we have a clear typology of the fivefold we can then use it as an interpretive key in order to discern motifs and themes that associate the different aspects of our nature with aspects of the fivefold. If APEST archetypes are mysteriously woven throughout human identity, organization, and culture in the form of common grace, then where exactly did they all come from? What are their roots? As we pursue answers to these questions, we will begin to recognize the divine source from where all 5Q scenius came from in the first place.

• The Metaphysics of APEST

We are now going to consider what I believe is the most significant aspect of the prehistory of the whole 5Q system ... that it is rooted in the very being of God himself! Even though this of course precedes the archetypes as they manifest in creation and history, I have left this section on the theology of APEST to the very end of this chapter mainly to serve as something of a climax to the backstory of 5Q. I feel this to be a great discovery. The reader should be immediately aware of the significance of this in giving 5Q a sense of symphony in the highest order. Here we will see how God himself informs and shapes all the expressions of APEST.

5Q Latent in the Image of God (Imago Dei)

The first clue to the divine origin of 5Q can be found in the first few chapters of Genesis. It has continued to intrigue us in that it enables us to gain insight into the archetypal aspects of what it means to be human, to be made in God's image, and to live in relation to God. Again, once we have a clear typology of the fivefold, we can use it as an interpretive lens in order to be able to discern motifs that associate with different aspects of our nature. Right at the roots of creation, we are told that men and women in their very being reflect aspects that are derived from their Maker and mirror something of his nature and character. The so-called *imago Dei* can be viewed using a 5Q lens to help us recognize that in some real but mysterious way APEST is derived from God himself. These are among others:

- **Relationality:** The desire to "know and be known" reflects in some sense the inherent human desire for righteousness (right relationship), personal intimacy, and for covenantal relationship. Using APEST as a hermeneutical key we can say that this in some way reflects distinctly *prophetic* as well as *pastoral* concerns and motifs.

- **Agency:** Humanity is given the command to rule and subdue, exercising vice-regency (under God) over the domain of earth. This kingdom agency reflects *apostolic* and perhaps *evangelistic* concerns.

- **Rationality:** The human capacity for logic and reason has always been understood as part of the *imago Dei*. In relation to 5Q, it lends itself to the acquisition of wisdom associated with the concerns of the *teacher* and the systems awareness of the *apostle*.

- **Creativity:** Our ability to reflect God's good creation in our actions can serve all the fivefold functions equally, but might express itself more fully in the more entrepreneurial and innovative instincts of the *apostolic* and *evangelistic*.

- **Responsibility:** This involves the inner capacity to choose between good from evil, to obey or disobey, and comes with the related ability to make right judgments and choices. This likely energizes *prophetic* and *educative* (teacher) capacities within the fivefold.

- **Language and communication:** This is important throughout, but *apostles, teachers,* and *shepherds* are likely to be especially attentive to communication and community.

It's important to note here that all humans have all these dimensions as part of their nature as image bearers.[25] While these are markers of universal human nature, not all people express these in the same proportion and measure; some aspects are highlighted in some in a way that is not in others. But all have the latent potential of relationality, rationality, language, morality, agency, etc.

5Q with a Christological Twist

The case for a legitimate systematic theology organized around 5Q becomes unavoidable when we consider that Jesus—who the Scriptures assert is the very image of the invisible God (Colossians 1:15) and the pure reflection of his nature (Hebrews 1:1–3)—actually redeems and blesses the fivefold through his incarnation, death, and resurrection (more on this in the following chapters). Jesus as the Word of God (Logos) is the best statement of God we will ever have. And the historic faith asserts through the doctrine of the two natures (divine/human) of Christ that whatever happens to Jesus happens to, and inside of, God, because they are one in essence.[26] By virtue of his two natures, Jesus makes the necessary connections and therefore provides the theological center of meaning to the people who follow in his Way.

We also affirm Jesus is the most definitive revelation of God given to humankind. As God's self-revelation then, Jesus forever defines what we understand to be true of God. It is Jesus who gives us the eyes to behold God's gracious hand in all his works. We understand that everything, including 5Q, is transformed in Christ into its true wonder and re-established to its true purpose.[27]

If this is so, then Jesus' particular expression/formulation of the fivefold—what I have called J-APEST—represents, and in some way mirrors, the nature and purposes of God. If the fivefold types are indeed represented and embodied in Jesus, then it is inevitable that it is also a reality rooted in God, for they are one. Why would we be surprised that APEST indeed is grounded in God? ... Jesus *is* God.

Pondering the mysteries of God's work in the world, Paul declares, "For from him and through him and for him are all things. To him be the glory forever!" (Romans 11:36). All things are derived from God and lead toward the triune God. More particularly, God as revealed in Jesus is the ultimate source (Colossians 1:15–20), as well as the ultimate purpose (*telos*) of all creation (Ephesians 1:18–23), including of course the various archetypes and domains.

The revolutionary claim here is that the APEST archetypes, forms, patterns and purposes are sourced in nothing less than the very being of the Father himself and expressed in the life and ministry of God's Son and communicated in the Spirit. As far as I am aware, no one has made this claim before, and so I submit it tentatively and humbly, but I think the theological logic is completely consistent with an orthodox understanding of the doctrine of creation and redemption in and through Christ.

5Q as Common Grace

Consider the following: Throughout our history, Christians have over-whelmingly believed that creation in some way, albeit fallen, bears the fingerprints and the traces of God.[28] Why does looking (and really seeing) a flower remind us of God? It is because a flower does contain, and witness to, the Creator's glory and making. Theophany happens in all arenas of life and not just in beauty but even in the cruelest of suffering. All creation bears some analogy to God (*analogia entis*). I have already made reference to the doctrine of *vestigia Dei* but it is well worth repeating in this context. The roots of this doctrine are found in the many biblical references to God's ongoing purposes and relation to his creation. It was first developed by Augustine, developed by Thomas Aquinas, and is now assumed to be part of the Christian understanding of the world. It teaches that the world having been made by God bears deep within its nature, structures, and its very being, the ongoing "traces of the Creator"—"God's fingerprints" pressed into nature and evident in human nature and history. Furthermore, not only do these vestiges exist, but they are available to us through reasoned investigation and reflection.

The Bible is full of metaphors of creation that somehow reflect our ongoing relationship to God (e.g., Psalm 19; Romans 8; Jesus' parables). The historic faith believes that God as Creator still continues to uphold his creation. Creation is continually dependent on him and reflects his ongoing work in his world (Hebrews 1:2–3).[29]

> The greatness and abundance and generosity of God are evident in his work: "The heavens are telling the glory of God; and the firmament proclaims his handiwork" (Ps. 19:1). Therefore, even though creation provides the stage rather than the plot for the

divine plan, creation has its own power of testimony. Guided by revelation, we can read nature as preaching many truths that scripture teaches ... Creation does not teach us the good news of God's offer of fellowship with him, but the patterns of nature provide apt reminders and powerful symbols of the purposes of God revealed in the calling of Abraham, the giving of the law on Mount Sinai, and the life, death, and resurrection of Christ.[30]

C.S. Lewis likewise believed that God is there in the creative processes that go on all the time. In his book *Miracles,* he points out that in the feeding of the five thousand and in the turning of water into wine, Jesus was just doing what God does all the time. In every vineyard, God turns water into wine. In every ocean, lake, and river God multiplies the fishes. In every grain field, God multiplies the loaves. Jesus was just doing a shortcut past the natural process, doing what God always does but in a sharply pointed way, illustrating Jesus' own deity and ongoing involvement in the everyday. The whole world is in his hands and bears his imprints and ongoing activity.[31]

Recognizing that we have to be very humble when working from analogy, I do believe we can use APEST in the broadest way possible—as a hermeneutical key—to try to ground it in aspects of who God has revealed himself to be. I tentatively suggest that one can trace direct lines from the fivefold functions *given* to the church by Jesus, back through the created archetypes, through the *imago Dei,* and from there find their origin and source in aspects of God.

Or to reverse the order: we can see APEST flowing from God into creation, its source in the being of God; 5Q is then expressed in shadow form in the archetypes as strands which are in turn woven together by Jesus into the very fabric of cultural and spiritual life of the church, and from there to the lives of all of his people in every sphere and domain of society. In other words, we can say that because they are rooted in the being of God, the fivefold archetypes evident throughout creation and history have ontological weight. I suggest therefore, that in 5Q, we not only have a rough outline of a new way of systemizing theology, we have the rudiments of a metaphysics of APEST. This is a big development, Padawan, because once APEST is connected to God in this way, we are dealing with truly primordial forces at work in our world.

God is ...

Using 5Q as an interpretive lens then, we can say that we can find the roots of APEST in various dimensions of God's nature. Consider the following ...

The roots of the **apostolic** are grounded in the fact that God is:

- the source of all things—the origin and fount of all existence
- designer, creator, and foundation of all
- the sent and sending God

- the source of pure will and purpose—and therefore the source of meaning
- the electing and predestining God—he works all things for good
- sovereign King over all creation
- the judge—he measures all and judges justly

The roots of the **prophetic** are grounded in the fact that God is:

- faithful—his word and nature are utterly true and dependable
- revealer—God always takes the initiative in communicating
- holy—pure and transcendent (wholly other)
- personal—pure relationship to be understood in terms of I and Thou
- passionate—God does experience holy love and anger
- covenantally related to his creatures—God is loyal and binds himself in relationship
- the source of meaning—the ultimate meaning of the world is found in the purposes of God
- omnipotent—he is powerful beyond measure
- worthy—of true worship
- transcendent Spirit—while he is immanent within creation, creation cannot be identified with him

The roots of the **evangelistic** are grounded in the fact that God is:

- savior and redeemer—he seeks out and saves that which is lost
- gracious—the source of mercy and all gifts
- abundant—his divine love flows out of his infinite abundance
- the source of true joy—rejoices in himself
- pure relation—he invites his creation into relationship
- lover and elector —he pursues his people and purposes
- sent—in himself, Jesus Christ, and the Spirit

The roots of the **shepherding** are grounded in the fact that God is:

- trinity—he exists in community-in-relationship (perichoresis)
- fully present in all things (divine immediacy)
- comforter—he has compassion and concerns himself with his creation
- known in intimacy—he knows (*yada*) us and likewise is known in immediacy
- righteous—he is in himself perfectly ordered and rightly related
- merciful and forgiving—it is his nature to be merciful
- love—and the ultimate lover
- family—he is the divine parent; we are his children
- shepherd—he reveals himself as a shepherd (Psalm 23, Psalm 80:1, Genesis 49:24)

The roots of **teaching** are grounded in the fact that God is:

- all-knowing—nothing is not known by him
- logos (Word)—and the source of reason in human beings
- glorious—he manifests himself in all things
- prescient—he has direct knowledge and foreknowledge of all things
- good and beautiful—and the source of all truth and beauty
- whole and complete in himself—his "system" is perfectly and ecologically balanced
- wise—he is the source of all wisdom and understanding

If we were to really index the fundamental qualities of the fivefold types with essences in the revelation of the Godhead, I would humbly suggest that:

- the **apostolic** best represents and expresses the *eternal purposes (sentness-missio) of God*
- the **prophetic** best represents and expresses the *holy covenantal heart of God*
- the **evangelistic** best represents and expresses the *saving mercy of God*
- the **shepherding** best represents and expresses the *loving communal embrace of God*
- the **teaching** function best represents and expresses the *infinite truth and wisdom of God*

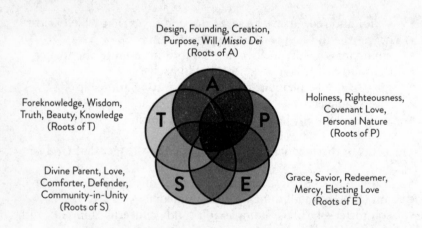

Figure 4.5 Theological Roots of the Fivefold in God

Now try imagining the sheer spiritual power that exists in the epicenter of the various circles above. There is a lot of spiritual power in 5Q theology. Here indeed are the divine roots of fivefold scenius—a part of God's nature and genius embedded into the whole world and expressing itself throughout.

I've tried to maintain soft eyes here and not to be forceful with the categorization. From what I can see, there is not a lot missing here from what is included in our more traditional ways of understanding the doctrine of God. This is just a different way of *organizing* and categorizing the same theology. If we consider 5Q as system, then we can acknowledge that the roots of APEST are ...

- grounded in God himself (*Theology*)
- laced by God throughout his creation (*Cosmology*)
- incorporated fully by Jesus into his perfect life (*Christology*)
- made real in and through the life of God's people (*Ecclesiology*)
- activated through the work of the Spirit (*Pneumatology*)
- fulfilled in God's eternal purposes through his *ecclesia* (*Missiology and Eschatology*)

This idea of having a "systematic theology" of APEST has far-reaching implications for how we understand and apply the fivefold categories. Grounded in God, laced into creation, redeemed by Jesus, granted to the church, lived out in the lives of its saints, to the glory of God—here we have a "system" that goes as deep as it does wide. The meta-idea that I talked about in chapter two just gained a whole lot more theological validity than we ever thought possible.

Viewed in this way, the theological significance is very hard to avoid indeed.

Conclusion

The aim of this chapter was simply to make a case for seeing APEST as an intrinsic part of God's original creation order, laced throughout society, and embodied by various people who function as exemplars and heroes to the society in which they live. APEST forms part of what the Bible means by *archons*: concentrations of power, core ideas, and cultural forces that are latent within culture and exert an abiding influence over the course of human affairs. Though damaged by the Fall, these archetypes continue to exercise significant sway over cultures and individuals in every time and place.

We now move from these more *generic* and universal understandings of APEST to see how they are perfectly embodied and exemplified in the particular life and ministry of Jesus. We will see how J-APEST encapsulates the multifaceted dimensions of his person and work in a way that is as profound and holistic as it is simple and elegant. In the chapter following the next, we see how APEST is then *given* (bequeathed as ascension gifting) to the *ecclesia*—the Body of Christ. These Body gifts are much more Christologically-nuanced than the more general creational archetypes because they are always expressions of the active ministry of Christ through the Body of Christ.

Onward to Jesus ...

Chapter 5

The Hero's Journey: The Movement that Jesus Started

If you want to know who God is, look at Jesus. If you want to know what it means to be human, look at Jesus. If you want to know what love is, look at Jesus. If you want to know what grief is, look at Jesus. And go on looking until you're not just a spectator, but you're actually part of the drama which has him as the central character.

—N. T. Wright

Our heroes carry our aspirations, our ideals, our hopes, our beliefs ... This is what makes heroism so important: it reflects our own sense of identity, our combined emotions, our myths.

—Rollo May

Since man could not come to God, God has come to man, identifying himself with man in the most direct way. The eternal Logos and Son of God, the second person of the Trinity, has become true man, one of us; he has healed and restored our humanity by taking the whole of it into himself.

—Kallistos Ware

Not surprisingly, an exploration of archetypes in human society is similar to the idea that myths are foundational to both personal and group identity. Joseph Campbell has aptly demonstrated the ongoing power of primary myths (defining narratives) throughout human history. For my purposes, I just want to highlight a particular aspect of myth and relate it to the role of Jesus, and this is what Campbell called "the mono-myth" or "the hero's journey." Heroes are persons, alive or dead, real or imaginary, who possess characteristics that are highly prized in a culture and thus serve as models for behavior.

According to Campbell and others (e.g., C.S. Lewis, J.R.R. Tolkien, C. Vogler), the hero's journey has a definite pattern and mythic structure. These are easily discernable in Tolkien's *The Lord of the Rings* and in Lewis' *The Chronicles of Narnia*, but actually form the structure of all myth and great story.[1] Once you know what to look for, the pattern is universally evident. In fact, according to Campbell, the hero's journey can be broken down into three sections with various sub-stages in each section. These are: *Quest* (or Departure), *Ordeal*, and *Return*. The Quest includes the hero being summonsed and sent, venturing forth on the journey. The Ordeal comprises the hero's initiation, wounding, battles, setbacks, and various adventures along the way, and the Return encompasses the hero's return home with the elixir of life—the special knowledge and powers acquired on the journey.[2] Campbell described it this way:

> A hero ventures forth from the world of common day into a region of supernatural wonder: fabulous forces are there encountered and a decisive victory is won: the hero comes back from this mysterious adventure with the power to bestow boons on his fellow man.[3]

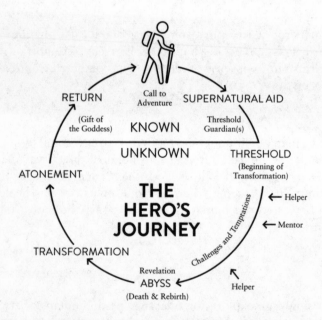

Figure 5.1 Joseph Campbell's Monomyth[4]

This story is as ancient as time itself, and it carries huge significance for every culture everywhere. If you think about this in terms of your favorite action movie for instance, you will be able to discern all the stages in the hero's journey, from *The Bourne Identity* to *The Matrix* and anything in-between. In many ways, myth is the Story behind and within all stories. And it permeates history, religion, and culture. As Balthasar said:

> Divine grace ... is secretly at work in the whole sphere of history, and thus all myths, philosophies, and poetic creations are innately capable of housing within themselves an intimation of divine glory.[5]

Paul, particularly in his apostolic-missionary function, is fully attuned to the underlying religious significance of ancient pagan religious myth as a rich metaphor for Christ's death and resurrection. For instance, in Acts 17:16–34 (esp. v. 23) he is in all likelihood referring to some myth of a dying and rising God, probably the god Ceres. Ceres (from where we get our word "cereal") was the Corn King that was believed to die and rise again with every new season. Paul uses the internal logic of the narrative to make a direct appeal for the parallel in the Jesus story. This is because of the abiding value of monomyth as a metaphor for the gospel. Listen to the master storyteller C.S. Lewis here:

> In theology as in science, myth supplies not answers but an experience of a larger existence than we can know cognitively. Such an experience touches depths the intellect cannot reach and conveys, to children and adults alike, the sense that this is not just true, but Truth.[6]

J.R.R. Tolkien once suggested to C.S. Lewis that the gospel sounded like a reframing of the Corn King myth because *Christ was a myth that had become fact*.[7] Christ lived (and so fulfilled) the myth that was already hidden in culture. Or, as Lewis scholar Louis Marcos says:

> Perhaps the reason that every ancient culture yearned for a god to come to earth, to die, and to rise again was because the Creator who made all the nations placed in every person a desire for this very thing.[8]

And, if that is the case, then does it not make sense that when God enacted his salvation in the world through Jesus, he did it in a way that deeply resonated with the desire that he put in all people?[9]

Once we have acknowledged this archetypal pattern of myth, it's not hard to see the hero's journey pattern fitting the characteristic pattern of Jesus' story—Jesus is sent on a mission, embodying the APEST identities; Jesus labors and suffers for the cause and gains a devoted following; Jesus overcomes and achieves victory; Jesus bestows the blessing of the fivefold (see Figure 5.2). In a word, Jesus is our true "hero" and serves as the primary Christian prototype ... the heroic form, perfected man in whose image we are being remade (2 Corinthians 3:18).

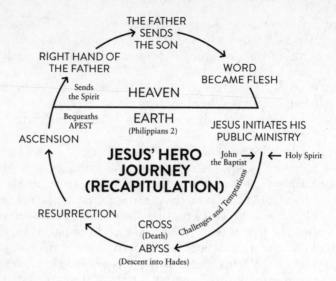

Figure 5.2 Jesus' Hero Journey

• Jesus as Triumphant King

Having identified and clarified the idea of creational archetypes of APEST, as well as the stages of the hero's journey, we are now in a position to better grasp the meaning of what has been called the "ascension gifting" described by Paul in Ephesians 4:8–11.[10] But to understand the ascension gifting properly, we need to grasp the cultural reference of the victor's parade and then consider how exactly it is that Jesus perfects and redeems the fallen archetypes in order to bequeath them to his people.

Scholars universally acknowledge that the imagery in Ephesians 4:8–10 is drawn from recognizable public ritual/events in the life of the various city-states of the Roman Empire existing around the time when the New Testament was written. So when a ruler or a general who went forth on a mission (cf. Quest) to conquer or defeat an enemy returned in triumph to his home city (cf. Return), the public were all invited to attend the victor's parade in celebration of the triumph. As the ritual precursor to a big party, the victorious champion would display the various spoils of war (of treasure and slaves) as part of the victory parade. But what made these parades extremely popular events is that the victor would also generously distribute much of the bounty with the public. The various "triumphal arches" in the cities throughout the world have their roots in this enduring cultural practice.

This archetypal pattern provides Paul with exactly the image that he needs to make sense of the so-called ascension gifting. In this passage, Jesus is portrayed as "descending" into the world; he is victorious and "takes captivity captive" and subsequently in his "ascension" leads the victory parade and bestows the boon on his people. The metaphor describes our victorious Lord who, having plundered the enemy, quashed the rebellion and disarmed the vanquished powers, so brings peace and salvation to broken humanity (cf. Colossians 2:15).

What is intriguing and revelatory in this case is *what* is retrieved from the vanquished rebellion and bequeathed to the citizens of Jesus' kingdom. The context requires that we see that Jesus actually takes the unredeemed APEST archetypes from the created order and redeems and remodels them in the image of his own humanity. It is these now recapitulated "victory gifts" that he subsequently bestows on the *ecclesia* (church) as its permanent possession—like the triumphal arches, the living testament of his victory.[11]

The mere fact that Paul attaches his teaching on APEST to the highly significant event of the ascension of Christ already gives it substantial theological weight. The Ascension is no everyday event; it is a vital aspect of Jesus' resurrection, involving his return to his Father, the sending of the Spirit, and his ongoing role as King and Judge, and of course his commissioning and constituting of his church:

> Therefore there can be no other basis for Christian discipleship and ministry than the resurrection for it is none less that the ascending and exalted Head of the Church and of mankind who distributes the charisms [gifts] and missions of discipleship (Ephesians. 4:7–11).[12]

• Reconfiguring the System

Having recognized the hero's journey in the sending, the descent, and the ascent of Jesus, we are now in a better position to understand exactly *how* Jesus redeems the archetypes and gifts them to the church. And here we are well-equipped by an ancient New Testament teaching on the meaning of Jesus' incarnation, life, death, and resurrection, called *anakephalaiosis* (Greek) or *recapitulation* (Latin) theory.[13] Although the term is derived from the New Testament itself, it was Irenaeus and the early church fathers who actually further developed the doctrine. Recapitulation teaches that Christ is the new representative man who, as the second Adam, succeeds where the first Adam failed.

One of the main New Testament Scriptures upon which this insight is based is in Ephesians 1:10 where Paul says,

> [God's purpose is, in] the fullness of the times, that is, the summing up [Gk. *Anakephalaiosis*, literally *"to restore in the new head"*] of all things in Christ, things in the heavens, and things on the earth.
>
> *Ephesians 1:10 (NASB)*

In Colossians 1:15–23 Paul further formulates the gospel in terms of recapitulation/reconstituting all things through his death on the cross. And very significantly, in Romans 5, Paul states that the work of Christ as the Second Adam reinstates his lordship over a fallen creation by living a fully human and obedient life. As we can see from these important texts, recapitulation is seen to be an inextricable part of the gospel itself.[14] Stanley Hauerwas (referencing Yoder) observes:

> The confession that the Messiah has been placed by God above and not within the cosmology and culture of the world means that under his lordship the cosmos finds its true meaning and coherence. In Colossians the powers are rightly understood to be not merely defeated but reenlisted in their original purpose to praise God.[15]

In Jesus, the rationality of the world and of history is dethroned and put to work in advancing his work through the church.

Through man's original and ongoing disobedience, the evolution of the human race has gone terribly awry, and the course of its wrongness could neither be halted nor reversed by any human means. But Jesus Christ, the true human being, perfectly carried out and realized in obedience the purposes of God. Jesus thus *consecrates* human history and culture in his own authentic living of it on behalf of the fallen race.[16] Playing on the word "recap" (as in recapitulation), theologian Peter Leithart calls Jesus:

> the Father's "summary statement" ... the Logos of the Father—*the logic or purpose in and through which the whole divine economy is conceived and implemented* [italics mine].[17]

Similarly, N.T. Wright, following Irenaeus, reads Christ's work of redemption in terms of what he calls *reconstitution;* meaning that Christ acts in a representative fashion to reconstitute the nation/people of God.[18] Humanity is perfectly restored and history effectively "rebooted" in Christ. And this, grasshopper, gets us to the very core of the teaching on recapitulation.

Now back to the significance of all this to 5Q; apply Jesus' recapitulation specifically to the fivefold archetypes. Along with all other varied dimensions of humanity, the fivefold APEST archetypes existing in fallen humanity are taken up into the very person of Christ and are thereby redeemed and reconfigured in and through his perfect life and his holy offering on the cross! APEST is hereby verified, reformulated, and elevated by Jesus. In the act of recapitulation itself, in becoming the Second Adam, Paul teaches us that Jesus becomes the new *Head* (Gk *kephale*, Lat. *caput*) of the human race and is explicitly called the Head of his Body, the church (Ephesians 4:15).[19]

We can say therefore that Ephesians 4:8–11 teaches that Jesus takes the pre-existing fivefold archetypes and (along with all the various other orders of creation) recapitulates them in true obedience to God. In so doing, Jesus gives APEST its most definitive and exemplary expression.[20] In other words, Jesus embodies APEST in a way that God originally intended, thereby sanctifying/reconsecrating the fallen archetypes. Having done this in his incarnation and cross, he then "gifts" them (Ephesians 4:7) to the Body of

Christ, where they are embedded into the very genetics of the church and subsequently lived out in different individuals in different times and places as their unique callings.

Jesus Offers the World Back to the Father

One might even say that if, in the logic of monotheism, worship is essentially *offering the world back to God,* then we can view recapitulation as the *way* in which Jesus takes all humanity—including the fivefold archetypes— reconsecrates it and then offers it all as worship to God. The church is the central part of the offering that Jesus the High Priest makes to the Father! Jesus worships the Father through the ongoing redemptive ministry of the Body of Christ, whose very purpose is to extend his mission in the world (cf. Ephesians 1:22–23, 1 Corinthians 15:21–28).[21]

And so we have traced the implications of Jesus' hero journey in the form of his incarnation; his exemplary life; his suffering; his redemptive work on our behalf; his ascension and subsequent return to the Father, for the benefit of humanity. We affirm that by ascending to the Father he bequeaths the now reconstituted APEST archetypes to the community that is called to be his embodiment in the world. We now have all that we need, to do what he has intended ... we are perfectly equipped. It remains for us to remember the enormity of the graces we have been given and live into his purposes in and through us.

Note that 5Q is somehow involved at every point of this whole schema, but is meant to be the treasure of the church who are the people indelibly marked by the person and the way of Jesus. If we break up, or bypass, or purge elements of the fivefold, we mess with the constituting design of the church and introduce a fatal flaw into the life and the capacities of the Body of Christ.

And so now we turn to the implications of J-APEST for the Body of Christ.

Chapter 6

Embodiment:
The Fivefold Modes of
Jesus' Presence in the Church

In the past God spoke to our ancestors through the prophets at many times and in various ways, but in these last days he has spoken to us by his Son, whom he appointed heir of all things, and through whom also he made the universe. The Son is the radiance of God's glory and the exact representation of his being, sustaining all things by his powerful word.

—Hebrews 1:1—3

The church is empowered by a certain communion with Christ which allows some measure of his perfected spirituality and destiny to be repeated or re-enacted in our lives.

—George Hunsinger

This distribution of royal gifts and ministries [APEST] is not a substitute for the Messiah's presence but the mode of his being present.

—Markus Barth

Thus far we have been focusing on one aspect of the work of Jesus in establishing and equipping his people for their mission in the world. We have seen how Paul's teaching on recapitulation (*anakephalaiosis*) helps us understand how it is that Jesus establishes the fivefold at the very core of the church's purpose. But still more must be said about the defining role of Jesus in the *ecclesia*. We look to Jesus to find out who we are and what we are called to do. The church's very existence, identity, purposes, and function are all inextricably bound up with who Jesus is and what he has done.

Bonhoeffer rightly reminds those that claim Jesus' name that:

> Action in accord with Christ does not originate in some ethical principle, but in the very person of Jesus Christ. This is because everything real is summed up in Christ, who, by definition, is the origin of any and all action that is in accord with reality.[1]

New Testament faith is directly related to the unfolding purposes in Christ—Head and Body:

> The work of the Holy Spirit in making that inner life of faith "living and personal" has to do not with an abstract truth but with the "personal truth of God made flesh in Jesus Christ" and this must include a reception of all that Jesus gives to his people in the form of his gifts.[2]

Jesus *is* God's agenda for the church and for the world. Jesus reconstitutes the world in his perfectly lived life and the result is his church. The church is meant to be humanity as God intended it to be—a humanity modeled completely on the pattern of Jesus. As the people forever defined by Jesus, it behooves us to continually realign ourselves with our Founder, Lord and Redeemer.[3] So let's look at Jesus again and reaffirm the centrality of his presence among his people.

• Jesus is the Agenda of the Church

Apart from simply affirming what Christians have always believed about Jesus (that although he is eternal God, he was enfleshed in human form; and that he lived a perfect and exemplary life; that he died to redeem a lost and broken world; that he was vindicated by God in his bodily resurrection; that he has ascended to effective lordship at the right hand of the Father; and that he will return to redeem his people), I simply want to highlight here those aspects of Christ's person and work (Christology) as they directly impinge upon his people ... the Body of Christ.

First, it is worth touching base with just one selection from Paul to get a feel for the New Testament vision of the absolute significance of Christ for the entire cosmos but also and perhaps especially for the church:[4]

> For he has rescued us from the dominion of darkness and brought us into the kingdom of the Son he loves, in whom we have redemption, the forgiveness of sins. The Son is the image of the invisible God, the firstborn over all creation. For in him all things were created: things in heaven and on earth, visible and invisible, whether thrones or powers or rulers or authorities; all things have been created through him and for him. He is before all things, and in him all things hold together. And he is the head of the body, the

church; he is the beginning and the firstborn from among the dead, so that in everything he might have the supremacy. For God was pleased to have all his fullness dwell in him, and through him to reconcile to himself all things, whether things on earth or things in heaven, by making peace through his blood, shed on the cross.

Colossians 1:13–20

Please take note, reader, because this is vital to understand how 5Q is central to the church's life and purposes. Firstborn … head … supremacy … all things—the language is comprehensive and symphonic. He brings all things together and gives them their true meaning. He is the Symphony of the Ages.

This is no reductionist, privatized, "Jesus-in-my-heart" type piety; here we are given a vision of the universal and cosmic significance of Jesus. Jesus is here worshipped as the organizing principle of the entire cosmos! He is also at the same time Head of his Body, the church. He so impresses himself on his Body that it is impossible to separate the two. The Jesus who rules the universe is Lord of the church. The church is not a mere historical effect of Christ; she is his "fullness" and his "Body." Therefore, to encounter Christ the Head, one will need also to encounter the Body of Christ—for they are indivisible.

The church is the one place on earth that Jesus is taken with the utmost seriousness. Why? Because it is in our relationship with Jesus that the very life, identity and purpose of the *ecclesia* is at stake. This is what I call Christ// Body of Christ—the belief that the Body is the immediate recipient, the living index, of the life and ministry of Jesus. Jesus the Messiah—everything about him, his person, and his work, *without reduction*—sets the primary template for the movement that claims his name.[5] Or as Stanley Hauerwas says, "the whole life of Jesus is to be understood as determinative for the whole life of the church."[6]

Furthermore, the church is the chosen instrument through which Christ may continue to work and to bear witness to himself. If the church is the primary agent of Jesus' kingdom, then every aspect of the culture of the church should reflect him in some way or another. In fact, one can perhaps say that the church is dysfunctional to the degree that it lacks focus on Jesus. I suggest that this lack of conformity to our Lord lies at the root of much of our malaise.

If we take the pattern/form of Jesus as determinative for every aspect of his Body, then it stands to reason that the life of his people must be directly formed around the life and teaching of Jesus. And it is this necessary correspondence between Jesus and his people that sets the primary template for the culture and expression of the church. He is the Archetype and we are to be the reflective image (e.g., Romans 8:29; 2 Corinthians 3:18) that are together and individually being *conformed* to his likeness.

If we can agree on this—and how could we who are called to be Christlike disagree?—then anything that is said hereafter about the relationship of Christ to the Body of Christ ought to make perfect sense.

In order to remain true to this unique calling, churches (and individual disciples as well) need to constantly undergo the process of returning to Jesus to assess whether we are faithful to him, whether we rightly express his person and extend his work.

> By the grace God has given me, I laid a foundation as a wise builder, and someone else is building on it. But each one should build with care. For no one can lay any foundation other than the one already laid, which is Jesus Christ.
>
> *1 Corinthians 3:10–11*

Or as George Beasley-Murray put it, "The apostles were commissioned to carry on Christ's work, and not to begin a new one."[7] This is as true for us as it was for the original apostles.

• The Five Identities/Purposes of Jesus

Having established the centrality of Jesus for the identity and purposes of his people, we are now ready to look at the actual ministry of Jesus through the prism of each of the APEST categories to see how he both fulfills and redefines them. Once we have identified 5Q as perfectly exemplified in the life and ministry of Jesus, we can then see how he grafts these into the foundations of the church. There is real value in seeing these as identities, or divine *personas*, which Jesus reconstitutes and bequeaths to his people.

There is much gained in seeing Jesus through the lens of the five identities.[8] The more facets we can view, the better we can grasp the unity and significance of the inspiration.[9]

Jesus is the Exemplary Apostle

It always amazes me how Christians have become not only alienated to the word-concept "apostle," but also have little understanding of what this signifies in both Jesus' ministry as well as that of his church.[10] The result of our failure to grapple with the meaning of the word means that we have largely failed to conceive of Jesus as the quintessential apostle, and yet this is precisely what he claimed to be on occasions too numerous to list.[11] And so we need to return to the basic definitions; the word *apostello* (and associated words) literally means "one who is sent" and basically refers to an empowered, ambassadorial agent[12] that acts on behalf of a sending ruler or king.[13] It carries with it a distinct mission,[14] an envoy sent with full legal permission[15] to act on behalf of the person who sends the apostle. Therefore, reception of the apostle is equivalent to reception of the authority (e.g., king, governor, owner-merchant) that sends him.[16]

Jesus certainly defined himself as God's empowered agent on a particular mission. In fact, nowhere is the central idea of "apostle" clearer than in

Jesus' defining statement of his mission. He experienced himself as *sent* (lit "apostello'd") by his Father to fulfill the eternal purposes of God, to be accomplished in his messianic vocation. He is the Son, the Messiah,[17] and as Lord of history he is God's sent one—his Kingdom agent/apostle. This apostolic dimension of Jesus' ministry therefore touches on the very purpose and mission of God in the world.

Jesus was sent to change the religious order thus far and to spark a movement of world redemption through his life and ministry (Matthew 11:11–15). He is the Founder-Leader of the people who claim his name. Toward the end of his ministry in Israel, he confers his own sentness upon the *ecclesia;* the movement is thus birthed through his apostolic ministry. The so-called Johannine Commission ("As the Father has sent me, I am sending you" John 20:21) is one of the definitively *apostolic* texts in the New Testament.

So now if we ask the question of whether or not Jesus was an apostle, actually the answer is a *no-brainer!* Of course he is! He is not only *an apostle*; he is by our confession the prototypical Apostle in all of God's purposes:

> Therefore, holy brothers and sisters, who share in the heavenly calling, fix your thoughts on Jesus, whom we acknowledge as our apostle and high priest.
>
> *Hebrews 3:1*

Jesus is the Exemplary Prophet

Walter Brueggemann, in his seminal book on the prophetic ministry is absolutely clear that Jesus is "the fulfillment and quintessence of the prophetic tradition."[18] It's hard to imagine anyone who would not be able to identify Jesus as a prophet ... in fact the quintessential one, who reveals himself as the Word of God.

The first words of Jesus' ministry relate to what is called the fullness of time; Jesus announces that in him, the time is fulfilled. It's God's now-time (*kairos*), and God's Kingdom is pressingly present in him (Mark 1:15). Jesus comes to break the power of human sin and demonic evil as well as to render justice and righteousness (Luke 4:14–20). Jesus brings God's judgment on the world and also at the same time is the new center of God's salvation (e.g., John 2:15, 5:22, 9:39; Acts 10:42, 17:31). As God's Son, he knows the Father's will and fulfills it entirely (John 5:19, 5:30, 12:49). The very covenant relationship between God and his people is being restated and reframed in Jesus (Matthew 5–7). He seals the New Covenant by his blood. Nothing less than repentance and faithfulness is required to enter into the God-relationship (Mark 1:15). People are called to hear and obey (e.g., his common refrain, "him who has ears to hear let him *shema* [hear-obey]," (Matthew 11:15; Luke 8:8; Revelation 13:9). In Jesus, the medium is the message. He is the Word of God in the flesh (John 1:1–14); the Faithful

One (Revelation 1:5); God's New Covenant, calling people to return to God, to live righteously (Hebrews 2–5) and render worship to God (Matthew 4:1–11). He is the perfectly obedient Son who renders perfect faithfulness (the Lamb of Revelation). He lives life in perfect union with the Father and the Spirit. He is the obedient Son of God and perfect Word of God. Is Jesus a prophet? *No-brainer!* He is God's prototypal example of what a true prophet is meant to be.

Jesus is the Exemplary Evangelist

We are not as familiar with naming Jesus as an evangelist as we are some of the other fivefold identities and functions. And yet once we state it, it becomes a glaringly obvious aspect of Jesus' ministry.

Portraying Jesus as the exemplary evangelist highlights his work of announcing and demonstrating the good news of the Kingdom. He does this in and through every aspect of his ministry. Jesus offers every person and community, everywhere, a valid opportunity to be directly challenged to a radical reorientation of their lives, a reorientation which involves both deliverance from slavery to the world and its powers, and embracing Christ as Savior and Lord (Luke 4:18, 4:43, 7:22, 16:16, 20:1).[19] Jesus is the "true Myth," the story fulfilled, and the deliverer.

Evangelistic motifs in Jesus' ministry are interwoven throughout what we call the saving work of Jesus on our behalf. The death and resurrection of Jesus usher in a new era of salvation. If his dying on behalf of the lost human race highlights the distinctly priestly (substitutionary and mediatory) aspects of Jesus' work on our behalf, the Resurrection highlights the evangelistic (proclamatory) dimension of salvation as good news for the whole world.

But it is in the actual life and teachings of Jesus himself that we get the clearest revelation of his calling by God as the Evangelist. Throughout the whole chapter of Luke 15, Jesus makes what must surely be the definitive case for the meaning of his own evangelistic ministry: He speaks of ardently searching for a lost coin, of leaving 99 sheep to go find and save the one straying sheep. The chapter ends with that most memorable of good news passages in the humble return of the prodigal to his loving father's welcoming embrace—an embrace which ends with a party, the most proclamatory of social events.

Perhaps the clearest we get to Jesus declaring a personal "mission statement" is in Luke 19:9–10, where Jesus responds to Zacchaeus, declaring that "today salvation has come to this house, because this man, too, is a son of Abraham. *For the Son of Man came to seek and to save the lost*" (italics mine).[20]

The strongest way we must affirm the primal calling of Jesus-the-Evangelist is to simply reaffirm what Christians have always affirmed—that Jesus not only proclaims the evangel, he actually is the Evangel. Jesus is the good news (Ephesians 2:14), the Savior. Is Jesus an evangelist? *No-brainer*, of course! Jesus is *the* Evangelist that defines all evangelism.

Jesus is the Exemplary Shepherd

Imagery inspired by calling Jesus the Good Shepherd is well established in our churches, both historical and contemporary.[21] As one of the primary "I Am" passages of Jesus intertwined throughout John's Gospel (John 10:11), there could be little debate that it has profoundly impacted our understanding of both Jesus' ministry and ours in light of it.[22]

Jesus is our High Priest, the Chosen One who mediates God-knowledge and restores the broken relationship between God and the human race. He is the true Shepherd of Israel (2 Samuel 5:2) who rules his people as a protector and guide. He is both Healer (Luke 7:22) as well as Reconciler of a broken world (Ephesians 2:14; Hebrews 1–4). Jesus opens all to relationship with the Father and thus provides us entry into the family of God. He has great compassion on the broken and the excluded (Matthew 20:34; Luke 7:34). As the Suffering Servant, he identifies with the broken human race. As Good Shepherd, Jesus protects the weak and defends their cause (John 10). As the true human, Jesus reconciles people, redeems them, and creates a whole new community in himself—his *ecclesia* (Ephesians 2–3)—which he continues to care for, direct, and protect. He is the "Shepherd and Overseer of your souls" (1 Peter 2:25). He binds all who follow him to learn the love of God, in and through loving others, in the context of ordinary life lived as humble service and worship to God. But he is always *with* and *among* his people, guiding and protecting (Psalm 23; cf. Matthew 28:20).

Is Jesus a shepherd? *No-brainer!* As we have seen, he says so himself in no uncertain terms. But he also demonstrates, in an exemplary way, the true meaning of all pastoral calling.

Jesus is the Exemplary Teacher

Christianity has a long tradition of understanding Jesus as Rabbi, Guide and Teacher—so much so that it hardly needs any emphasizing at all. What we have not always fully understood, however, was the very particular "way" in which Jesus brings wisdom and understanding to his people. He is not some detached lecturer. He is himself "the Way," and he shows us what a lifestyle based on truth looks like (John 1:17, 14:6.) In Jesus, ethics *becomes* ethos—a way to live. He discipled his followers by actually living life with them—he was their Master and Rabbi, and they lived under his word and authority. He is the Word Made Flesh—both the Revealer and that which is revealed: God's Truth (John 1:1–14, 14:6, 17:25–26; Romans 16:26). He is the fulfillment of the Torah (Matthew 5:17). His authority is such that he can redefine the Torah itself (Matthew 5:21–22, 27–28, 33–34). Jesus is sent by the Father to show us a new way of being human (John 10:10). He is the Light of the world, and as such he ushers in the true knowledge of God (John 8:12, 12:26). Paul affirms that Jesus is the source of all true knowledge and wisdom when he prays for the new disciples of the early church, that they would "have the full riches of complete understanding, in order that they may know the mystery of God, namely, Christ, in whom are hidden all the treasures of wisdom and knowledge" (Colossians 2:2–3).

Drawing deeply from the teaching metaphor, it was John Stott who apparently noted that Jesus was at once the teacher, the classroom, and the curriculum. Is Jesus a teacher? *No-brainer!* Of course he is the Teacher; one by which all Christian teaching is measured.

J-APEST: The Onefold Medium of the Fivefold Message

It is actually very easy to affirm that indeed Jesus is the exemplar of each of the APEST ministries. In fact, his life would not be understandable without all five elements or motifs present. We can therefore say that in Jesus the medium is the message. He is the fullness of APEST in its perfected form. He is the perfect expression of the five key identities/personas. He embodies APEST culture fully and as such is the fractal in the system. This is not a forced reading and should not be hard for anyone to see.[23] The fivefold typology allows as to "see" the key motifs in the life and ministry of Jesus and enables us to emulate them in his church. Observe what happens when you bring them all together in a summary statement:

- As Messiah, Jesus both experienced (and proclaimed) himself as being sent into the world as the chosen messianic agent of God's eternal mission. He followed the path that the Father had set for him. He lived perfectly by the demanding dictates of the kingdom of God; he reframed the terms of reference by which God was to be experienced and accessed; he extended the boundaries of God's claim thereby initiating the worldwide messianic movement that was to become known as Christianity. *He is the great Apostle.*

- Jesus was fiercely and uncompromisingly prophetic. Almost everything he said was tinged with the deep spiritual pathos related to covenantal concern with faithfulness to God. He unremittingly exposed the fundamental breakdown of covenant obligations of God's chosen people; he named injustice and railed against unrighteousness; he exposed the ungodly toxicity in misguided religion. He cast out demons, spoke truth to power, confronted evil and unrighteousness. *He is God's perfect Prophet.*

- Jesus proclaimed good news for the poor, forgiveness for all sinners, and salvation for the lost. Signs and wonders confirmed his witness. He opened the doors to all those previously excluded through religion and politics. The masses experienced him as genuine good news. Ultimately, he paid for this redemption with the sacrifice of his very life. *He is the greatest Evangelist ever.*

- He worked to include the previously excluded people into the covenant community and in so doing creates a new family, one not exclusive to Israel but open to all who love Jesus. Everything about him radiated concern for people and for the establishment of true human community and relationships. His healings and his miracles demonstrated God's grace, mercy, and concern. They were prefigurations of the heavenly union. *He is the perfect expression of the Shepherd, the Lover of his people.*

- He taught people wherever and whenever he could. He chose, instructed, and guided disciples (at various levels of intensity), teaching them his Way and the ways of the God of Israel. He actually recast the Torah by fulfilling it. His teachings were eloquent simplicity-beyond-complexity and were therefore accessible by the simplest and the wisest alike. The medium of his life was its message: the Truth and Light. *He is the greatest Teacher ever.*

At this point I want to point the reader to the rationale of 5Q and why Jesus—and specifically J-APEST, the Jesus-shaped expression of APEST—is actually the key to seeing the system. Remember in chapter two, I noted that using Ephesians 4:1–16 as an interpretive lens (a hermeneutical key) enables us to see what was already present in the revelation of Scripture but which we were previously unable to see because we lacked the perceptual categories to be able to understand what it was that we were seeing. Well, having noted how Jesus reconstitutes the APEST archetypes through his perfect life; and having observed how it is that he perfectly embodies these identities/purposes and provides us with the exemplary definitions and meanings of APEST, we are now ready to see how Jesus is related to 5Q and how this impacts us all as his chosen people ... the Body of Christ. Consider the following diagram:

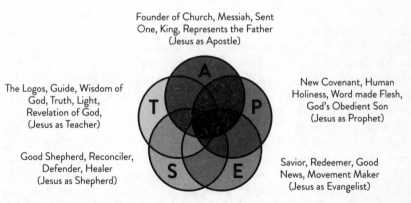

Figure 6.1 J-APEST: The Jesus-Shaped Expression of APEST

Jesus cannot be understood apart from all fivefold identities. Clearly all five APEST motifs are unmistakably present in Jesus' life and together comprise his ministry. Think of them as the constellation of Christological identities and purposes that come together in Jesus. Not surprisingly, then, the New Testament gospel clearly has all these motifs in them—mission/

purpose, the prophetic call to repentance and relationship, the proclamation of good news of salvation, adoption into God's family, and direct access to the true knowledge of God. But they are only in the church's core proclamation because they are first and foremost part of the very life, ministry, and teachings of our Founder and Lord.[24] 5Q is simply a way of indexing the manifestation of Jesus' presence in his people. Jesus is indeed the key unlocking the power of 5Q because he is its defining Center.

• Bringing the Head and the Body into Alignment

I will make a case in the rest of the book as to why the 5Q system is a key to renewal of our ministry and suggest ways on how to code it deeply into your church or organization. But here I simply want to embed the all-important idea that Christian ministry is based on, and derives its authority and authenticity from, its foundation in Jesus Christ. Note that this is going to sound mystical because in fact it is mystical. So follow closely, *Padawan*.

The church then is not only God's redeemed people, but they are that human agency by which Jesus extends his own ministry into the world. *The church carries out the work that Jesus started and it does it in a way that is consistent with who Jesus was and how he went about his own ministry*. And here we come to the great New Testament doctrine of the Body of Christ.

Nowhere is Jesus' connection to the church and its ministry more emphasized than in Paul's teaching about the Body of Christ. It is for this reason that we have to let this profound Pauline metaphor do its work and enrich our understanding of who we are and how we are to function in the world. The metaphor itself is a critical key to understanding the nature of the relationship between Christ and his people in general, but more particularly the Body metaphor helps us see how 5Q is embedded into the church's genetic code and how it should shape the resultant culture and activities in the community. We must grapple with the implications of this phrase, the Body of Christ, live into it, and let it do its work to make us more responsive to our Lord.

Perhaps the first way we can get a sense of the enduring connection between Christ and the Body of Christ is to link the words Christ//Body of Christ, Messiah//Messianic, and Christ//Christian. Look at how the words naturally respond to each other. It is this indissoluble association of the one with the other that the metaphor "Body of Christ" is meant to confer.[25] Balthasar rightly notes that while the church is not Christ, she can claim for herself and for the world no other pattern than the pattern of Christ, which leaves its stamp in her and shapes her through and through.[26]

Secondly, note the direct associations of the language itself (the *Body* of Christ) with the theology of the Incarnation: In the Incarnation, God's Word became flesh ... it was embodied. Dietrich Bonhoeffer rightly understood the incarnational aspect when he said that the church is "the form of Christ in the world."[27] Jesus himself is thus indelibly imprinted upon the whole people of God. Jesus fleshed out what God is like; now it is our responsibility to flesh out what Jesus is like. We must not try dodging the very concrete implications of the imagery; we do not merely represent Jesus—in some real way we are meant to actually *embody/incarnate* him.

So vital is the connection with Christ and his Body that we can say the church itself—not any particular church sacrament or ritual, but rather the concrete and collective body of people that comprise the *ecclesia*—is the real presence of Christ in the world.[28] This people is therefore a totality which carries Christ through the ages and in so doing makes Jesus present in the world. Applied to fivefold-thinking we can say that 5Q is essentially a living sign of the dynamic activity of Jesus in and through his people.

The church is empowered "by a certain communion with Christ which allows some measure of his perfected spirituality and destiny to be repeated or re-enacted in our lives."[29] So much so that we can legitimately say that if Jesus is the incarnation of God, then the church (individually and corporately) must in turn be particular and local incarnations of Jesus.[30] Augustine is ascribed as saying that, "A Christian is: a mind through which Christ thinks, a heart through which Christ loves, a voice through which Christ speaks, and a hand through which Christ helps." This is as true corporately as it is individually. The miracle is that he actually chooses to abide with/in any particular people.

Thirdly, note that the Body belongs to Jesus Christ. He is its Head/Source and stamps it with his personality and character. The Body of Christ is "the complement of Christ; that which completes Him; which fills up by its activities the work which His withdrawal to heaven would have left undone, as the body completes the head."[31] Jesus Christ continues to be Head of the Body of Christ. According to Frank Viola, there are five abiding aspects related to the idea of Christ's headship:[32]

1. As the head, Jesus seeks to express his character and nature through his body.
2. As the head, Jesus continues his earthly ministry.
3. As the head, Jesus directs both the church and the work.
4. As the head, Jesus nourishes his body.
5. As the head, Jesus is the source of the church's life.

Once again by viewing things through the prism of the Head/Body metaphor we can see that the purposes and agency of the church is inexorably bound to the person and work of the Lord Jesus. We might simply say that the church is the concentrated expression of a culture that is birthed and maintained in Jesus.

Fourthly, following the logic of the body metaphor, we can say that all Christian ministry originates with, and must be indelibly shaped by, and modeled on, Jesus. There is a very particular culture that emerges when the church is truly indexed to Jesus. The authentic Jesus-shaped church will not only do the kind of things Jesus did, but it will do it in conformity to the way in which he did them. "The life and self-offering of Christ perfectly expresses what it is to serve God and man. All Christian ministry flows and takes its shape from this source and model."[33] Karl Barth likewise taught that because the church is the "earthly-historical form of Christ's existence" it necessitates a corresponding *con-formity* of the life and ministry of the church to that of the life and teachings of the church's Founder.[34] The Body of Christ ought to be directly indexed to the person of Christ.[35]

Fifthly, the metaphor of a healthy body is meant to convey an understanding of a symphony composed of many parts. A *diseased* body by definition defeats itself and fails to become what it could be. And just as a symphony or a jazz quartet collaborate to create an emergent sound, so too the various parts of Jesus' body create a super-abundant form of synergy that can be called variously "fullness," (*pleroma*) "maturity," "perfection," "wholeness," "built up in love," etc. by Paul in the Ephesians 4 text. In a very real sense, we not only need each other in order to be ourselves, but we really need each other at a whole new level if we are to be the Body of Christ.

Remember the problems of reductionism here. The idea of the innate synergy of the whole Body of Christ should never be underestimated because God's purposes are meant to be embodied in a community that lives by his word—Christian discipleship is always ecclesial. Synergy, as you know, involves the interaction or cooperation of two or more agents in a system to produce a combined effect greater than the sum of their separate effects. In the math of the Body it means that $1 + 1 + 1 = 5$ or more. Jesus has intended that we are better and more effective together than we can ever be apart—that is why we are called to strive to maintain our God-given unity. The Body of Christ is a synergistic synthesis composed of many parts.

Finally, note that a body implies a certain agency and capacity to do certain things. It exists to extend the purposes of the organism. The Body, like all bodies, is designed to fulfill a certain function. It is *purposed* to do what only it can do. "The Church is the receptacle of His powers and represents Him on earth."[36] Tim Keller agrees. In *Center Church* he affirms that firstly "Jesus Christ has all the powers and functions of ministry in himself" and that subsequently it is "*this* ministry that is distributed in and through his church."[37] The Body of Christ is designed to extend the purposes of Jesus in the world.

All these dimensions of the Body of Christ are supercharged with significance when we consider that Jesus himself acted in accordance with a fivefold pattern and purpose. We have seen that he not only recapitulated and redeemed the creational archetypes, but that he perfectly embodied and expressed all five APEST identities and purposes. He modeled them in their perfected and holy form. His life is literally saturated with 5Q—he is its true gravitational epicenter. If Jesus expressed his ministry through the medium of APEST, how much more should the church, if it is to be truly conformed to him? Surely if it's a significant part of the ministry of Jesus, it should be a significant part of his Body. We should expect a corresponding fivefold pattern in the Body where Jesus, and no other, is the Head.

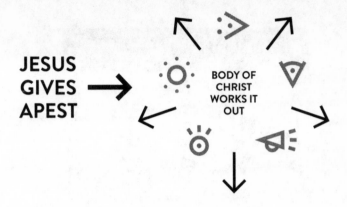

Figure 6.2 From J-APEST to APEST: The Body Works Out what Jesus Puts In

Here again we are able to discern the nature and source of the scenius of the Body. Jesus puts it in so we can work it out.

Making APEST Unavoidable in the Life of the Body of Christ

This direct correspondence between Christ and the Body of Christ (Messiah// Messianic) is powerfully reinforced with the help of important teaching in the social sciences called "the routinization of charisma." Max Weber, who came up with this theory, noted that all movements are started by an exemplary "charismatic" leader with a vision that rallies and catalyzes the movement. But starting a movement and sustaining it are two different things. If the movement is to be able to thrive and continue, the charisms (the vision, capacities, and functions) of the founder must be passed on from founder to the organization itself. And so power and function are distributed into various roles, rituals, and structures in order to make the founding charism "routine" throughout the life of the community. If this does not happen, for whatever reason, the movement will simply not survive the passing of its founder—this is known as "founder's trap." Routinization is a powerful truth evidenced in the vast history of movements and institutions.

Applying this directly to the imagery of Ephesians 4:1–16 we can say that by recapitulating APEST and subsequently bequeathing it to the Body of Christ, Jesus is effectively *routinizing* fivefold ministry into the life and fabric of the *ecclesia*. In his ascension, Jesus' own ministries and identities (J-APEST) are effectively parsed out and implanted into the primal foundations of the church. The question of how the church functions as the fullness of Christ in the world is thus given concrete expression.[38]

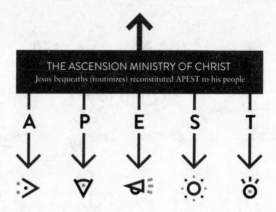

Figure 6.3 The Ascension Gifting: Routinizing APEST in the Body of Christ

Allow me to illustrate the importance of the routinization of charisma by reference to an example of the defining role that founders play in the movements that they start. This will also give the reader a clue as to how 5Q is manifested, and what happens when it is actively excluded or suppressed.

Let's look at the pattern of one of history's most remarkable movement makers ... John Wesley. When working with various Wesleyan denominations (who I like to call "Wesley's children" ... Methodist, Nazarene, Wesleyans, Salvation Army, various Pentecostals, etc.) I always ask them to consider the utterly remarkable person that lay at the root of their own respective movements. Presumably, Wesley still continues to inspire because all forms of contemporary Wesleyanism continue to exist to *somehow* embody the energy, vision, capacities, and character of their founder, John Wesley. So, for instance, if some organization claims to be Wesleyan, you ought to expect a correspondence between Wesley//Wesleyanism.[39] So far, so good. All agree.

Then I ask them to think of Wesley in terms of each of the APEST types. Was Wesley an apostle? The answer is ... of course he was. He not only called himself an apostle on various occasions but was arguably the most outstanding expression of apostolic ministry in Western church history! He certainly started a movement, the most explicit symptom of his apostolic agency. The traces of his apostolic gift, though severely diminished in current Methodist circles, are nonetheless still evident: he built an adaptive system around a common DNA and pattern that rapidly went to scale and that involved all of God's people in every domain of society—the rest is history. So, *check the "A" box.*

I then ask, was Wesley a prophet? The answer? Of course he was. Once again, probably one of the most remarkable prophets in the history of the church: His teaching on social and personal holiness is probably one of the most mature expressions of the prophetic in our history. In the prophetic mode, he called all hearers to decision before God. Furthermore, he called for direct personal (covenantal) knowledge *of* God not just knowledge *about* God. Wesley worked tirelessly against the social ills of his day—he is credited as the founder of the original trade unions, a movement to protect workers from exploitation; he dignified women by recognizing their equal agency; he was active in the abolition of slavery, etc. Wesley was a mature prophet on steroids. *Check the "P" box.*

Was he an evangelist? Again, he was probably one of our very best. He personally rode thousands of miles on horseback to proclaim the gospel to tens of thousands in places that religious folk never bothered to go. He is arguably England's greatest evangelist, but in terms of evangelistic impact in America in his own day, he is second only to George Whitfield. It would not be an exaggeration if we said that millions of people have come to know Jesus through his ministry and the movement he started. *Check the "E" box.*

Was he a shepherd? Well, not so much. But he did design and initiate a system of caring for the poor and the broken that is still working today, and he most certainly believed in the importance of the church in mission. He certainly never undervalued the shepherding function. Ironically, even though it was Wesley's weakest, the pastoral function is probably the one most evident in the various Wesleyan denominations today. *Check the "S" box.*

Was he a teacher? Here again, yes ... and while it is not probably his highest APEST capacity, he was more than adequate—way better than most of us—and his teachings are still highly influential today. And most importantly, he was committed to the ongoing task of discipleship. He not only designed a system around discipleship and disciple making, but he developed copious amounts of sermonic teaching material that are still doing the rounds in Wesleyan circles today. *Check the "T" box.*

So we have in John Wesley a super-gifted man who manifested very high 5Q! All Wesleyans know and appreciate this about Wesley and so they are proudly affirmative of his 5Q capacities.

The subversive nature of this exercise should be obvious. Given that now that the vast majority of Wesleyan denominations actively suppress the APE side of the fivefold equation, how do Wesley's contemporary children expect to be able to extend the movement Wesley started if they no longer believe in, or legitimize, the full fivefold typology that lies at the very core of their own movement/s? Or in terms of routinization, how do they expect to be able to carry on the work of the founder if they now deny, and in fact cannot even name let alone define, the very capacities that enabled Wesley to be truly remarkable in the first place? The answer? They can't. Almost all these denominations are now in decline.

What happened? Well in terms of APEST dynamics they have managed to "un-routinize" their founding charisms and subsequently named the now-reduced capacities as the new normal—the "two orders of ministry"! After the remarkable success of what is called Early Methodism, following the Christendom template of ministry they bought into that fatal flaw of abandoning the fivefold typology. Consequently, they are now condemned to recurring Sisyphean despair in their attempts to fulfill their own sense of identity and mission exemplified in their amazing founder. Cessationist Wesleyans therefore have effectively cut off the very branch they were sitting on. Or to change the metaphor slightly, they severed their roots in the founder's ministry. This is what I'd call a *movement killer* of the first order.[40]

And here is the kicker: Wesley is only a pale reflection of the original fivefold template exemplified in Jesus, the real Founder of the Christian movement. Wesley was only effective or for that matter legitimate, insofar that he mirrored the APEST represented perfectly in Jesus!

It is worth mentioning a more current example of a highly gifted leader in the contemporary church—that of Pope Francis. I have found myself somewhat fascinated by this remarkable man and have started reading his material and observing his ministry. I have no doubt that he has all of the five APEST functions operative in his ministry: He has the joy of a great evangelist who invites all to know Jesus (he is quite *the* evangelical Catholic), he has the driving passion and vision of an apostle, the critique of the system and the love of the poor of the prophet. He is also a humble and caring shepherd, as well as a very eloquent teacher. It's been a long time since Catholicism has someone with primary APE giftings in the role of Pope.[41] I honestly believe that it is for this very reason that he is bringing renewal to the worldwide Catholic Church. The challenge will be whether or not his particular embodiment of APEST is recognized as such, and adopted more fully into the Catholic Church so that the renewal they are currently experiencing might be "routinized" and continue beyond Pope Francis.

• Let me Hear your Body Talk ...

As the Founder and Designer then, Jesus provides us with the exemplary pattern of behavior against which all other corresponding models, patterns of discipleship, ministry, and leadership in the movement are to emulate. Jesus provides the model of humanity and service by which all disciples are to be evaluated and legitimized. It's like a spiritual template of sorts—a pattern of behaviors that, once discovered, helps us better understand ourselves and others. And here's the critical thing in relation to 5Q: Jesus' person and work are the perfect embodiments of APEST. Conformity to Christ in the Body of Christ must also therefore reflect the fivefold nature of Christ's ministry, if it is to be authentic ministry!

Similarly, the fivefold must feature in individual discipleship because discipleship is essentially formation in Christ. To become a mature Christlike person then, would mean engaging all the elements of fivefold latent in our living relationship with Jesus. Actually, this idea of becoming like Jesus lies at the heart of all genuine spirituality and discipleship. Imitation of Christ can therefore take the form of the imitation of the fivefold as it is expressed in Christ. Disciples follow their master in all things (Luke 6:40). One of the most clarifying definitions of ministry then, *is doing the kind of things that Jesus did for the same reason that he did them.* Now think of this in terms of the *fivefold.*

So how does the ministry of Christ, and with it his fivefold ministry, get into the church? To answer this, we need to recall briefly the primary imagery of Ephesians 4:1–16—that is in his ascension Jesus "has given" (vv. 7, 11) to his Body its inherent callings and functions so that the church APEST may mature (vv. 13, 15) and in so doing "attain to the whole measure of the fullness of Christ" (v. 13). In other words, APEST is not only the mode of Jesus' presence among his people, he gives APEST to the church that she might grow, mature, and "attain to the fullness of Christ"! So perhaps the central idea of Ephesians 4:1–16 can be portrayed as follows:

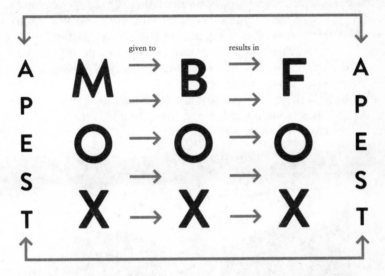

Figure 6.4 Ministry of Christ (MOX) Given to the Body of Christ (BOX) Which Results in the Fullness of Christ (FOX)

There are huge implications here for both you and your church/organization—this is a Yoda-moment so please pay attention to the following logic: We have seen how Jesus lives, fulfills, and exemplifies the APEST types in his life and ministry. We have also seen that in his ascension, Jesus confers (routinizes) the now-redeemed and perfected APEST functions to the Body of Christ with the explicit intention that these be expressed throughout the church's life and discipleship. As the diagram above shows, the Ministry of Christ is given to the Body of Christ so that it might attain to the Fullness of Christ!

But here's where the rubber hits the road for most readers and their respective churches or organizations: Assuming the logic of 5Q portrayed thus far, and assuming that the core purpose of the church is to extend both the meaning and impact of Jesus in the world, then we must honestly answer the question, *can we extend Jesus' ministry if we are only operating in a truncated twofold, ST form of ministry?* To restate this in another way for clarity: If Jesus clearly operated as APEST, do we think we can extend Jesus-impact if we have any less? And once again we see how tampering with the APEST typologies has damaged our capacity to be faithful witnesses ... *New Testament ministry in the Body of Christ cannot be done with anything less than all the dimensions inherent in Christ's own ministry.* Without full APEST expression, a church cannot expect to logically extend Jesus' ministry in the world; neither can it attain to the fullness of Christ or achieve its purposes/mission—it will inevitably have dangerous gaps in its culture. And herein, folks, lies a huge amount of the church's dysfunction! We are trying to extend Jesus' ministry with only two of his at-least-five functions! In fact, as we shall see later in the explorations of the 5Q marks of the church, I believe that many of the church's dysfunctions can be traced back to one or more of the fivefold functions being absent from the equation.

Conversely, restoring APEST is *almost* a silver bullet in the renewal and mission of the church— and this is because Jesus really *is* the answer to all our problems—the silver bullet. But to get at the solution you are going to have to deal with Jesus! I am totally confident in saying this: restoring mature APEST functionality *will* bring life-changing renewal to your own ministry, your church or organization.

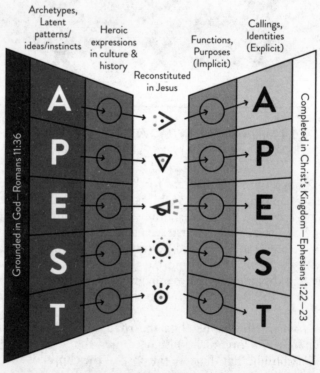

Figure 6.5 The 5Q System

Now, with these powerful images and ideas reverberating in your heads, recall the key graphic (Figure 6.5) introduced in chapter two. What do your soft eyes now see?

We have now come to the end of section one, which was to provide a thoroughgoing rationale for the total scenius of 5Q portrayed visually in the key graphic. If I have done my work well and have been a good custodian of the ideas bequeathed to me, you will by now see the sheer elegance and genius in the fractal pattern that has its roots in the Godhead and is now bestowed on the church (and all creation) in the form of the fivefold functions and callings. You should also feel some sense of awe at the theological weight that is built into the entire 5Q system. You should also feel the internal pressure of 5Q derived from its presence, its latency, as Jesus presses us to conform ourselves with the logic and pattern of his own ministry—the invisible church asserting itself again. You should also sense that it does provide something of an answer to the missional crisis we now face in Western contexts.

The time has come to awaken it in your life and in your community. And, as I have already said, Jesus has irrevocably given these to the church. They are there by the Word of God; they cannot be removed even if the most ardent cessationist wanted to remove them. What is more, these fivefold functions can all be identified, measured, and developed! Any adjustments (positive or negative) at this point will have exponential impact throughout the system.

It is now vital that we begin to look into this latter aspect; namely, the nature of the fivefold functions and callings, and why it is fruitful to focus on them. We turn to the practical implications with the understanding that the health of the church itself, the capacity to get the job done (its ministry), and of course the overall maturity of the church are at stake in a correct appropriation of APEST typologies. To this we now turn.

SECTION 2

• LIVING THE IDENTITIES •

The "perfect" Christian is the perfect proof of the truth of Christianity: in the Christian's existential transparency, Christianity becomes comprehensible both in itself and to the world. ... The saint [that is, the holy human being] is the greatest defense of the Christian religion.

—Hans Urs von Balthasar

Your beliefs become your thoughts. Your thoughts become your words. Your words become your actions. Your actions become your habits. Your habits become your values. Your values become your destiny.

—Mahatma Gandhi

The business of the church is to "remember" the future. Not merely to remember that there is to be a future, but mysteriously to make the future really present.

—Herbert McCabe

Chapter 7

Eph4Us: The Fivefold Functionality of the Church

The church proclaims the Gospel in order to awaken faith in Jesus Christ, provoke commitment in the Spirit, make Christ present in society, and carry on the cause of Christ.

—Hans Kung

The Christian ideal has not been tried and found wanting. It has been found difficult; and left untried.

—G.K. Chesterton

Do or do not. There is no try!

—Yoda, *The Empire Strikes Back*

In this chapter, we are going to move from a more strictly biblical-theological exploration to a description of ways in which we can begin to embed 5Q into the very life and practice of your local church/organization. This is where the fivefold rubber begins to hit the organizational road.

Even though largely marginalized throughout the thinking and practices of much of the Western church tradition, the *phenomenon* of APEST (in function as well as vocation) has been ever-present in our various renewals, movements, revivals, and heroes in history.

Viewing through the 5Q lens, one can say most of the renewal movements over time have involved a recovery of one or more of the five functions: For instance, in terms of the Catholic orders, the Franciscans involved a recovery of the prophetic and shepherding function. The Jesuits are largely an apostolic order, the Benedictines a teaching order, the Carmelites the mystical-prophetic, etc. In Protestant circles, many of our sending-mission agencies were similarly recoveries of previously excluded APE functions. Our so-called "para-churches" were often birthed in an attempt to recover lost functions; so for instance Campus Crusade (Cru) has strong apostolic-evangelistic edges, Navigators evangelistic disciple making, Intervarsity largely evangelistic-teaching, World Vision the prophetic, etc.

As for various people who have heroically embodied the various APEST callings consider: St. Patrick (apostle/shepherd), Francis of Assisi (prophet/apostle), Teresa of Avila (prophet/teacher), Martin Luther (prophet/teacher), John Calvin (teacher), John Wesley (apostle/prophet), Catherine Booth (apostle), Dietrich Bonhoeffer (prophet/teacher), George Whitfield (evangelist), Billy Graham (evangelist), Mother Teresa (shepherd), Martin Luther King Jr. (prophet). What other biblical categories of leadership best accounts their contributions? How do we explain these using our reduced categories of ministry? They break the box because we cannot simply profile them as classic pastors or professors. But as we shall see in this chapter, the Body would not be faithful, let alone survive, without the various historical expressions of APEST throughout the life of the church.[1]

• The Five-Dimensional Church: Of Functions and Callings

Much of our sense of destiny and purpose lies in finding our unique calling. I wholeheartedly believe that each disciple is obligated to strive to understand and live into his or her own calling as Christ has apportioned it (Ephesians 4:1, 7). I also believe that APEST is the best way of getting a handle on precisely that calling. I am convinced that clarity in relation to our relative callings can be adequately illuminated as well as developed by use of the fivefold typologies.[2] Certainly, each one of us can, and ought to, develop something of a personal and unique APEST portrait—a picture of one's unique identity and destiny in and by Jesus.

But, having said this, as you hopefully will have realized by now, I believe that 5Q is actually much bigger than simply providing the vocational profile of individual people at various times in the church—although it certainly includes that. As I have tried to lay out, 5Q is grounded in the being of God himself; woven throughout the creation orders in archetype, myth, and hero; recapitulated in Christ; and subsequently bequeathed to the church, to be expressed in and through the lives of its saints for the glory of God and the edification of his people. The individual saints—you and me, and other people called to serve Jesus—are therefore at the far end of a very deep and ancient redemptive process. Individuals are simply particular expressions of a grander universal unfolding of God's purposes in creation and church. APEST is so much bigger than little old me finding my ministry mojo—as important as that is!

We have already noted that Jesus is the exemplary expression of APEST. He is also the Head of the Body, the Giver of these "gifts" to the church. He embeds his fivefold identities (personas) into the life of his Body. These in turn form the backbone and structure for the purposes of the church. And because Jesus is ever-present in the church, and because APEST is the very means by which it attains to Christ's fullness, we can confidently say that the fivefold functions are actually implicit in the church's identity, purpose, culture, and mission. They are *implicit* because Jesus is present at the heart of the church's life and purpose; 5Q is likewise coded into the very core of the church's purpose. The next chapter will apply these insights in the form of identifiable "marks" of the church.

And so take a look at our guiding map of 5Q again. Note where functions are located and how they got there. Also note APEST is an intrinsic part of the operating system (OS), and therefore it provides the primary platform from which the various personal callings (apps) are launched. The Body of Christ as a whole is the true recipient of 5Q. The church is the platform from which all believers are empowered to fulfill their callings. It's pure scenius!

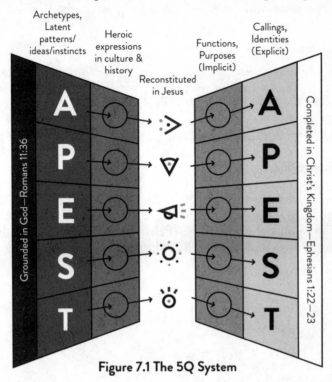

Figure 7.1 The 5Q System

Let's Get Functional, Functional

I have already mentioned that in this book I am focusing on the fivefold functions—and the relative *dys*-functions brought about by corruptions in the fivefold system. In doing this, I am choosing to focus on the identity and purpose of the church as a whole entity, rather than on individual vocations. In doing so, I am exploring the organizational functions that in turn create the organizational culture wherein healthy expressions of the fivefold callings actually take place. The *functional* lens therefore opens up new perspectives of the collective, organizational aspects. The *vocational* lens allows us to see APEST as necessary for the healthy discipleship, development, and releasing of potential of each of God's wonderfully unique people.

This focus on functions ought to have the effect of highlighting the importance of individual APEST callings as *expressions of the church's innate purpose and functionality*. The dimension of personal callings—what I call *explicit* APEST—are therefore the concrete, particular ways in which the functions already given to God's *ecclesia* are expressed (made explicit) through the lives of the many individuals that make up the church in different times and places.[3] That these fivefold functions are manifested in various individuals in different times and places is simply a demonstration of the prior fact that they are already embedded into the Body of Christ itself![4] In some ways, one can thus see calling (vocation) as an individual and personal expression of the fivefold functions given to the Body.

Functions-Dysfunction

Just as the human body is made up of numerous interdependent and interrelated functions (cardiovascular, nervous, digestive, etc.), so too the Body of Christ needs all five APEST capacities in order to be truly functional. Anything less than five functions operating interdependently must inevitably lead to system fatigue and dysfunction. Or, to change the metaphor slightly, think of a motor vehicle operating on less than all its cylinders. If it's not operating according to design specification, then it will be an ineffective vehicle that will eventually fail.

A church that is not operating on all five APEST "cylinders" is to that degree significantly disabled as a body, and God's purposes through it are frustrated if not outright opposed. Deficiencies and imbalances in the fivefold system damage the entire system. Recall this graphic from chapter one.

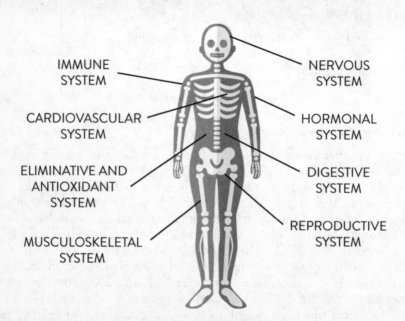

Figure 7.2 The Systems of the Human Body

When the church is referred to as a body, it immediately evokes the idea of systemic interconnectivity. In the same way that body parts cannot exist independently of the body itself, so too church function and individual vocation are inextricably related to each other. To remove one is to undermine all the others. We need all five to mature. So for example, we can say that every church is called to the ongoing task of evangelism; however, in a particular church some are actually called and identified as evangelists. The specific role of that evangelist expresses one of the functions, and therefore one of the important purposes, given to the church by Jesus. The function precedes, and provides the implicit platform for, the individual callings and expressions. In other words, the callings presuppose and make explicit the functions already given to the Body (implicit) by the ascending Lord.

Therefore, whatever one thinks of various *APEST individuals* being called apostles, prophets, teachers, etc., it is just about impossible to separate the implicit *APEST functions* out from the New Testament understanding of the church itself without the whole thing unraveling. Even if one might be cessationist in terms of individual callings, it's not possible to be cessationist in terms of the organizational functions and still claim to be *biblical*. Who can debate that each APEST *function* is still given to all of God's people in every time and place and as a whole? Who would doubt the ongoing validity of these? Why would we even want to? Is not the whole church called to be apostolic (missional), prophetic, evangelistic, and so on? It would be foolish to deny that these remain the core purposes of all churches in every context. For instance, even people who deny the personal role of the apostle see *apostolicity* as one of the universal marks of the church—the church is said to be one, holy, catholic, and *apostolic*.

To drive the point home in relation to all the fivefold functions, we can say that without the apostolic function we would undercut the missionary purposes of the church in every age and context; deprived of the prophetic function the church would fail in its obligation to stand against unfaithfulness, unrighteousness, and injustice wherever these are found; without a deep sense of the evangelistic purpose the church would not feel itself obliged to proclaim good news in a bad-news world; without its community-building capacities (S) the church would not even exist as a viable entity in society; without the pedagogic functions (T) we would lack appropriate knowledge and wisdom, and so would be quickly lost or become dangerous fanatics. Because it is the Body of Christ—the literal embodiment of Jesus in the world—the church itself is *always* called to be missional, prophetic, evangelistic, pastoral, and wise.

This function/role distinction ought not to be too strange because it in fact is part of an organization. All organizations need certain distinct departments (e.g., product design and development, marketing, human resources), each responsible for highlighting and executing its share of the various functions necessary for the whole organization to thrive. Each department has a distinct function within the whole, and within these departments there are roles that are filled by people selected to fulfill these roles effectively. For instance, the marketing department is the right context for the role of a marketing manager; the job of Chief Financial Officer is filled by an appropriately suited accountant.[5]

But before we parse out the fivefold categories more thoroughly, let me once again differentiate between *functions* and *calling*.

Function: The actions or activities assigned to a particular person, thing, or organization; functions embody the purposes for which something is designed or exists.

Calling: Distinctly personal; involves a strong inner impulse toward a particular course of action especially when accompanied by conviction of divine influence linked to personal destiny.

And remember, for the purposes of this book, I will use "functions" to describe the more corporate, organizational, dimensions of APEST, and "callings" to describe how each function would be expressed through the actual lives of individual believers. Calling is therefore the personal living expression of individual destiny as well as corporate function.[6]

CAPACITIES		OBJECTIVES
PRACTICES		DUTIES
ESSENTIALS		EXTENSIONS
INSTINCTS		AGENCIES
PURPOSES		GENERATIONS
SENSES		MISSIONS
ROLES		ACTIONS
CATEGORIES		SERVICES
FUNCTIONS		DIMENSIONS
IDENTITIES		TYPES

Figure 7.3 Synonyms for Functions

Another very important point: Although I am articulating these functions and callings in terms of the church, *in no way do I imply that these are limited to the organized worshipping community alone.* Because these archetypal functions and callings are latent throughout human culture, they are to be expressed and lived out in any of the spheres and domains where disciples are called to live out their faith. This is especially true for Christians because when your spiritual calling intersects with your broader vocation, you are fulfilling your particular mission and destiny as a disciple. And so, while in this book I am focusing on church-based APEST here, it has direct correlations to the other domains. I believe that all forms of organization can be developed and maintained using a fivefold perspective. I therefore encourage the reader to courageously translate these ideas into non-church settings.

• APEST Functions Defined

Having defined what a function is, we can now move on to developing a working description of each of the fivefold functions along with the associated callings:

Apostolic-Apostle

In writing the foreword to *The Permanent Revolution*, the preeminent theologian Darrell Guder notes: "Especially crucial for missional ecclesiology today is the *recovery of the apostolic function in the church* [italics mine]." He goes on to say that:

> It is this ministry that ensures that the church is always centered on its calling to be the agent and instrument of God's mission and that everything it is and does relates to and demonstrates that calling.[7]

Seminal missiologist Hendrik Kraemer agrees:

> The Church is, by its nature and calling, in the first and last instance an apostolic body ... By "apostolic body" we mean that the Church is "sent" into the world, has a specific mission: it has a message for the whole world that must be heralded.

He goes on to note that without a genuine understanding of this fact *there can be no real understanding of the Christian church*.[8] Perhaps Emil Brunner nails the apostolic dimension of the church in his famous aphorism, "The Church exists by mission [viz. apostolicity... *being sent*] as fire exists by burning."[9] Apostolic organization, as far as it relates to the church itself, will likely embody the practices that Ralph Winter calls the sodalic functions.[10]

The Apostolic Functions/Purposes of the Church

All these theologians highlight the defining aspect of the apostolic: to maintain and develop the *sentness* of the church. And given that mission is clearly a central aspect of the church's purpose, the function is absolutely indispensable if the church is to remain true to her calling.

"Apostolicity," therefore is the inbuilt, culturally embedded drive to ensure that the church is faithful to its missionary calling.[11]

The apostolic function exists to:

- **extend Christianity.** The driving logic of *apostolicity* is the extension of the Jesus movement in and through the lives of the adherents, as well as establishing the church onto new ground. The apostolic function will therefore highlight those aspects of the church's purpose that develop its missional capacities and prioritize the church's sentness to the nations.

- **maintain movement.** Because of the dynamic and advancing nature of the *ecclesia*, the key apostolic metaphor for the church is that of a dynamic, adaptive, advancing, integrated movement that can extend itself over time and across geographical regions. This is no static understanding of the church. In other words, apostolic ecclesiology is distinctly *movemental*.

- **maintain focus on broadest purpose/mission.** The very term "apostolic" (sent/purposed) hints at one of its own core purposes, namely to constantly highlight the ultimate purpose(s) of the organization—the mission of the church in the world.

- **design scalable organization.** Because organization is essential to all forms of community and dynamic movements, the apostolic needs to develop the necessary organizational bias, as well as cultivate the necessary culture, around the extension of the movement as a whole. Therefore, we can say that the distinctly apostolic perspective of the forms, functions, and purposes of the church will be dynamic, adaptive, innovative, reproducible, and scalable.

- **maintain compliance around core DNA (meta-ideas).** Another irreplaceable apostolic function involves the constant elucidation of the meta-ideas that in turn sustain the core identity and message of the organization. To change the metaphor to genetics, the apostolic function involves guarding the very DNA of the movement which is always subject to various misunderstanding, dilution, or hindrances. DNA is critical to movemental health, extension, and integrity. Taking the apostolic function seriously requires that the movement ensures ongoing compliance with the core ideas that, if weakened, will damage the capacity of the movement to hold together over time and distance.

- **maintain paradigm and vision.** In many ways, the apostolic vision of the church is the most comprehensive one, in that it sees the whole system and not just the parts. As such, it defines reality in the broadest possible terms. It is what the New Testament calls "foundational" because it is the one that is able to meaningfully include all the others. This "big picture" vision, because it articulates the systems story at the heart of the church, will make sense of all the other functions.

- **plant the gospel.** Planting the gospel is the surest litmus test of apostolicity. We are never commanded to plant churches, but we are to plant the Jesus story in ways that create the basis for Christian community—the church (1 Corinthians 3:6). Churches grow out of the encounter with Jesus through the gospel. Associated with this is:

  o **development of new congregations.** Planting the gospel will generate new communities founded on Jesus, his gospel, and his lordship. If any church is not planting new congregations, or never has, it is a sure-fire sign that it is deficient in the apostolic function. Therefore, almost all aspects involved in generating new congregations and nurturing their growth are primarily associated with the apostolic function.[12]

o **innovation of new forms**. When churches are planted in new cultures (cross-cultural and/or subcultural) they will need to be able to generate new forms to suit the different cultures. A genuinely apostolic church needs to somehow support the innovation of new forms in multiple contexts.

- **cultivate entrepreneurship**. Because of the missionary function of taking the gospel on to entirely new ground, entrepreneurial aspects of the organization will also likely be associated with the apostolic function.[13] Entrepreneurialism requires a culture of permission-giving, and the encouragement to take risks, fail, and learn from failure.

- **maintain healthy translocal network**. Because the distinctly apostolic metaphor of the church is that of an expansive movement across entire regions, they require the organizational structure of a translocal network. Just like a flight control center, everything is moving at the same time, so keeping the lines of communication open is absolutely critical. Likewise, to maintain healthy burgeoning regional networks, meaningful relationships across the system become crucially important. The apostolic function therefore nurtures rich communication between the various players, outposts, and agencies throughout the network.

- **maintain movement-wide unity while cultivating diversity**. There is a lot of diversity of people, race, status, and cultures in expanding movements—just look at the New Testament church. The apostolic function is the one most responsible for the essential unity of the church as it grows and matures (e.g., Ephesians 4:1–16). The apostolic is therefore quick to respond to elements in the movement that threaten its common life and create systemic dysfunction.

- **maintain systemic health**. Furthermore, apostolic understandings of the church will also be systems-aware and have a view to the big picture. The apostolic function will therefore involve maintaining overall system health and keeping the various members of the living body as connected and functional as possible.

- **mobilize effort**. The apostolic function also involves mobilizing all the agents in the system. In other words, the church's apostolicity requires that all disciples be "in the game" and appropriately equipped and empowered to be God's representative people in the world. This involves recognizing the agency of all believers and is clearly related to leadership development and deployment.

The Calling/Role of the Apostolic Person

The apostolic person is therefore the person who most corresponds to the functions described above. As in all the APEST callings, no single apostolic individual would likely express *all* the functions above, but I believe a mature expression of the apostolic will embody many in an exemplary way.

In the power of the Holy Spirit, the apostolic person is imbued with an innate sense of the big-picture purpose of the organization. In its mature, idealized, leadership form, the apostle (*sent one*) is the person most responsible for the overall vigor, as well as extension, of Christianity as a whole, primarily through direct mission and church planting.

Not surprisingly, apostolic types tend to favor the entrepreneurial edges of the church and have a natural capacity for adventure; they tend to be less risk-averse than those who fall under other forms of ministry and leadership. Following this pioneering instinct, they are the ones most likely to engage at the edges of the organization, to innovate, and to extend the faith into new ground. They therefore provide the "catalytic, adaptive, movemental, translocal, pioneering, entrepreneurial leadership needed to spark, mobilize, and sustain movement(s)."[14]

Apostles have an irreplaceable purpose in maintaining ongoing missional capacities, generating new forms of *ecclesia*, and working for the continual renewal of the church/organization.

The mature apostle will tend to have a more developed sense of the church/ organization as a living *system* comprised of essential parts, or subsystems. This involves being the developer and custodian of the meta-ideas (DNA) that determine the health of the system. Because of this they can play a vital role in the design and the leadership and health of organizations.

Prophetic-Prophet

The church is called to be a prophetic community by its very life and witness. We can say that the prophetic calling and function is absolutely crucial to the unique purpose of God's people in the world. As his people, we are to be the one place where God, and everything he stands for, is revered, cherished, and obeyed.

The Prophetic Functions/Purposes of the Church

I have spent many years pondering the nature of the prophetic function, and from what I can see throughout the Bible, the prophetic function has two primary dimensions or orientations—what I call the *vertical* and the *horizontal*.

The *vertical prophetic* relates to those functions and instincts concerned with maintaining constant attentiveness to God—of guarding the covenant relationship God has with his people. It is the preeminently God-oriented function. It is sensitive to situations where this life-giving, irreplaceable relationship is damaged or broken.

The *vertical* prophetic function exists to:

- **maintain God-orientation.** The vertical prophetic will tend to cultivate a culture of God-centeredness through worship; it will also highlight the need for listening prayer and for responsible and responsive obedience to God.

- **engage with Pathos.** God feels things deeply. He is passionate, and his holy passion involves complex dynamics between his unshakable love, his compassion for his creation, his jealous protectiveness, as well as his profound wrath against sin and injustice in society and unfaithfulness in the church. Engaging God's pathos means feeling what God feels. It therefore inevitably involves experiencing grief, pain, joy, rejoicing, anger, love, compassion, mercy, judgment, and the like. In spite of the pain and holy discomfort that it brings, the church is called to remain open and malleable toward God.

- **encounter God.** Some of the key bodily metaphors used in the Bible itself to describe the prophetic might help us categorize the type. For example:

  o **Ear.** The prophet is described as, or experiences himself as, an "ear," the primary organ of human receptivity, attentiveness, and obedience. The Word of God is heard, but it is only rightly understood when it is obeyed.

  o **Eye.** The "eye" highlights the prophetic capacity for spiritual insight, as well as its opposite—blindness. Instead of simply trying to see God, the prophetic is an attempt to see as God sees. As such, this deals with the church's receptivity to a holy vision and imagination.

  o **Mouth.** The prophet as "mouth/mouthpiece" highlights the prophetic call to forthtell the Word: to proclaim, to speak on God's behalf, and to be willing to suffer the same painful rejection that the Word of God itself does. Because of the immediate association with God, prophetic speech and action will tend to be passionate, motivational, ethical, and often corrective.

  o **Heart.** A particularly important function of prophecy involves being willing to feel what God feels—to experience things from God's perspective. The prophet is not afraid to experience what we might call "the heart of God." The appeal of the prophet is primarily to the heart—the source of the all-important capacity for imagination, trust, values, and volition. If things go wrong at the level of the heart, they go wrong everywhere. The prophetic therefore guards the collective heart of God's people.

The *horizontal prophetic*, on the other hand, as the metaphor suggests, are those aspects that highlight our relationships with others and the world as part of our obligations to God. The covenanting God requires that we be a holy, just, and righteous people as he is holy, just, and righteous.

The *horizontal* prophetic function exists to:

- **highlight covenant obligations.** A covenant is a two-way relationship and is not morally or spiritually neutral. The church is the one and only agency on earth which submits to the Triune God and exists to obey him. The prophetic function therefore always highlights the un-relentingly existential, moral, and ethical nature of that responsibility that arises from any authentic encounter with the living God.[15]

- **serve as a reminder of covenant love.** Prophetic functions are not just about demand and obligation; prophetic ministry is also a constant reminder of God's abiding love (*hesed-agape*) and of his covenant grace that saves.

- **call to repentance.** If, as Bonhoeffer says, to know God is to change, then it is the prophetic function that embeds in the *ecclesia* a constant willingness to learn, unlearn, and relearn. In a rebellious world, this inevitably includes a focus on ongoing repentance. The prophetic is also unrelenting in its call to repentance because it understands the importance of maintaining a relationship with a holy God—as well as the rebellious and sinful nature of the fallen human heart.

- **speak truth to power.** One of the key functions of the prophetic is to constantly expose the pretensions of human power and its abuses. This is particularly true of political, economic, and religious institutions. The prophetic is particularly harsh on false religion and hypocrisy.

- **maintain sensitivity to spiritual warfare.** The prophets in the Bible were the ones most attuned to the power of the spiritual in daily life—witness the book of Ezekiel or the Revelation of John for an example. Because of this, the prophetic function involves an acute sensitivity to spiritual warfare.

- **distinguish true and false worship (idolatry).** People tend to worship things, people, and ideas as replacements for God—this is what the Bible terms idolatry. The prophetic function is therefore strongly iconoclastic in relation to all distorted values and false forms of worship. In fact, there is a very likely correlation between the loss of the prophetic voice in history and the rise of toxic and ritualistic religion. The prophet makes sure that the relationship with God remains very personal and direct.

- **champion justice.** One cannot worship vertically if one is living unjustly (see, e.g., Isaiah 58; Amos 5:1–27). Issues of justice, such as concern for the poor, the marginalized, and the downtrodden, are derived primarily via the prophetic function given to the church. The prophetic prioritizes consistent ethical action and deeds of goodness. God's people are to love righteousness, to do justice, and to walk humbly before God.

- **call to holiness.** The covenantal relationship requires a requisite holiness in God's people: "Be holy because I, the LORD your God, am holy" (Leviticus 19:2). The call to righteousness (meaning *right relationship* with God and others) and to an ethic of holiness remains a central prophetic concern.

- **communicate urgency**. The sure sign of prophetic ministry is that it creates a sense of urgency around core ideas. Urgency is a very important aspect of a healthy organization.

- **demonstrate prefigurative community**. The prophetic form of community is what we can call *prefigurative* in that it lives into an ideal in a radical way that provides a compelling picture of what can be. It lives out God's justice, holiness, covenant loyalty, faithfulness, and so on.

- **develop learning through questioning**. The prophetic function creates the conditions of holy discontent, which leads to a pursuit of methods and practices that are more consistent with who God is.

Most prophetic activities will be either vertical or horizontal, or when genuinely integrated and mature, will express both. And so we can see that the prophetic function itself codes prophetic sensibilities into the church. It becomes a community wired to "listen to" and "hear" (i.e., obey) God's Word.

I also believe this twofold distinction helps highlight the limitations of reducing the prophetic gift into either the mystical-charismatic dimension or the social justice activist types. In the Scriptures these ought to belong together, less we end up in mumbo jumbo or dry activism. The *passivist* (wait on God) and the *activist* (act for God) tendencies are the two sides of the covenant/kingdom coin. This is also true of the Wesleyan emphasis on *social* as well as *personal* holiness; in a mature biblical expression of the prophetic, the two belong together.

The Calling/Role of the Prophetic Person

The prophetic function in turn sets the agenda for the job description of prophetic people. Those graced with the prophetic calling will do all they can to listen to God, see what he sees, feel something of what he feels, speak and act on his behalf, and call people to faithfulness and obedience. JR Woodward calls prophets the "heart revealers" in the *ecclesia*.[16] In my experience, they make the best worship leaders and artists of all the fivefold types.

Prophets are often agitators for change. In the name of greater faithfulness they will tend to ask pointed questions that highlight God's call, the gap between our obedience and his will, and our responsibility to act accordingly. Outside the *ecclesia*, prophetic men and women are agents for broad cultural change, social justice, and incarnational integrity. They are the God-oriented mystics who call all people to attend to the voice of God, wherever and however it reveals itself.

The prophetic vocation is likely the most difficult of all the APEST callings, partly because of the personal vulnerability involved (God is "dangerous" ... he is a consuming fire) but also because the prophetic word, like the Word of God that the prophet seeks to represent, is often rejected by people who prefer their own ways. The prophet is likely the loneliest of all the vocations and the one most open to misunderstanding. I think this is why Jesus calls us to especially respect the prophets in our midst (Matthew 10:4–42).

But because of the close association of the prophet and the unfolding of the will/heart of God, along with the innate subjectivity of this message, prophets can potentially be volatile and divisive people—especially when their gifting is immature and undeveloped. New Testament prophets are therefore put under significant restriction and are subject to corporate discernment and discipline when necessary—we are told to test all prophecy, as well as to hold "false" prophets to account (1 Corinthians 12–14; 1 Thessalonians 5:20–21; 2 Peter 2:1; 1 John 4:1ff.). The Body truly benefits from mature prophets who follow in the way of the Suffering Servant—the subversive and hidden agent of God.

But prophetic people following in the way of Jesus cannot be moralistic and grouchy religious naysayers; like Jesus, they are also harbingers of eschatological joy and hope, heroes of the faith, declarers of God's abiding love for his people no matter what, people who find their primary comfort in God himself—the intimacy of the prophet's connection to God is its own reward.

Evangelistic-Evangelist

At their core, the evangelistic aspects of the church relate to their unique status as people whose very existence is brought about through living into the original and originating message of the *ecclesia*—the gospel of the kingdom. Evangelism is essentially the task of getting the message out and getting a positive response from the audience. In many ways, the evangelistic function is the church's inbuilt marketing department.

Seminal missiologist David Bosch offers us a packed description of the church's evangelistic purpose:

> We may, then, summarize evangelism as that dimension and authority of the church's mission which, by word and deed and in light of particular conditions and a particular context, offers every person and community everywhere a valid opportunity to be directly challenged to a radical reorientation of their lives, an orientation which involves such things as deliverance from slavery to the world and its powers; embracing Christ as Saviour and Lord; becoming a living member of his community, the church; being enlisted into his service of reconciliation, peace, and justice on earth; and being committed to God's purpose of placing all things under the rule of Christ.[17]

The Evangelistic Function/Purposes of the Church

Leveraging off Bosch's great description, I would add that the evangelist function exists to:

- **communicate.** The evangelistic function enhances the capacities of the whole church to be able to communicate the unfolding story of the church in compelling, accessible, and understandable ways.

- **elicit response.** It elicits a response from the audience—effectively "closing the deal."

- **create an invitational culture.** Related to the "taste and see" aspect of the previous function, an evangelistic culture invites people to experience what the church is pointing toward. In this form, it is inherently attractional.

- **sneeze the movement message.** Evangelism involves the infectious sharing of the movement's core message. This is done both inside and outside the community of faith. The message itself must remain compellingly related to real existential human issues so as to retain its infectious and timeless nature. The message is viral and can readily be passed on. A church without an evangelistic function is definitely on its way to death, precisely because the gospel (the evangel) is what brings new life.

- **ensure cultural relevance.** Evangelism makes rich use of popular culture (symbols, language, narratives, and ideas) to find the gospel-keys into the heart of the immediately surrounding culture (not necessarily cross-cultural).

- **develop sticky messaging.** The sticky message is simple, surprising, emotive, and creates enthusiasm. The evangelist ensures the "stickiness" of the core message of the church—the evangel, or the cause of the organization.

- **present the value proposition.** It is vital that all understand the "value proposition" that is the church of Jesus Christ. To use the words *marketing*, *sales* and *promotion* does not cheapen but rather highlights the irreplaceable importance of the function for movemental forms of church.

- **create branding.** Branding involves the management of how the organization is being perceived and experienced. Because it is concerned largely with the communication and reception of the message, evangelistic functions will need to include the issue of branding and brand consistency.

- **value the individual.** Evangelism takes individual people very seriously. Each person is a vital part of a network in the broader society. Each person is an object of God's eternal compassion.

- **demonstrate catalytic witness.** Because of this external focus, evangelism is an essential catalyst for people movement. It's not just about verbal proclamation but is also committed to the *demonstration* of good news in word, sign, and deed. Evangelism is therefore witness to the good news of the reign of God in Jesus.

- **recruit to the cause.** Sociologically speaking, evangelism is all about recruitment to the cause. Cultivating an innate evangelistic sensibility therefore requires making sure that the message is transmitted well and is received by the recipients in ways that draw them into the saving story of Jesus. But recruitment is not just about "saving people." It also describes the general capacity to draw people into the various other functions of the church in mission.

The Calling/Role of the Evangelistic Person

The whole church, in fact all Christians, are to be involved in extending the message of the church. But some are called to embody and exemplify evangelism in the community. These are the evangelists.[18] Evangelists are exceptional recruiters. The most obvious outcome of the ministry of evangelists is that people are enlisted to the cause of Christ. In other words, the church grows. Evangelists have the capacity to get significant buy-in from their hearers. They are persuasive, infectious people with appealing personalities.[19] In terms of the diffusion of ideas and the spread of movements, they are the persuaders—people with significant negotiation skills. They tend to have an indefinable trait that goes beyond what they say and makes others want to agree with them. For this reason, evangelists are agents of conversion.

Evangelists tend to be great social connectors—the kind of people who can link the rest of us up with the world: "They have a special gift for bringing the world together," as Malcolm Gladwell puts it.[20] They have a capacity to make connections with people in a way that demonstrates social as well as emotional intelligence. In many ways, their function is therefore genuinely priestly, in that they mediate between God and people as well as between people and people. Evangelists also have an affinity for the gospel that makes them adept at applying it to people's unique experience and circumstance.

They really are positive, *good news* people. The sharing of good news is an inextricable part of their capacity to understand people and make connections. Not only do they have strong relational affinity, they also have a great capacity to translate the gospel into the prevailing culture in ways that make a lot of sense. This too is an intrinsic aspect of priestly ministry: mediating the knowledge of God, sharing good news, and inviting people to join the story.

Outside the organized faith community, evangelists tend to be entrepreneurs, excellent communicators, motivators, marketers, and enthusiastic storytellers.

Shepherding-Shepherd

The ideal of a good shepherd is widespread throughout the Bible (Psalm 23) as is conversely the image of a bad one (Jeremiah 21). The shepherd, the one who cares for his sheep, symbolizes one of the ideal forms of political dominion in Israel. The Lord tells David, "You will shepherd my people Israel, and you will become their ruler" (2 Samuel 5:2). Following the many archetypal biblical cues, fulfilled and exemplified by our Great Shepherd, the shepherding purposes given to the church will tend to be those associated with social connectivity in the community and the church's purpose to be an agent of God's healing—helping people to develop resiliency and protecting them from damaging influences.

The Shepherding Function/Purposes of the Church

The shepherding function or purpose of the church exists to:

- **enrich communal experience.** At its core, the *ecclesia* is a community gathered in adherence to Jesus—the recipients of his saving, reconciling, and healing grace. The shepherding function exists to enhance the communal dimension of the community. Friendship, mutuality, reconciliation, and devotion in the midst of life together demonstrate a better way to be human together.

- **develop social bonding.** In many ways, the shepherding functions develop the necessary attachment and bonding to the movement and its purposes in the world. The focus therefore falls strongly on developing loving relationships that mirror the love of Jesus in the world. In a sense, the shepherding function is the ecclesial equivalent of an organization's human resource (HR) department.

- **demonstrate credible witness.** It was Lesslie Newbigin who said that the greatest evidence for the power of the gospel is the life of a community who is willing to live by it.[21] The shepherd purpose of the church will be then to nurture just this form of alternative society of local disciples witnessing to the blessings of the kingdom of God.

- **protect the Body.** Healthy communities are notoriously difficult to develop and maintain. Because each member of the community is capable of sinful actions and each community is made up of selfish people, community life is inordinately vulnerable to damage. Therefore, like the Good Shepherd, shepherding will serve to protect the church from influences and people that will destroy it from the inside out. More often than not, these forces are inside the church; the shepherding function will at times therefore need to be able to identify, correct, and discipline errant members.

- **promote and facilitate healing.** This highlights the healing and restorative dimensions of the gospel of Jesus. This function spans from practical care of the sick and feeble, to prayer for healing, to counseling and reconciliation in broken relationships—a very important aspect of healthy community.

- **encourage shalom and wholeness.** The biblical idea of peace (*shalom*) involves not just an absence of conflict, but also the active experience of harmony, restoring of wholeness, and the experience of godly prosperity.

- **champion inclusion and embrace.** The members of the church are chosen by Jesus and not by societal trends and preferences. The church is a new humanity made up of all classes, ethnicities, and genders, united together in Jesus and called into his Body. There is a deep respect for the poor and the excluded.

- **assist in discipleship in the Way.** This function requires each church to assist its members in living consistent lives in the everyday. The local church is in essence a disciple-making system where everyone is committed to following Jesus in the context of all of life. Perhaps one of the best ways to articulate the essence of the shepherding function is summed up in the word *formation* in the way of Christ, lived locally and communally.

- **enable human flourishing.** The shepherding function creates a culture and an environment where people can thrive and flourish and reach their full potential as creatures made in the image of God.

- **cultivate the family of God.** One of the main goals of the shepherding functions is to draw people together and reconcile them together as a redeemed family. The functions look to restore God to the people as *father* and to each other as *brothers and sisters*. Family is God's plan A, and the shepherding functions highlight the empathetic nature and loyalty that keeps families together.

- **cultivate rich and loving community.** Scripture is clear that one of the main ways the world will know us is by our reputation as a loving community (John 13:35). Deep and meaningful relationships with one another, along with a strong value for each person's story exemplify the shepherding functions that seek to create and maintain healthy community.

The Calling/Role of the Shepherding Person

At its core, the shepherd is the vocation tasked with creating and maintaining healthy community, promoting the common good, encouraging people in the faith, and ensuring the welfare of the people as well as the broader society in which the community abides.[22]

Shepherds pay close attention to their immediate environment, noticing details about people and the state of the community. They necessarily have strong empathic aptitudes and heightened capacities for meaningful friendships and relationships. To be a good shepherd in any reasonable sense of the word would be to know all the names and the stories of the people in one's immediate care. Although this does not exclude a broader shepherd-of-shepherds (*pastor et pastorium*) role that occurs in a larger pastoral organization, it does highlight that calling oneself a pastor or shepherd yet not knowing the personal details of the particular people in one's orbit probably disqualifies one from being a shepherd in any meaningful sense of the term.

Because of their great sense of and need for cohesion and unity, shepherds will find it disheartening when people leave the community—for good or not-so-good reasons. People, even (or perhaps especially) the most unlikely, most vulnerable, and most insignificant ones, matter to shepherds.

Teaching-Teacher

The teaching function has roots in the scriptural tradition but came to prominence in Israel's exile, as the people of God had to cultivate a distinctive worldview in a hostile context—hence the role of the rabbi by the time of Jesus. Other than that, its roots are in Israel's wisdom literature, whereby people were schooled in seeing the world through the eyes of faith.

The Teaching Functions/Purposes of the Church

The teaching function of the church exists to:

- **bring wisdom and understanding.** At its core, the teaching function is focused on acquiring wisdom and understanding in the community of God's people. This is achieved partly by cultivating a culture of curiosity and the pursuit of insight and learning, as well as through the interpretation and explanation of the Scriptures. In the New Testament, the church is meant to be its own seminary, a place of learning, and is directly responsible for the teaching function.

- **develop worldview formation and maintenance.** Christianity has a distinctive "take" on the world. There is such a thing as a biblical mind. It means seeing the world as God sees it, as described in the Scriptures. One of the key purposes of teaching is the development of a philosophy congruent to Scripture and workable in life.

- **cultivate a love of the Scriptures.** The Scriptures are complex and rich documents that require devoted and loving study in order to see their true beauty. The teaching function seeks to reveal the beauty to all within the church.

- **ensure theological discourse.** One of the key aspects of the teaching function is to ensure ongoing *theo-logos* (God-talk) through engagement with the primary texts of the movement among all the members of the community.

- **develop resources for learning.** A critical aspect of the teaching function is to communicate ideas through the various media at hand. This also involves developing useful tools, writings, liturgies and practices that can embody ideas.

- **integrate life and thinking**. Good teaching not only informs; it also *forms* people in an ethos ... a way of discipleship. For theology to be truly grasped, it must be lived. We must become the truth that we seek to convey. The medium must become consistent to its core message. This involves lifelong learning and practice.

- **transmit ideas**. It is very important for the church to be able to transfer its worldview and ideas to individual people, and through them, to different generations and cultures.

- **develop traditioning**. This involves the development of a "tradition" (*paradosis*) or learning that can be handed down from one generation to another, which creates a legacy of those ideas. The articulation of this tradition is an important aspect of the teaching function.

- **create a culture of lifelong learning**. The teaching function creates a passion for learning within the community. Teachers create a culture that values and creates pathways for learning, and makes learning accessible to all. Learning is lifelong because we are continually being transformed, as well as continually exploring and discovering ever-greater depths of God.

The Calling/Role of the Teaching Person

As we can see, at its core the teaching function is about mediating a particular type of practical wisdom and philosophical understanding nuanced by the biblical worldview. A teacher therefore will largely be concerned with helping people gain insight into how God wants them to see and experience their world. As such, they will seek to bring theological truth and shape the consciousness of God's people to be consistent with that truth.[23]

In many ways, teachers are similar to prophets and apostles in that they deal with ideas that shape life. The difference perhaps is that teachers are concerned more about broad comprehension and systematic understanding as opposed to faithfulness to the covenant (prophets) and the nest of more foundational and formative (meta)ideas for which the apostle is the assigned custodian. Teachers often do not have that sense of urgency that drives the apostolic and the prophetic functions.

From a biblical perspective, teaching is not about speculation in and of itself (idealism); rather, it is about the ministry of ideas in action (ethos), that is, discipleship or formation. Teachers cannot teach what they do not know, and they cannot lead where they will not themselves go. Therefore, biblical teachers must have real participation in the ideas they propose.

Bringing it All Together

Summarizing all this in a table might look like this:

Table 7.1 Comprehensive List of Functions and Possible Expressions of Callings

APOSTOLIC / APOSTLE

APEST Functions (Purposes)	APEST Callings (Roles)
· Seeding the DNA of the church through mission and works that extend the movement · Maintaining an abiding commitment of sentness (mission) throughout the organization · Extending the missionary impact of the church · Maintaining compliancy around core ideas and culture (DNA) · Networking translocally · Maintaining paradigm and vision · Maintaining a strategic commitment to church planting strategy and pioneering leadership · Ensuring organizational agility, adaptability, and scalability · Mobilizing leaders, resources, and churches · Maintaining a sense of the big picture which makes sense of the small issues · Priming the organization for innovation and entrepreneurship · Developing capacities for appropriate risk-taking (develop "anti-fragile" organization)	· Missional leaders · Movement starters · Church planters (though not all) · Innovators · Pioneers · Custodians of the DNA of the Church · Entrepreneurs · Organizational architects and designers · Cross-cultural missionaries · Founders of organizations/movements · Guardians of the organizing ideas (DNA) · Designers and architects · Networkers · Culture creators · Missional trainers · Research and development workers · Consultants · Ambassadors (agents and representatives) · Quality controllers

PROPHETIC / PROPHET

APEST Functions (Purposes)	APEST Callings (Roles)
· Maintaining the God focus/orientation throughout the organization through prayer and worship · Maintaining covenantal bonds throughout church/organization (love, passion, and responsibility) · Cultivating commitments to social justice and commitments to respect the poor · Engaging in spiritual warfare · Speaking truth to power · Encouraging repentance to maintain the God-relationship · Questioning the institution where it becomes inhuman, self-protective, and/or oppressive · Developing learning through questioning · Maintaining the moral and spiritual witness of the community · Maintaining the "soul" of the organization · Fueling passion for the cause · Renouncing idolatry and false forms of worship · Maintaining the integrity and authenticity to the founding values · Maintaining and cultivating a holy imagination of life under God's rule and covenant · Developing prophetic sensibilities in leaders and ministers · Developing prefigurative communities that witness to God's presence and purpose · Maintaining self-critical insight in the organization and the people	· Call to repentance and faithfulness · Intercessors · Social activists and campaigners · "Passionary" (maintaining the soul and passion of the organization) · Worship leaders · Questioners of the status quo · Holy rebels/dissenters · Incarnational missionaries · Innovators of new forms · Poets · Artists · Musicians · Prayer and deliverance ministers · Local activists · Non-violent protesters · Aid and development workers · Problem solvers · Detectives · Mystics · Insightful/deep thinkers · Whistle-blowers · Investigative journalists

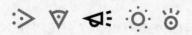

EVANGELISTIC / EVANGELIST

APEST Functions (Purposes)	APEST Callings (Roles)
· Developing an invitational and welcoming culture (enhancing attractional capacities) · Proclaiming the core messages of the organization/church · Championing cultural relevance of organization and message to primary audience · Developing the stickiness and simplicity of the core message · Entrepreneurial · Developing evangelistic culture · Ensuring Evangel(ical) theology and ethos · Maintaining cultural relevance · Developing evangelistic leadership and ministers · Maintaining connections with outsiders · Maintaining positive, life-affirming and redemptive "vibe" in the community	· Recruiters to the cause · Contagious agents of the message · Singers of the organization's song · Spreaders of the message · Apologists · Entrepreneurs · Salespeople · Communications and media workers · Marketers · Storytellers · Leaders of large and expansive organizations · Journalists · Networkers · Event producers and directors · Deal-makers

SHEPHERDING / SHEPHERD

APEST Functions (Purposes)	APEST Callings (Roles)
· Cultivating a loving and caring community · Being the extended "Family of God" · Including the unloved and marginalized · Ensuring bonding among the followers in the Jesus movement · Cultivating wholesome relationships in community · Developing a loving culture · Developing a high EQ Culture · Championing a commitment to discipleship · Ensuring the appropriate protection of members (inclusion/exclusion) · Maintaining relational glue · Developing and maintaining pathways for maturity and discipleship · Enacting communal discipline · Creating a place of healing · Developing pastoral leadership and ministers	· Defenders and guardians of the community · Pastoral carers · Spiritual directors · Community developers · Networkers (relational) · Healers-counselors · Spiritual directors · Human resource workers · Recreational workers · Social workers · Police and defense personnel · Conveners of community · Liturgists (communal worship)

TEACHING / TEACHER

APEST Functions (Purposes)	APEST Callings (Roles)
· Fostering a learning culture—the church is its own seminary · Developing resources for learning · Developing active learning experiences through engagement with God and World · Cultivating a culture of curiosity and the love of insight · Explaining and interpreting the Scriptures · Articulating the theology-philosophy of the group · Transferring ideas across generations · Providing instruction in the Way · Fostering wisdom and intelligence · Developing a philosophy congruent to Scripture and life · Training wise and informed leaders and ministers	· Mediators of wisdom and understanding · Instructors/trainers · Managers of meaning · Mentors/coaches · Educators · Theologians · Philosophers · Guides for the perplexed · Writers · Thinkers · Truth-tellers · Researchers

Just to highlight the power of functionality, consider all the functions down the left-hand column. If a church has a way to cover all these, how rich it would be. You essentially here are witnessing the power of a 5Q organization. This church is doing the work!

Consider how important these various functions are for the life of any healthy organization, let alone the church. How could you operate without them? And it is worth reminding ourselves that God has already given us all that we need to get the job done—this includes the fivefold. The good news is that all five functions/callings are like seeds latent in the system. They are already there by virtue of the defining Word of God. This is a liberating idea—all the potential for a tree is actually already in the seed; we don't need to mess much with that. What we need to do is simply focus on the environment that will allow the seed to flourish.

• About Arrested Development

Because it is the active way of expressing the Body of Christ, the fivefold system is all about the symmetry, proportion, and interdependence of the functions. When one function (or person) dominates the others, it must have a detrimental effect on the whole Body. In their useful book on missional leadership, Briggs and Hyatt note that churches with a dominant function, or that are led predominantly by a certain type of leader, tend to flavor the whole ministry with that function, as well as the spirituality of that church.[24] This often creates an unhealthy bias that disrupts the spiritual ecology of Jesus' body. So, for instance:

- Churches with a strong apostolic bias tend to break new ground, constantly pushing the bounds of creativity in ministry and forging ahead into new territory. In these communities, spirituality tends to be experienced as something dynamic, adventurous, and innovative. However, when the apostolic is dominant to the exclusion of the other types, the organization will be task-driven, demanding, and alienating.

- Churches with a strong prophetic bias tend to speak truth to those in power and do well at justice-oriented ministry. In these churches, spirituality is equated with care for the poor, the marginalized and the outsider. These churches will also call forth a passionate response to God in worship and prayer. They will also engage in spiritual warfare and discernment of spirits. However, when the prophetic is overdominant, the community can be outright whacky, overcritical, demanding, moralistic and judgmental.

- Churches strong on evangelism and led by evangelists tend to be characterized by a heart for those who don't know Jesus and have a strong emphasis on evangelism. In these churches, spirituality is equated with a heart for the lost and telling others about Jesus. When dominant, the church will feel like an Amway convention, relying on marketing methodology, charismatic leaders, and will very likely be shallow. The church will tend to be pushy, opinionated, and aggressive.

- Churches led by leaders who are strong on shepherding tend to do well at loving each other and caring for the needs of the Body. Spirituality will be strongly communal and relational. But when the shepherding function dominates the others, the community can become risk-averse, co-dependent, cloying, exclusive, overprotective and cautious.

- Churches with a strong teaching function tend to be well-informed, wise, patient and committed to discipleship. But when the function is dominant, the church will likely be an over-intellectual, objective, knowledge-based community where right doctrine is seen to be more important than rightdoing. Such a church is likely to be controlling, anxious, fussy and doctrinaire. In these teacher-dominated communities, spirituality can easily be equated with listening to sermons and acquiring Bible knowledge.

In human development theory, this type of imbalance in either people or in human systems is called precocious development, and it is generally considered to be a disorder with an associated pathology.[25] Think of a child who is freakishly overdeveloped in one dimension of life (e.g., math or art) and ends up relying too strongly on his or her overdeveloped capacities, failing to develop the other essential aspects needed for proper functioning in the world. For precocious people, then "holistic maturity is very difficult due to the over-reliance on their strengths and the arrested development of the other areas. True maturity requires integration, which is difficult when the over-developed strength mimics wisdom but masks deep immaturity. Literally, therapy and inner healing are needed to bring health and wholeness."[26]

One does not have to look very far to see evidence of a one-dimensional and immature approach to organization. For instance, a precocious apostolic leader/church will always tend to see the organization's problems as being caused by a lack of more distinctly apostolic approaches, whereas the real answer might well be that the group needs more by way of the self-correcting dynamic of one or more of the other four functions. So, for instance, to an apostolic person the answer is always more church planting and leadership training. To a teacher, the answer to the church's problems is always—yes you guessed it—more preaching and bible study, etc.

Think about it; so many evangelical churches seem to over-rely on the sermon (T/S) or put all their effort into the Sunday service (E/S) to the neglect of other vital functions of *ecclesia* such as evangelism, discipleship, mission, and covenant community. Attractional evangelism alone (E) over-relies on a particular and overused, entertainment-based method and loads that onto the Sunday gathering to the exclusion of the other functions of ministry. In all these cases the answer always seems to revolve around improving the sermon and getting people to the weekend service, as if more sermons and the latest worship music craze will solve the systemic problems of the church. This is reductionism at its worst! Churches operating like this not only fail to communicate the broader fivefold purposes and identities of Christ, but are precocious, disordered, deformed, and immature. Not pretty!

At its best, precocious asymmetry within the 5Q system creates a kind of obsessive narrow-mindedness that sees the purposes of the *ecclesia* in a constricted and exclusive way. The result is that the purposes of the church are reduced to merely one or two of the five necessary functions. At its worst, such a church can be dysfunctional and cult-like because it lacks the mutual self-correcting capacities inherent in the fivefold functions. This is hardly the image of the maturing Body of Christ given to us by Paul in Ephesians 4:12–16.

When will we learn? In order to be an authentic expression of the Body of Christ, each of the APEST functions need all the other functions in order to be healthy themselves (Ephesians 4:12–16). The real answer to our complex problems is seldom one-dimensional. The answer I believe is at least five-dimensional: the symphony of 5Q.

Another problem associated with APEST asymmetry is that the asymmetrical churches always end up attracting people who are like-minded and therefore asymmetrical. The one-dimensional teaching church attracts people who love to be taught and tends to alienate other forms of spiritual expression. This is seldom a good thing because such churches simply become vulnerable to groupthink or even mass delusion. This has happened way too often … witness the many one-dimensional charismatic/vertical prophetic movements of the last century. Or consider the asymmetrical mega-church that markets religion and ends up producing consumptive, dependent, underdeveloped, cultural Christians with an exaggerated sense of entitlement.

• Putting the Last Pieces of the Puzzle Together

The Body of Christ exists to extend both the logic and impact of the ministry of Christ in the world. If Jesus expressed his ministry in terms of the fivefold, then the church as the primary agency of the ministry of Jesus must correspondingly also have all the fivefold functions operative to do what Jesus did and to attain to the fullness of Christ. When we put it all together we can sense the wonderful symmetry that Jesus has built into the Body.

Perhaps the use of a table at this point will help us to see how far we have come in articulating the 5Q system. This will also provide us with something of a summary. Notice again that the functions and the callings exist on the far edge of the entire system. But they receive and carry forward the weight of the whole redemptive process delivered over to them in Jesus Christ.

(See Table 7.2 overleaf)

Table 7.2 5Q System in Overview

FUNCTION / CALLING:
APOSTOLIC / APOSTLE

Theological Roots (APEST in the doctrine of God)	Archetypes and Heroes (APEST patterns laced in and throughout creation)	Reconstituted APEST (Redeemed and exemplified in Jesus)	APEST Functions (Implicit) (Given to and coded into *ecclesia*)	APEST Callings (Explicit) (Practitioners)
Father, Creator, Sender (*missio Dei*), Sovereign, Designer, Judge, Source	Founder, General, Agent-envoy, Visionary, Pioneer, Adventurer **Examples:** Pioneers, Breakthrough designers, Innovators, Entrepreneurs, Visionaries, Embodiments of purpose-mission, Paradigm shifters, Cultural architects, Movement-makers, Systems thinkers, Business Leaders, Problem-Solvers, Imagineers, Start-ups	Founder, Messiah, Sent one, King/Head, Messiah, God's kingdom agent, Establisher of genetic code/DNA, Establisher and builder of his church, Commissioner of his people	Organize around sentness, Maintain integrity of paradigm and DNA, Translocal networking, Entrepreneurial capacities, Church planting, Scale and scalability in organization, Innovation and risk-taking	Church planters, Innovators, Entrepreneurs, Cross-cultural missionaries, Organizational designers, Regional networkers, Cultural architects

FUNCTION / CALLING:
PROPHETIC / PROPHET

Theological Roots (APEST in the doctrine of God)	Archetypes and Heroes (APEST patterns laced in and throughout creation)	Reconstituted APEST (Redeemed and exemplified in Jesus)	APEST Functions (Implicit) (Given to and coded into *ecclesia*)	APEST Callings (Explicit) (Practitioners)
Holy, Faithful, Incarnate Transcendent, Covenantal, Just and True, Omnipotent	Seer, Warrior, Poet, Reformer, Iconoclast, Meaning-maker **Examples:** Artists, Poets, Shamans, Ethicists, Activists, Liberators, Meaning-makers, Iconoclasts, Revolutionaries, Advocates, Existentialists, Anarchists, Hackers, Spiritualists, Mystics, Environmentalists, Whistle-blowers, Feminists, Aid workers, Psychologists, Politicians, Futurists, Quality controllers	Word made flesh, God's New Covenant, Faithful Son, Prophet (speaks and acts for/ as God), Calls to repentance, The way/truth/light, Demonstrates perfect holiness and faithfulness, Speaks truth to power (both religious and secular), Ushers in *kairos* time, Radical ethics of the kingdom	Maintain God focus/orientation, Require conformity to covenant obligations, Demonstrate right faith/ fullness, Develop prefigurative community, Bring words of knowledge, Give prophetic insight	Intercessor, Social activists, Questioners of the status quo, Worship leaders, Holy rebels, Ethical leadership

FUNCTION / CALLING:

EVANGELISTIC / EVANGELIST

Theological Roots (APEST in the doctrine of God)	Archetypes and Heroes (APEST patterns laced in and throughout creation)	Reconstituted APEST (Redeemed and exemplified in Jesus)	APEST Functions (Implicit) (Given to and coded into *ecclesia*)	APEST Callings (Explicit) (Practitioners)
Savior, Redeemer, Gracious Giver, Lover, Merciful	Messenger, Achiever, Believer, Guerilla-leader, Champion, Storyteller **Examples:** Mobilizers, Recruiters, Negotiators, Sales, Media workers, Achievers, Marketers, Organizers, Miracle-workers, Communicators, Preachers, Dealers, Raconteurs, Journalists, Motivational speakers, Networkers, Buccaneers, Public relations	Savior, Message-messenger, Redeemer, The way/life, Proclaimer of the gospel, Embodies good news, Demonstrates the reign of God, Recruits followers, Bearer of love and hope (Israel's Messiah), Seeks and saves the lost	Recruit culture, Maintain commitment to Gospel theology and ethos, Invitational, Maintain cultural relevance, Inspirational	Recruiters to the movement, Storytellers, Spreaders of message (communicators), Apologists

FUNCTION / CALLING:

SHEPHERDING / SHEPHERD

Theological Roots (APEST in the doctrine of God)	Archetypes and Heroes (APEST patterns laced in and throughout creation)	Reconstituted APEST (Redeemed and exemplified in Jesus)	APEST Functions (Implicit) (Given to and coded into *ecclesia*)	APEST Callings (Explicit) (Practitioners)
Community in Trinity, Comforter, Immanent, Intimate Knower (*yada*), Divine Parent, Compassionate	Caregiver, Defender, Peacemaker, Helper, Servant, Selfless, Healer **Examples:** Elders, Lovers, Guardians, Loyalists, Humanizers, Parents, First responders, Cultivators, Mediators, Military, Counselors, Health-workers, Priests, Community workers, Human resources, Police	Good Shepherd, Healer, Reconciler, Protector/Guardian of the community (lays down his life), The life, Reconciler, Healer, Establishes true community, God's righteous one (*Tzaddik*)	Cultivate loving and caring community, Protect members, Maintain relational glue, Develop pathways for maturity / discipleship, Create place of healing, Shalom	Pastoral carers, Spiritual directors, Community reconcilers, Relational glue, Healers-counselors, First responders

FUNCTION / CALLING:
TEACHING / TEACHER

Theological Roots (APEST in the doctrine of God)	Archetypes and Heroes (APEST patterns laced in and throughout creation)	Reconstituted APEST (Redeemed and exemplified in Jesus)	APEST Functions (Implicit) (Given to and coded into *ecclesia*)	APEST Callings (Explicit) (Practitioners)
Omniscient, Prescient, Truth, Beauty, Wisdom, Logos (Reason)	Sages, Thinkers, Observers, Philosophers, Guides, Scientists **Examples:** Coaches, Instructors, Investigators, Information workers, Professors, Educationalists, Mentors, Disciplers, Theoreticians, Debaters, Engineers, Researchers, Theologians, Accountants, Forensics, Legal workers	Rabbi, Logos, The truth, The way, Light of the world, Our teacher/guide, The Word made flesh, God's wise judge, The fulfillment of the Torah, The riches of knowledge and wisdom	Foster learning culture, Develop resources for learning, Articulate the theology-ideology for the group, Provide instruction in the Way	Instructors, Theologians, Philosophers, Guides, Writers, Thinkers, Truth-tellers

It is also pretty easy to discern that each one of the five major functions is critically important to the health of the others. Each actually needs the other to make the whole work. (The church really is a body after all.) Together they represent Jesus' ministry in a way that they cannot in isolation from the other. That we have sought to negotiate our way in the world without three of the five functions (by elevating teaching and shepherding and neglecting evangelism, the prophetic and the apostolic) accounts for so many of the problems we face in the church. In the next chapter I will seek to make a case as to how the fivefold system, based as it is on the ministry of Jesus, provides us with distinguishing "marks" (metrics) of the church. This in turn will provide us with a real approach to both diagnose our ills and where necessary, to cure the disease. To this we now turn.

Chapter 8

Marking the Body

People in any organization are always attached to the obsolete—the things that should have worked but did not, the things that once were productive and no longer are.

—Peter Drucker

All our ecclesiologies are inadequate and out of date. Nearly all of them have been constructed in the light of a static concept of the Church as something given, something which already exists. Much attention has been concentrated on external "marks of the Church." As far as I know, no one has yet set to work to think out the theology of the Church in terms of the one thing for which it exists.

—Bishop Stephen Neill

Church is not what we do; it is what God does, although we participate in it.

—Eugene H. Peterson

In a commencement speech given at Kenyon College in 2005, David Foster Wallace told the following story:

There are these two young fish swimming along, and they happen to meet an older fish swimming the other way. The older fish nods at them: "Morning, boys, how's the water?" The two young fish swim on for a bit, and then one of them looks over at the other. "What the heck is water?"[1]

The immediate point of this fish story is that the most obvious, ubiquitous and important realities are often the ones that are the hardest to see and talk about. We don't know who actually discovered water, but we are pretty sure it wasn't the fish. *The fish is blind to its own wetness because it has never lived anywhere else*; it has nothing else with which to compare its own experience.

One of the strangest things about human consciousness is that it seems that the more fundamental things are to our existence, the less consciously aware we tend to be of them. Question the truth of this? Well then, answer the following: While we all have a "self," an ego, try describing it in a way that makes sense to you and others. Another example is that although we all have some sort of existence, or "being," try briefly defining these concepts. What about "life"? What really is it? We are all apparently alive; you would think that we could sound off a definition in no time. Yet even the most self-aware of us find it hard to give an adequate description of any of these.

Ask the average Christian to define the church, and you will likely have a similar response. Even those who have been raised in the church will struggle to elaborate beyond even the most basic of descriptions and in accordance with the prevailing paradigm. But it is concerning, not only because this lack of awareness exposes deficiencies in a sense of biblical identity and purpose, but also because it demonstrates how the standard reductionist formulations have become limiting prisons for the church's collective mind.

In what follows, I am going to suggest that the fivefold typology, based as it is on Jesus, and coded into the very constitution of the Body of Christ, provides us with one of the most accurate ways of *identifying* the church and *measuring* its maturity and effectiveness.[2]

• On Your Marks ... When is a Church a Church?

So, how *do* we know when a group calling itself "church" really is a church? How can we reliably gauge whether a community claiming to be an *ecclesia* really is an authentic expression of "church" as the Bible understands it? How is the church different from any other social grouping? In other words, the *marks* are the *defining characteristics*, the *distinguishing features* that mark us off as different. They are also a theological metrics of sorts and can be used as a "dashboard" of the organization to assess where things are at in the system.

How does this relate to APEST? Recall the discussion in chapter six about the Christ//Body of Christ dynamic—that the church is meant to correspond to Jesus and be conformed to him. We saw in his ascension, that Jesus bequeaths APEST once and for all to his Body. The Body therefore is the direct, corresponding recipient of Christ's own fivefold ministry. In its very constitution/foundation therefore, the Body of Christ is designed to *em-body* and extend the full ministry of Jesus himself. In the 5Q system we can better grasp the nature of our purpose (why?), the strategic functions needed (what?), and the distinct motivations and vocational shapes of the various people who are called (who?) and will better understand the tactics or methodologies that pertain to each type (how?).

According to the standard dictionary definition, to "embody" means to "be an expression of, or give a tangible or visible form to, an idea, quality, or feeling." To embody something is to make it concrete and real. This means that what is being expressed must be observable; it must be able to be measured as a distinct activity. According to Ephesians 4, as we have seen, the Body must be able to demonstrate full APEST functionality to be a mature and authentic church! In fact, APEST is to be its living, ever-evolving, maturing, form. *APEST is therefore a super effective metric on the church's authenticity as well as its effectiveness.* Leadership guru Seth Godin rather wryly notes that "measurement is fabulous. Unless you're busy measuring what's easy to measure as opposed to what's important."[3] 5Q is a way of ensuring that you are measuring that which is essential and important. And it is worth noting at this point, that as organizational experts always reiterate … what you measure improves, and what you celebrate gets repeated.[4]

So, What's in a Definition?

It is this measurability that brings this whole conversation into relation with what the church has traditionally called "the marks of the church" (*notae ecclesiae*). Marks are the quantifiable quality-characteristics that differentiate the *ecclesia* from other communities, like the local pub, the sports club, or the mosque. They indicate whether or not a congregation is authentic and is in fact a genuine church of Jesus Christ—they serve as checks of authenticity. For instance, the true church is not just any other worshipping community (like a mosque or a Sikh temple); the church's worship is thoroughly distinguished by its devotion to God in Jesus Christ. The marks are inherently phenomenological in that they are the means by which any group can be readily recognized as an authentic church—or not.[5] In other words, you cannot just read about the marks; you must be able to observe them.

Marks are also in a sense our most basic definitions. They set the most foundational criteria by which we operate. This is because definitions create a mental image that eventually becomes a consciousness, which in turn leads people to act in various ways. Whole paradigms are formed by primary definitions that determine what is considered real among a group of people.[6]And so while it might seem obvious, when it comes to the church, with its distinctive purposes in the world, really good definitions become vital, and really bad ones fatal.

Always the Same or Always Reforming?

In order to propose the APEST as valid marks of the church, I have to come out and say why I believe the prevailing marks of the church are utterly inadequate. First, let us briefly consider the marks put forward by the Roman Catholic Church.

The Roman Catholic Church sees the marks of the church as *one, holy, catholic,* and *apostolic*. Derived from the Nicene Creed, these terms are seen to describe the church of Jesus Christ and its mission in the world. Emphasis in the Catholic system is on the elemental, ontological *essence* of church, but because the idea that to be a mark implied concrete expression, these too need to be visibly present and observable. For example, to be truly one and catholic (universal) there must be visible unity of structure and confession. For the Roman Catholics, this means compliance with Catholic sacraments, hierarchy, and authority. Therefore, any religious community that does not accept this is thereby deemed inauthentic. Hence Catholics will not share in Communion with other Christian faith expressions. Apostolic succession, the papacy, the magisterium, and other Roman Catholic conceptions all come into play. It is this complete identification of the true church to Roman Catholic polity that is unacceptable to most Protestants and other non-Catholic expressions of Christianity.

Aside from the highly institutional dimensions of Roman Catholic ecclesiology, I think the Nicene marks are genuinely big ideas and definitely helpful. Most significant perhaps is that Catholics do hereby recognize the sentness (apostolicity) of the church as one of its distinguishing marks. I'd take these over the standard Protestant marks (see below) any day.[7]

In order to distinguish their movement from Catholic hegemony, the Protestant Reformers concluded that there are only two (or three) marks of the church: the right preaching of God's Word and the right administration of baptism and the Lord's Supper. (Some in the Calvinist tradition add church discipline as one of the marks.) So according to standard Protestant theology, this is how you spot a church: When you see the two sacraments (or "ordinances") being practiced, and where there is biblical preaching, then voila, it is a true church of Jesus Christ! *Talk about an underwhelming description of the movement that Jesus started!*

Actually, this comes as no surprise because this is *exactly* what almost all Christians think the church really is ... buildings, clergy, and ritual/programs! That's precisely the message we have been giving them all along. Even more appallingly, this is exactly what non-believers think the church is as well. They have got the message because we have communicated these reduced understandings for so long, and so effectively, that they have become prisons of the mind of both Christians and non-Christians, insiders and outsiders. *Hoorah*—the Great Commission is thus fulfilled!

I apologize for the biting tone here, but I am always flabbergasted at how ridiculously reductionist and short-sighted the Protestant marks really are. Honestly, of all the doctrines handed down to us through our traditions, I can think of few more that are so uninspiring, clerical, and useless. Why do I say this?

Firstly, it's what's *left out* of these Protestant marks that really matters. There doesn't necessarily need to be an explicit mention of God, Jesus, or Holy Spirit to be considered an observable mark/metric (how can these be measured anyhow?), but whatever happened to a metrics defined by concrete expressions of love, discipleship, evangelism, mission, service, worship, or community? Not only are these not mentioned in the traditional marks, I would suggest that they are not even implied![8] The traditional marks leave us all with the strong impression that preaching and the practice of the two sacraments in a Sunday service are all that is required for us to be a church because it is precisely these that are being measured![9] There are glaring holes in this depiction/reduction of the church.

Secondly, these marks presuppose the active presence of a clerical/priestly class to mediate the sacraments and do the necessary preaching. In mainline Protestantism, the only way any Christian can "handle" the sacraments/ ordinances is to be ordained. By insisting on the priesthood of all believers, the Reformation rejected the "priestcraft" of Catholic sacramentalist tradition only to create another form of Protestant clericalism and religious sacramentalism every bit as elitist and entrenched as the Catholic ones.

Thirdly—and related to the above—it seems that the only place one can actually come into contact with the sacraments/ordinances is on a Sunday gathering of the church, and intermittently at that, as in many cases baptism and Communion are not celebrated every Sunday. Think about this: By enclosing the sacraments/ordinances into formal worship gatherings conducted only by ordained clergy, we effectively "institutionalize" grace, locking it up in a stained-glass institution. George Hunsberger, himself a Reformed theologian of note, has lamented that the Protestants' marks of the church have left us with an understanding of the church as "a *place* where certain things happen." Therefore, the church is defined primarily as a place where a person must go to hear the Bible taught, to participate in the Lord's Supper and baptism, and, in some cases, to experience church discipline.[10] Given that Jesus explicitly said that worship would no longer be limited to a specific location, and even less a building (John 4:20–24), what do we really think he would say to our restriction of grace to the confines of a religious institution?

How can we possibly have used these profoundly inadequate marks to characterize the Holy Spirit empowered, transformed and transforming people of God in the New Testament and history? How do they possibly describe the transformative phenomenon of the people-movement living out the faith in the context of ordinary life, going from house to house and city to city, by innovatively proclaiming the gospel of Jesus in diverse cultural contexts? How can we square these domesticated and all too churchly marks with the dynamism of New Testament spirituality and church? If our vision of the church and its ministry really comes to this—to the orderly administration of churchly sacraments, pulpit preaching, and perhaps some discipline—then all I can say is, "God help us!"

Ranting aside, if we accept an axiom of organizational theory—that we are perfectly designed to achieve what we are currently achieving—then applying the APEST test to the traditional marks, we can say that the church is *actually perfectly designed* by shepherds and teachers to produce shepherding and teaching outcomes.[11] The organizational bias of the inherited form of church organization is in a real sense a reflection of the consciousness of the people who designed it in the first place!

It's a classic example of the precociousness I discussed in chapter seven. The precocious asymmetry within the 5Q system has created an obsessive narrow-mindedness that sees the purposes of the *ecclesia* in a constricted and exclusive (APE)ST way. The church's structures and practices subsequently mirror the mindset of the people that produced it. In other words, what we see today among churches is exactly what you would expect to see arising from the predominant consciousness and logic of the shepherds and teachers who have effectively commandeered self-understanding of the church for hundreds of years now. This is the church predefined and seen with the hard eyes of the Christendom understanding. The traditional marks then turn out to be proof of the exclusion of distinctly APE understandings from our inherited understanding of church.

The problem is that all the other functions and purposes of the church have been edited out as if they no longer exist or are needed.[12] But I ask the reader again, how can you *define the church* without mission and extension (A), covenant obedience (P) and proclamation of good news (E)? I'm genuinely amazed that we have uncritically retained the traditional marks for so long. They ought to be finally discarded as obsolete—and even dangerous—relics of the thinking derived from our European Christendom past.

I fully realize some people will be offended by this. Some will consider calling traditional church theology to account tantamount to challenging God himself. This is because by overly sacramentalizing the human organization and cultural forms of the church, we have put it beyond criticism. This is unfortunate. Church insiders simply assume that the tradition got it right and that it should just be accepted on faith. It's a case of the holy fish not being able to see the church for all the holy water. I would argue that we can actually observe the end result of the church that has defined itself with the traditional marks. Just look at the form of church which came up with them in the first place! I don't think I am being too harsh when I say that, from a missional perspective at least, the predominant European church is an utter disaster!

All I ask is that you unharden your eyes in order to see again what it means to be an authentic expression of the Body of Christ. I ask that you firstly remember the dangers of reductionism in times of transition and crisis, then *prayerfully* and *honestly* reconsider how we can continue to justify the current, significantly reduced "marks" on the basis of the intrinsically missional (i.e., purposive) logic of Scripture itself. Beyond this, I would ask you to try and discern what is explicitly missing in the traditional formulas. What do you think is the result? It is what is *missing*—remember reductionism here—that makes the whole difference as to whether the church is being true to its total calling.

• Get Set ... The Fivefold Marks of the Church

Let me restate going forward that to be effective, the very concept of the marks requires that they be *clear, observable signs*—in effect, a *metrics*—by which all people can recognize a church as founded and led by Jesus.

As a metric system, think of the 5Q marks (and the associated 5Q Systems Test) as something like a sound mixing desk which allows the sound engineer to balance the inputs and outputs thus creating a truly symphonic sound. Balance in the fivefold, both in inputs as well as outputs, equals harmony. The true and authentic church must have all the marks *visibly* and *demonstrably* present. So the ministry and leadership mix ought to reflect a harmony of all five functions.

But how do I come to the claim that the fivefold purposes of the church might actually provide us with the best set of marks by which to assess the legitimacy of the church as church? Well, to answer this we simply need to summarize the logic of this book so far.

As we saw in chapter six, any legitimate understanding of the church must be established on the active presence, primacy, and lordship of Jesus Christ. In other words, *no Jesus*, then there is *no Church!* The church is the one community that claims him as King and Savior. This is the central, defining aspect of the church. Everything else flows from this center:

> The fact that Christ is this center—and not, for instance, merely the beginning, the initiator of an historical form which then develops autonomously—is rooted in the particular character of the Christian religion and in its difference from all other religions. … The plausibility of Christianity stands and falls with Christ's, something which has in essence always been acknowledged. For even the doctrine of the *notae Ecclesiae* [marks of the church] has never seriously been intended to be taken in isolation from Christology: *the notae are the properties which are exacted by Christ's promises and which can be discovered in history as the fulfilment of Christ and as proofs of his living power* [italics mine].[13]

Beyond affirming the utter centrality of Christ, I have made a strong case that not only is Jesus *the* exemplary expression of APEST, but that the APEST functions and callings given to the church are the actual means by which he expresses himself through his people. Or as Markus Barth has stated, the five ascension gifts are actually *the mode of Christ's real and active presence* in the church.[14]

Finally, we saw that the five functions or purposes "given" to the church must be identified and developed if we are going to fulfill our calling as the Body of Christ. APEST is also the very means by which the church "attains to" the fullness of Christ, integrates and "becomes mature."

APEST as the defining marks of the church therefore presents us with an outstanding, ready-made, inbuilt, and theologically robust, way to assess the church's overall spirituality, ministry, and effectiveness. And we are effectively making an assessment against the ultimate benchmark of all Christian ministry—the ministry of Jesus Christ himself. Having then identified relative strengths and weaknesses, we can then go on to develop appropriate leadership and organizational strategies to suit. We can also ensure ongoing effectiveness by redesigning organizations along APEST guidelines. 5Q thinking offers an almost perfect solution to long-term problems brought about by reducing Christ's ministry in the church to unbiblical proportions.

The shift from recognizing five functions to then using these as five marks of the church is a natural one. If we wanted to know if a congregation was actually an *ecclesia*, we would need to be able to observe whether or not it exhibits all the fivefold functions in some discernable way. Allowing for relative strengths or weaknesses of different churches, when a church does express all fivefold functions, then we can be sure that Jesus' ministry is being increasingly extended through the community. If one or more of the marks are missing or seriously diminished, then we have cause to question that congregation's capacities to be a viable and authentic expression of the Body of Christ. And so, *voila*, there we have it, APEST are the marks of the church!

So, using the liturgical cadences of confessional language, we can say that the true church is expressed in the following characteristics or marks:

- **The founding mark**: The community that rightfully belongs to Jesus Christ—the people called, sanctified, redeemed, by the Father through his chosen Messiah, Jesus. The church is called the embodiment of Christ in the world. By the power of God's Spirit, the church exists to represent him, to participate in his saving work, to conform its life to his and to live out every aspect of his message, and to extend his kingdom by whatever appropriate means possible. To the degree that King Jesus is actively present and revered in a community, there is the authentic church. (This is actually the foundation of the other five marks that follow and therefore more like something of a meta-mark that defines all the other marks. The church is thereby marked by the real and active presence of Jesus. This is the basic defining mark of the church which serves as a true foundation for the rest.)

- **The apostolic mark**: The people-movement that participates in the redemptive and transformative mission of God in the world. The true church experiences and seeks to live out its sentness (*missio*) in every way possible. Therefore, when a community engages apostolically in God's mission of transforming the world, it is authentically church.

- **The prophetic mark**: The holy people that stands for God in the world, calling all to faithfulness, to true worship, to receptive obedience to God and his word, and to the prayerful participation in the prophethood of all believers. When a community stands up for covenantal justice and calls all to the covenant love of God, to repentance, and to prayer, it is authentically church.

- **The evangelistic mark**: The Body of saved people that joyfully proclaim the good news and call all to experience freedom and salvation in and through Jesus. The church is the witness to, as well as a demonstration of, the presence of good news in the world. A community arising from God's yes of salvation, then, is authentically church.

- **The shepherding mark**: The family of God's redeemed people that nurtures a faithful, reconciled community that witnesses to the

Resurrection through its common life. The church witnesses to the new way of being human in Jesus Christ. When a community represents God's chosen, reconciled and reconciling, healed and healing family in the world, then it is authentically church.

- **The teaching mark:** The wise and intelligent people that passionately seek truth and share all the treasures of the wisdom, insight, and knowledge of God hidden in Christ Jesus, faithfully nurturing understanding and communicating truth in the world. When the knowledge of God is sought, treasured, and shared, there is an authentic church.

It is worth noting here that none of these marks are form-specific. How these are expressed will depend largely on the culture and context of the *ecclesia*. But it is my contention that wherever you have the *kind* of communities and people described above—where the marks are recognizably present i.e., the defining presence on Jesus, missional impact, covenant faithfulness, gospel proclamation, reconciled community, and deep wisdom—there you have a real, authentic, church. This is church as Jesus meant it to be! Anything less is less than a church.

Each of these marks stands for an inalienable function of the church, without which it could not fulfill its task in the world. Moreover, authenticity and faithfulness occur as each church or movement moves to increasingly integrate the disparate functions into one mature body. And so the scenius (the latent genius embedded throughout) of the church becomes increasingly evident for all to experience.

It follows that maturity is increasingly experienced as all five increasingly intersect and mutually inform each other, thus experiencing the systemic synergy of a truly functional Body. This can be viewed as follows ...

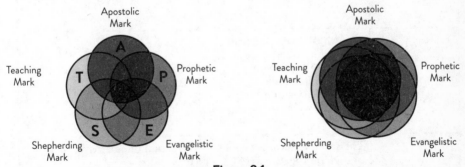

Figure 8.1
The Marks of *Ecclesia* (left)
An *Ecclesia* Experiencing Increasing fullness in Christ (right)

There's increased "Jesus space" at the center of the right-hand image! This enlarged space in effect signifies Jesus' active presence in the community. The more integrated the church is with APEST, the more mature they become through that integration, and the Church moves ever-closer toward experiencing the fullness (*pleroma*) of Christ.

	Mature Expression of *Ecclesia* (Mark)	The (Desired) Social Impact
Apostolic	Church as theologically consistent, missionally engaged in all of life, culturally dynamic, high impact, organizationally adaptive, scalable, and a church planting movement.	· *A transformed society* · Gospel saturation · A church unified in purpose and mission
Prophetic	Church as alternative society (a prefigurative community), with strong commitment to worship, prayer, spiritual warfare, holiness, justice, and incarnational witness.	· *A restored community* · A community/society living in covenant relationship to God · Respect for God's presence
Evangelistic	Church is an experience of Good News. It is a redemptive, infectious, culturally relevant, and always hopeful, people movment.	· *A redeemed community* · A growing movement · A thriving society built on restored relation to God · A grace economy built on sharing
Shepherding	Church is a human community that is reconciled, healed, forgiven, which expresses itself in loving relationships.	· *A reconciled community* · Loving human community · Reconciled across race, gender, age, nationality · A communion in Christ
Teaching	Church is a well-practiced community of learners with increasing self-awareness, understanding, and presenting wisdom for living well.	· *A wise community* · The Kingdom of Truth · Loving God with mind, soul, strength
APEST System	The sum of all these visions of *ecclesia* together = New Testament *ecclesia*!	The total impact of all these together = Holistic transformation

Table 8.1 Scenius and the Five Marks of the Church

5Q, Baby!

To drive the point home as to how important this all is, we have already noted that throughout church history all movements of spiritual and theological renewal are in some way related to the retrieval of one or more of the fivefold ministries. For instance, missional movements are essentially a recovery of the apostolic impulse; prayer and justice movements are manifestations of the prophetic impulse; revivals are an aspect of evangelistic; community and charismatic renewal is a recovery of the pastoral ministry; and theological renewals are largely related to a rediscovery of some lost motif in Scripture. Imagine if all five were taken seriously at the same time? Bring it on!

It should be relatively easy to now see that the church's problems derive from what is left out or missing in the APEST system. Simply remove, or significantly diminish, one or more of the marks from the equation, and there I wager you have a proportionally and correspondingly dysfunctional church. A church is a true church when it actively demonstrates its participation in *all* the fivefold functions/purposes to some degree or another. This is because all five marks, as genuine markers of an authentic church's identity and calling, must be *demonstrably* present, and in an increasing degree of fullness. A community that does not have all five marks evident is a community on its way to being a true church, or on its way out.

For instance, if a church excels at evangelism and teaching, but patently lacks the others in meaningful proportion, then the best that one can say is that it is a "para-church" (whatever that is) that evangelizes through apologetics and theology. But as it does not engage in corporate worship, new church planting, prayer-justice and discipleship, it is not an *ecclesia* as the New Testament would define it.

A church that suppresses the prophetic function is likely to be the kind of church that I grew up experiencing in racist South Africa, which legitimized apartheid long before it was a political theory applied through right-wing, nationalistic politics. The church had all but silenced its prophetic function—its capacity to attend to God, to experience his passionate heart for the poor, his desire to dignify the oppressed. This church was blinded to its own sin, lacking the capacity to speak truth to power. Was it an authentic church then? I will give it the benefit of the doubt in believing it to be an imperfect church made up of confessing believers, but to the degree that it diminished the prophetic mark, it increasingly became a heretical church.[15]

Heresy can therefore be understood as just another form of precociousness. And so we ought not to think that this is limited to the glaring sins of the apartheid church; *any* church that similarly fails to have a vital prophetic mark will fail in that aspect of its universal calling to be the faithful covenant people of God. I would suggest that this lack of prophetic capacity would also account for the almost systemic submission of the church to the power of money, nationalism, pride, consumerism, and many other forms of idolatrous enculturation to the prevailing culture.

Further, a church that fails to define itself by the mission of God in the world misses a fundamental part of its unique purpose to be a partner and agent of the kingdom of God in the world. Such a church will make no effort to transcend its own culture, will not be faithful to reproduce itself, and will inevitably be forced to define itself as a static institution rather than a dynamic movement. A church that refuses to recognize its own apostolicity is a church that is rebellious and disobedient to the commands and commissions of our Lord (e.g., Matthew 28:16–20; John 20:21). This is indefensible in terms of how Jesus originally designed his church to function. Without apostolicity (alongside all the other marks), we cannot ever be a true and authentic church.[16]

If we remove shepherding as a mark of authentic *ecclesia*, the resulting church is guaranteed to become just another diseased, wounding, and even hateful religion. A church that fails to create and nurture genuine healing community, one that does not care for all people irrespective of class, race, gender, and so on, is likely to result in a toxic, immature, judgmental, and unloving nest of people.

The church is more truly the church when there is a proportional demonstration of all the marks (Figure 8.2). The *fullness* of Christ is when all the functions are *fully* operative. In other words, the shaded in portion below is the "Jesus-space"; the zone of Jesus' operative presence in the ministry of the church.

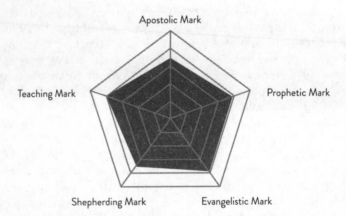

Figure 8.2 APEST Marks of Functional *Ecclesia* (Mature and Authentic)

Correspondingly, the church is increasingly inauthentic, and dysfunctional, the fewer marks it exhibits. This will be evident by the lack of proportion or symmetry in the pattern. The 5Q ("Jesus-space") in Figure 8.3 is much smaller and disproportional. So this is an example of what an unhealthy church would look like. Sadly, this pattern would probably describe the average evangelical congregation in North America.

Hopefully you get the point: All five functions are needed, and they must always derive their meaning and legitimacy as marks from Jesus' living presence and example at the center. All five are frontiers for ways in which each church should extend the ministry of Jesus in the world. This is what it means to be the Body of Christ.

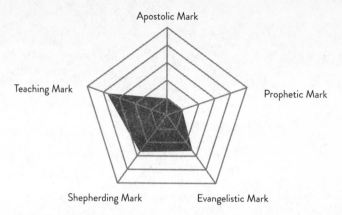

Figure 8.3 APEST Marks of Dysfunctional *Ecclesia* (Immature and Inauthentic)

The proposal is therefore that, to live into our collective calling, we adopt the APEST as marks of the church, and be willing to reconfigure the way we do church accordingly.

• Go! The 5Q Systems Tests: Diagnosis and Strategy

If the fivefold marks are the identifying characteristics and theological metrics by which we can be and become an authentic church, then our agenda has just become a whole lot clearer. Having a church APEST profile means that the church can now identify its relative deficiencies and strengths on the spectrum, and then develop resources and lead strategically from there. The marks therefore provide us with a theologically dynamic diagnostic tool, as well as a means by which to inform leadership decisions and develop organizational strategy.

Diagnosis and Strategy

Cast your mind back to the beginning of this chapter. There I suggested that if APEST are genuinely "marks" of the church, then they must by definition be observable. Because they are observable, and because each APEST is associated with certain functions, we can actually measure the marks both in terms of quantity and proportion as well as quality and maturity of expression.

To understand fully the significance of a powerful diagnostic tool, consider the use of magnetic resonance imaging (MRI). MRI allows the medical practitioner to get a 3D cross section image of an internal organ without the need for invasive surgery. Once a clearer picture is attained, then strategic and tactical decisions can be made. Such decisions are not based simply on hunches, as valuable as these are.

An organizational diagnostic similarly enables us to identify critical weaknesses sometimes invisible to external observation. But it can also show health and strength as well.

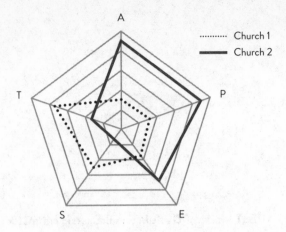

Figure 8.4 Comparative 5Q Diagnostic

As a church improves in its APEST functionality, as it moves from level one through to a level five in each function, it covers more area in the diagram. This is a way of visualizing increasing maturity.

Take a minute and do a blink test:

- Identify in your own mind where you are weak in terms of the fivefold purposes/functions of the church.
- Now identify where you think you are strong.
- Now ask yourself: In terms of broad strategy, what needs to be done?

If you are weak in evangelism, for example, you need to develop the evangelistic function, using tools and resources that suit the culture of your organization. It will almost definitely mean that you will have to improve the collective understanding of what evangelism is and why it is a non-negotiable function of the church. It will also likely mean a budget adjustment to suit. The church will need to find ways to contact non-believers, get its "branding" act together, and work on the overall communication of its message. Ironically, it will also mean that you will need to engage those with evangelistic gifts to get the necessary buy-in to the idea that everyone should be engaging with evangelism. There will likely be a whole host of other leadership decisions needed to get the evangelistic function up to scratch.

Now imagine being able to do a full and accurate 5Q Systems Assessment on the church that you are a part of or lead. I am also (along with many others) developing further resources for coaching and development around the 5Q system (details given toward the end of this book). Likewise, if a church planting movement is diagnosed as weak in the shepherding gift, then the long-term sustainability of that organization is surely in doubt. It might expand quickly, but because of weak bonds of human association, it will not likely last very long. Movements live off the commitments and sacrifices of the people that make them up. People who are recognized and loved in a movement that genuinely cares for them and champions their contribution will almost certainly give their lives for that movement. Take this human bonding aspect out of the equation, and immediately its sustainability will be called into question. Therefore, a system weak in the shepherding function must seek to remedy this deficiency.

One can even do a similar 5Q assessment on whole denominations and agencies. It would seem to me that Baptists, given their high commitment to Scripture, preaching, and evangelism will score higher in T, E, and with S coming in a likely third. But this only underscores a lack of functionality on the A and P. Pentecostal-Charismatic denominations will tend to highlight the prophetic, evangelistic, and shepherding functions but are likely more dysfunctional in relation to the teaching and apostolic functions. High Church and mainline traditions will likely emphasize the stability of the shepherding and teaching functions with a supplementary commitment to the lateral prophetic, but will likely have delegitimized the apostolic, evangelistic, and vertical prophetic, and so on. The reader is invited to think about his or her tradition with this fivefold analysis in view. What are its strengths? What are its weaknesses? And what is the result of being biased toward one area and weak in others? How does this play itself out in the history of your tribe?

Having done an APEST diagnostic and gained a clearer map of the distribution, concentration, and relative weaknesses of the purposes, leaders can go on to make choices and develop strategies to enhance them. Remember the mixing desk analogy. In a system, diagnosis and strategy are related to each other. And leadership should always remember at least two things here: First, focusing on developing one part does not mean that we should diminish the other purposes. Health is found in all five together. Second, the church has the answer already coded into it. Jesus really has already *given* us everything we need to operate in the fivefold categories. You don't have to search far to find the answer; it's right there hiding in plain sight. It's called the Body of Christ.

Chapter 9

Tools for the Trade

The Church is the place where the process of conforming humanity to the person and event of Christ is begun, the place where people dedicate themselves, in a faith that listens and obeys, to this event that is a person, are formed by him and seek through their existence to make him effective in the world.

—Hans Urs von Balthasar

Among the faithful Jews, the instruction (law) was graven on their hearts, always present before their eyes, written on their hands. Their entire being was thus structured by the law; their gaze recognized the law in the life of the world, the creation of divine wisdom; and finally the law was accomplished by their hands, by their everyday acts.

—Paul Evdokimov

Ideas should in principle always be seen as part of practices. ... Ideas enter into the bodily habitus expressed in practices.

—T. Engbert-Pederson

The poet and naturalist Henry Beston spent a year living on the great ocean beach of Cape Cod. One of the marvels he constantly witnessed on a daily basis was the instinctive movement of flocks of shoreline birds.

No aspect of nature ... is more mysterious ... than the flights of these shorebird constellations. The constellation forms ... in an instant of time, and in that same instant develops its own will. Birds which have been feeding yards away from each other ... suddenly fuse into this new volition and, flying, rise as one, coast as one, tilt their dozen bodies as one, and as one wheel off on the course which the new group will has determined. There is no such thing ... as a lead bird or guide ... By what means, by what methods of communication does this will so suffuse the living constellation that its dozen or more tiny brains know it and obey it in such an instancy of time?[1]

The bird constellations, and especially bird migration, remain one of nature's most marvelous mysteries. Brain size aside, it is hard to deny that there is something of a living parable in a flock of birds flying, something that hints of the mystery of innate sensibilities, latent instincts, diversity in unity, of reciprocal accord—ideas that are all equally evoked in the term "the Body of Christ."

Bodies are marvelous things. We know now that all bodies are themselves "intelligent" in that they have body memory and innate reflexes, and they involve numerous "instinctive" practices: heartbeat, breathing, balance, hearing, sexual desire, and the like. The wonderful thing is that our bodies are doing all these on a largely unconscious level. This is not as spooky as it sounds at first. Habits and practices of all kinds, good and bad, shape every aspect of our lives all the time. It's just that we are seldom conscious of them. Who thinks about walking or breathing?

If we believe in the mysteriously enduring power of the archetypes to shape culture, or if we take our cue from the inspiring and exemplary humanity of Jesus, or if we accept that the church's purposes are embedded into its very constitution, then we can say that 5Q is experienced in any congregation as something akin to an innate spiritual instinct. It *should* resonate deeply, but it should also shape behavior. APEST practices ought to create definite patterns throughout the life of God's people.

I have long believed and argued that Jesus has given his church everything it needs to get the job done. All the potentials for world-transforming movement are in every church in every age, not just the New Testament church. It is only in this way that we can account for the amazing growth and impact of the Chinese underground church in our own day, or other transformative movements in other times and places. The 5Q system can be considered as the Body of Christ's instinctive "body-knowledge." It not only consciously shapes our thinking through faithful theological reflection, but because it is latent it unconsciously directs our actions through practice.

This is not as strange as it might seem at first. The idea of latent potentials is evident in every human being at birth. When a baby is born, most of its physical capabilities are not present: She can't yet use language, walk, ride a bicycle, add and subtract numbers, or eat with a knife and fork. However, within her body she possesses the genetic codes that, with all the right conditions, will produce the physical development by which to carry out these capabilities. If that child is properly nurtured, in time, these abilities will naturally develop within her. She will organically grow into them. Why? Because they are organic to her species as a human being. They are the product of human life.[2]

Similarly with the Body of Christ: The potentials are already latent—they lie dormant until they are once again activated. Nowhere is this concept truer than in 5Q. APEST is part of the church's core DNA, written into its primary scripting, and therefore part of its instinctive codes. We don't have to "import" these capacities into the church; they are already there, *latent*. With the Spirit's help, our task is to live in accordance with this gracious givenness and to accept that it is a God-assigned pathway to maturity (Ephesians 4:12–13). When we live according to our intrinsic design, we will find that the ministry of Jesus through his people will get a whole lot more meaningful, sustainable, and impactful. This is church-by-the-book, ministry-by-design.

It is this relationship between high internal resonance and explicit social patterning that this chapter seeks to address. The idea here will be to try to connect the resonance that you should feel in regards to APEST functions and callings with the community in which you are called to express faith.

Organizational theorists talk about "communities of practice." These are formed by people who engage in a process of collective learning in a shared domain of human endeavor: a tribe learning to survive, a band of artists seeking new forms of expression, a group of engineers working on similar problems, a network of surgeons exploring novel techniques, a gathering of first-time managers helping each other cope. In a nutshell, communities of practice are groups of people who share a concern or a passion for something they do, and learn how to do it better as they interact regularly.[3]

All that is needed for a community of practice is a group of people identified by the common practices they share around a definite idea or theme. In the church this is called *discipleship*.

Discipleship involves being formed in the way of Jesus. It is the primary means by which we all become more like Jesus in both mindset and behavior, and it is the means through which he gets to live his life in and through his people. Fivefold-thinking provides an outstanding framework to engage with discipleship and create environments for this formation to happen. The APEST system can also be extremely beneficial in framing an organization, developing tools and training processes, creating holistic culture, and so on and so on. Fivefold-thinking can be applied across the whole church, each function focused on and specialized in by certain groups, or practiced by people in their callings both within and beyond the worshipping community. It is a powerful system that, if followed, can bring maturity in culture, structure and practice.

And the good thing is that human beings and communities are structured in a way that we need not only think our way into new ways of acting, but we can also act our way into new ways of thinking.[4] Indeed, action is a tacit form of knowledge.[5] By simply practicing certain functions, we learn more about them. For instance, a liturgy trains those who are shaped by it to follow in a certain way. The mental or social tools that we use to guide our actions each deliver a certain idea. Tools make ideas concrete by making them doable and repeatable. The idea gets into us through the sheer power of habit—we are changed as a result.

• But You Know it Don't Come Easy ...

The habits of institution that we have inherited through the European formulas are coded according to a different template than the fivefold one. Christendom churches have generally followed the Bishop-Priest-Deacons model, or the more generic Shepherd-Teacher model (the so-called two orders of ministry), or the Preacher-Elder model of the Reformed tradition. Most of these, as we have seen, have managed to assiduously script a full APEST typology out of the tradition. The net result is that we don't know how to even talk about APEST dynamics, let alone implement APEST. *We are out of touch with the more instinctive models laced throughout the book of Acts.*

As far as I can discern, to reconstitute APEST ministry in the church is going to require at least three levels of work:

1. The most basic and fundamental change needs to be bottom-up and take place at the level of *discipleship*. The main emphasis of biblical teaching is not on knowledge about God but rather emphasizes personal devotion to God, along with, imitation of, and obedience to him.[6] This imitation is to be attempted by following a right way of living. The word *discipleship* has its root in the word "to be a learner." Discipleship involves, then, the way in which one walks—the way that leads to an ever-increasing approximation of God's actions in the life of the disciple. Following this discipleship approach, the language, concepts, functions, and vocations associated with APEST must become second nature through practice. This is essentially what we in the Forge International tribe call "giving language and license"—we must give people new language, but we must also then give them the license to go and do what God has called them to.

   At this level, people must be able to discern and name their own ministry profile, while also understanding and cooperating with the other ministries in the Body. When people do this, they get in touch with their own sense of purpose and destiny. Also, if APEST is indeed a picture of Christ, then all disciples must grow in all these five qualities to be more like him. So we need to further grow in each of the five elements and not allow for people to just be good at one or two. Most training in gifts tends to promote a kind of specialization and leaves people saying, "I'm not gifted in that." The 5Q approach does away with the isolated individualism and recognizes the source and direction of the fivefold is Christ. (The vocational tools described later in the chapter, along with the statistically reliable APEST vocations test at www.apest.org, will go a long way to helping disciples connect with, and enhance, their own sense of calling.)

2. The next critical level that needs to be recalibrated to suit APEST dynamics is at the level of the *local church* or *organization*. This

will involve the leadership of the church/organization coding APEST dynamics into the living culture (the rhythms of the gathered and scattered community) as well as its organizational structures (the programs, policies, and procedures). The idea is to make APEST inevitable in the very culture of the organization/community and inherent in its structures, to gear the church toward greater conformity to Jesus' pattern of ministry and therefore to its own maturity and impact. I heartily recommend that you consider using the resource Tim Catchim and I wrote, entitled *The Permanent Revolution Playbook*. It is a great group resource.[7] (The tools related to "functions" and "culture" later in the chapter, along with the APEST functions test located at www.5Qtests.com and www.apest.org will also help leadership in this important quest.)

3. If the first two represent more local, bottom-up approaches to recoding along APEST lines, then the third one relates to the top-down aspects of systemic change. In order to effect system-wide change, leaders need to create a climate of legitimacy at *higher levels of the organization* through the integration of the APEST theology, language, and practice. Permission has to be given at the macro level for a denomination to engender APEST forms of function and ministry. This is, in my opinion, a mission-critical issue for denominational leaders to pursue if they wish to lead their organizations into a viable future, different from the current one, which is geared toward decline.[8] Once people in the movement are able to use APEST terms and express the functions without censure, new explorations and deepening of collective understandings of APEST can begin to take place.

Activating change through all three levels will have system-wide impact, and this can be accomplished by:

- enlivening lost truths
- legitimizing new concepts
- repenting of the obsolete (or incomplete) understandings of function and calling
- embracing change
- reshaping culture
- permitting risk
- celebrating progress as it occurs

Even more crucially it will involve *discipling not just individuals but the organization itself*—creating new habits and patterns of behavior for the whole system. This is the function of new assessments, tools, and practices along with an accompaniment of a coach or guide: at this level of re-scripting or re-discipling, practice does make perfect.[9] (Various levels of coaching and training in 5Q capacities is offered at www.5Qcentral.com)

Think about what it takes to learn to drive a car with manual transmission. The driver starts off with unconscious incompetence—not even knowing what she doesn't yet know. How often have you heard a teenager say, "How hard can it be?" Then comes reality in the form of bunny-hops or questions such as, "Where exactly is the brake?" But through determination, regularity of practice, conscious learning, and the help and guidance of a driving instructor, the task of shifting gears while driving through traffic and changing lanes becomes second nature—automatic, as it were. And then eventually comes the stage of unconscious competence—the moment when we arrive in the parking lot and think, "how did I get here?" It becomes automatic and unconscious.

And always remember: According to Paul, the wholesale recalibration of the church and its ministry along APEST lines means that his people, now and everywhere, might so "attain to the fullness of Christ" and become mature. Maturity is attained through decisive, meaningful, and habitual actions, even when conditions are difficult and old habits come all too easy. Paul helped Timothy "learn to drive" (1 Corinthians 4:17). Much is at stake—much more than learning to drive—so keep trying.

And so in what follows are suggested tools, practices, and processes to embed different aspects of the fivefold system at the individual, local, and system levels.[10]

• The 5Q Toolbox

Much of the information in this book has been about wrapping our minds, as well as the organizations we lead, around the pattern of 5Q that we have sought to trace in theology, culture, history, and in Christ and his people. Ideas are clearly an extremely important part of human consciousness, and we need to take them very seriously indeed. However, transformation happens less by arguing cogently about something new than by generating active new practices that shift the experience of the basis for reality. In other words, the best way of making ideas have impact is to embed them into the very rhythms and habits of the community in the form of common tools and practices.[11]

A tool is a mental device or physical implement used to perform an operation necessary in the practice of a vocation or profession. Each tool delivers a distinct function: A saw is for cutting wood, a hammer for nails, and so on.

Each of the tools suggested in this chapter—tools that have been created by myself and my 5Qcollective colleague Rich Robinson—will similarly deliver a certain impact.[12] A good craftsman has numerous tools and knows what each can, and cannot, do. Knowing one's tools, understanding the task at hand and having some clarity about the desired outcome, should determine the choice of the tool.

Because each of these tools focuses on a different dimension of APEST, I highly recommend you try as many of them as possible. However, I believe you will find that each of these will be useful at different times, and in different parts of the process. Get your teams trying these out.

Remember, all five functions/callings are like seeds latent in the system. All the potential for a tree is already in the seed; all we need to do is simply focus on the environment that will allow the seed to flourish. These tools and processes offer simple ways to focus on the environment in order to allow the seed to flourish.

Warning: Before you start any exercise below, be sure that each member of the group understands the basic definitions and distinctions of each of the fivefold functions/callings. (This much at least ought to be clear by now.) For instance, don't confuse evangelistic work with apostolic work just because an evangelistic work seems entrepreneurial. Entrepreneurialism as a skill can in fact serve each of the fivefold functions. Each participant should be able to know the broad difference between apostolic and evangelistic profiles. Perhaps another example of a category error is to equate preaching (usually associated with the pulpit) with the prophetic function. It might well be that preaching can be prophetic, but it can also be evangelistic, or used to teach the community. Preaching is just a medium; APEST is the message. Be clear with definitions and distinctions upfront.

The 5Q Systems Tests

There are two tests that can be used to diagnose and assess the quotient of 5Q in your organization; namely the 5Q Diagnostic Test and the 5Q Systems Test. The diagnostic test is a straightforward assessment of current capacities in relation to APEST. It can be used on multiple occasions to provide a diagnostic "picture" of the organization similar to the ones illustrated in chapter eight (page 138—the "APEST marks" diagrams). This allows leaders to assess strengths and weaknesses in leadership and in the organization and to develop strategies in light of the diagnostic.

The 5Q Systems Test is a more in-depth analysis that measures organizational awareness in relation to APEST in the organization. Built on the framework of stages of maturity and learning, it not only includes a diagnostic analysis but also provides a more complex and multidimensional one that indicates depth of both perception and practice.

Both tests are built squarely on the contents and ideas represented in this book. They measure organizational functionality. I suggest beginning with the diagnostic test and once people are more familiar with 5Q thinking, then move toward the systems test. You can access the tests at www.5Qcentral.com (or at www.5Qtests.com). Importantly, Jessie and I have written a book to help communicate the core ideas of 5Q which can be read by non-specialists. It's an accessible book that will help the average church leader grasp the importance of the test as well as understand how to interpret it. The book is called *Activating 5Q: A User's Guide to*

Understanding and Applying 5Q in Your Church or Organization.[13] I recommend that this book be read by staff and volunteer leaders in a church seeking to activate 5Q.

Personal APEST Portrait

This tool will focus on developing a "portrait" or profile of each person's particular calling but associating the APEST on a descending order. The best way to get a statistically verified picture of your vocational shape or portrait is to simply do the test online (www.apest.org or it can be accessed via www.5Qcentral.com). However, it is an enriching process when it is also done as a dynamic group process of communal discernment. So I highly recommend both test and process.

In order to honor how God calls and shapes people, there needs to be some deep personal reflection. And so each member of the group should do the following exercise before coming together as a group.

- Paul says in Ephesians 4:7 that each one of us has been given a measure of gifting from Christ. When you think about the measure of gifting that Christ has given you in each of the five APEST ministries, and what you know about the agreed definitions of APEST (for a refresh of APEST definitions see page 99), what would you say is your primary or dominant calling? What about your secondary calling? Fill out the image below with your primary APEST gifting in the largest circle, your secondary in the next largest circle, and so on. What does this say about you? Think of events and meetings in your own life that connect to your profile.

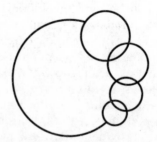

Figure 9.1 - APEST Personal Profile

- Once you have filled in the circles, consider taking the online test at www.apest.org to correct or confirm your initial impressions.
- Journal the insights that you gain from these exercises to share with the group.

When you come together as a group, create the necessary social conditions for each member to be able to share for up to 30 minutes. If you need to take a few meetings to get through the entire group, this ought to be seen as a valuable investment of time:

- Each member should *describe their portrait*; how they feel about it; and why they believe it to be an accurate reflection of their personal calling. In other words, let them share their story, their sense of calling, their defining experiences, and perhaps where their vocational passions lie. To model this, I suggest the leader goes first because people will have some experience of his or her fivefold profile.

- Then the rest of the group is invited to give *honest but loving feedback* regarding the portrait. Is it correct? Can the community confirm what the individual is saying? How, if at all, can it be adjusted? The important thing to realize here is that people get honest feedback regarding the nature of their influence on others. Because APEST is called a Body dynamic, we will only really know ourselves in relation to the other members of the Body of Christ. The truth is we cannot know ourselves in isolation from others; we can only know ourselves in relation to others—in community. This is an important aspect of the teaching about the Body of Christ in Ephesians as well as Corinthians.

- *Adjust the portrait accordingly*: Having heard the loving feedback of others, by submitting himself/herself to Body feedback, the person under review might need to adjust their individual profile accordingly.

- *The group prays for, and affirms the calling, of that person* and encourages them toward greater self-awareness and impact.

APEST Thinking Hats

The aim here is to learn how to think through the category of each APEST "hat" without having to name people vocationally. My source of inspiration here is a problem-solving tool, called the six thinking hats, developed by creative-thinking specialist Edward de Bono.[14] In de Bono's model, the six hats represent six modes of thinking, six different ways of processing information and coming to a decision. Most people tend to opt for one or another of these hats; we usually see things from a single perspective and tend to reject other types of thinking.

Apply the same idea to APEST, where each function is a hat. You can define a problem facing the team and work your way through the five thinking hats in trying to solve it. The exercise is like trying on five different colored hats. Each "hat" designates one of the fivefold modes of thinking. Under the "A" hat, everyone has to try to see the problem (and the solution) from the apostle's perspective—for example, the interest in missional extension, the guarding of the gospel and the church's DNA, the multiplication of disciples. Then put another hat on and see it in the light of, say, evangelistic intelligence and sensibilities, and so forth. This exercise helps people use their bases and phases without even realizing they are doing so (see below). Even someone whose vocation is different has the opportunity to understand

and practice each of the fivefold and appreciate its value. Approaching this exercise as a game means that no one needs to get defensive (it's a game after all); each type of thinking will eventually be heard.

Base and Phase

The aim of this tool is to help identify areas that need development in each of us and to prompt leadership to design a process by which all move toward maturity. 3DM, a movement that stems from the work of Mike and Sally Breen, developed "Basing and Phasing" as a great process by which everyone can become more aware of the Body dynamics of APEST and learn about themselves at the same time. Whilst the "base" was identified as an individual's primary APEST gifting, it was recognized that an individual would also experience particular "phases" in ministry, during which they would operate more distinctly in one of the remaining four APEST. The churches they led always saw the phase time as a time for learning provided at the prompting of the Holy Spirit to help each disciple learn more about leadership and ministry, and as an equipping necessary for the ministry and season that individuals found themselves in. As such, the base-phase process was more than just a tool; it was understood as the work of the Spirit in the life of the church to help develop maturity.[15]

Paul says the overarching purpose of APEST is maturity, and that maturity happens through the process of equipping. As my co-author and I say in *The Permanent Revolution Playbook*, the word Paul uses in Ephesians 4:12 for "equip" was in some cases used to describe the mending of torn fishing nets, while in other cases it was used to describe the process of setting a broken bone. Overall, the word carries the idea of increasing one's ability to function in a certain area. Paul is telling us that God gives each person APEST gifts so each individual in the Body of Christ can increase his or her ability to function within the five categories of Christ's ministry.

We all have a base ministry in which we feel most comfortable. This base ministry flows out of our primary gifting. In order to mature, we have to enter a phase where we receive training and experience in one of the other four ministries. It would look something like this:

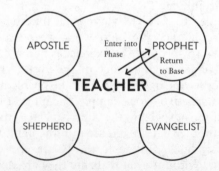

Figure 9.2 APEST Base and Phase

So, for example, teachers are not just designed for teaching. Everyone has all five APEST giftings to various degrees; maturity and fullness in Jesus comes as we move toward all five in us. For a teacher (T), growing toward maturity means learning to also function in the other four primary categories of ministry (APES).

Fill out the diagram, putting your base (primary) ministry in the middle of the largest circle. Based on life experience, write down which particular APEST ministries you have entered into—phases of equipping within the smaller circles. Then, with a few words, describe your growth experience in the box beside each phase.

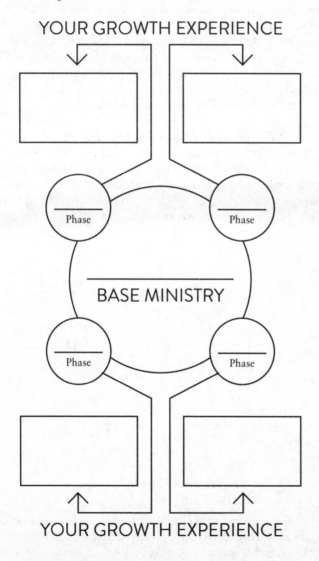

Figure 9.3 Base and Phase Exercise

Most often, we are not the ones who orchestrate a phase in our life; instead, circumstance or a relationship typically guides us into it. The goal is not to agonize about your deficits or lack of experience in the various APEST ministries, but to remain open to entering a phase and to embrace it when it happens. If the opportunity does not present itself, we can always seek out opportunities to learn from others.

APEST Inventory

The APEST inventory is perhaps the easiest to grasp because it is very close to the idea of "functions" pursued and articulated throughout this book and is one of the dimensions built into the APEST functions test.[16] As we have seen, there are very definite functions associated with each of the APEST systems. These can be observed and "tagged" accordingly with different colors to give a visual representation of relative strengths and weaknesses. By using the fivefold as a kind of inventory list, a church or organization can get a clearer picture of what it is and is not doing.

As a group, touch base with the list of functions on page 99. Then list all the major activities of the church/organization. Tag these activities in terms of A, P, E, S, and T. You can even give them a primary and secondary tag. So, for instance, a certain activity/program could be primarily evangelistic and secondarily apostolic; you can list this activity as "Ea." It's important that you are honest in your assessments—don't stretch activities to fit the criteria.

Having listed them, chart them on Figure 9.4.

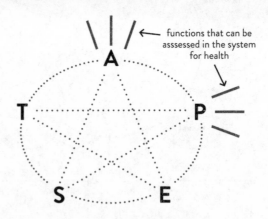

functions that can be asssessed in the system for health

Figure 9.4 APEST Inventory

Simply by listing the vision, values, and major activities of a church and categorizing them according to function, leaders can get something of an inventory of the church's overall functionality—and relative dysfunctionality. Notice the concentrations of activity and the deficiencies. Look for the symmetry or asymmetry in the system. Discuss the reasons for these and ask what can be done to fill in the gaps.

Some churches have used the fivefold as a checklist for each and every program or cell group. So, for instance, Northwood Baptist Church requires that every cell group check off deliberate activities related to all five functions in a given period, say, a year. This way each cell group, while perhaps majoring in one or two of the five, nonetheless is being discipled and groomed as a potential *ecclesia*.

APEST Perspectives

Mark Conner, a friend of mine from Australia, places an object (say, a statue) in the middle of a round table and asks people to share what they see. He notes that two things happen. First, everyone sees the object differently. Second, no one sees it accurately, since each only sees it from where he or she sits. Consequently, the only way everyone can see the object accurately is when each person listens to everyone else's perspective.

This exercise demonstrates that without multiple perspectives, we cannot develop an accurate view of the challenges and opportunities in front of us. This is true in every area of life and ministry—for problem-solving, decision-making, vision creation, and strategic planning.

The APEST Perspectives tool simply puts an idea, topic, problem, or subject at the center of the conversation and then invites each of the people present to describe what they see from within their predominant vocations, or from within the logic of the functions they represent. So for instance, if you put the term *gospel* at the center of the diagram below, how do you think an apostle's perspective might be different from, say, a shepherd's? What aspects would each of the APEST highlight? Now put the term *church* at the center, or *culture, organization, spirituality,* and so on.

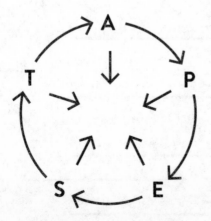

Figure 9.5 APEST Perspectives

If you're reading this book as a church leader, I'd recommend you put your core values through this process with your core staff, board/eldership and key leaders. Values help shape culture (whereas vision sets direction). Using this process and engaging the APEST perspective in this way will help your church to more maturely, holistically, and creatively express those values.

You can also use this tool for problem-solving, thinking through strategy, culture creation, planning, communication, key messaging, etc. It is also very useful for each team member to understand and respect the opinions of others and the perspectives from beyond their dominant gifting.

APEST Pipeline

In this exercise, the team needs to construct a profile of what they think each APEST calling should look like. Paint a picture of a competent practitioner of each of the callings. What mentality, behaviors, skills, and competencies would they possess (particularly emphasizing the competencies needed)?

As with a real pipeline, it is also important to consider where the blockages or leaks are, so the process should also involve anticipating what the particular stress points or struggles will be for each of the APEST in the training process.

Once clarified, the team then develops a model process (which includes a sense of the curriculum/content that would be needed) in order to disciple people into the ideal. In other words, what would the discipleship or apprenticeship process look like in each of the five categories?

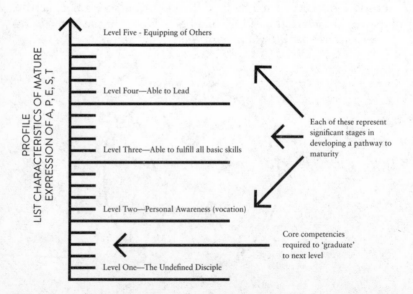

Figure 9.6 Competency-Based Process

The process developed ought to be articulated in terms of what is needed to acquire the competencies. Theory is passed on through coaching and practice, until each student can demonstrate mastery of the task or competency required.[17] This is important because it is closer to the process of discipleship itself. If you wish, you can use the outline in Figure 9.6 as a process for the team.

An APEST pipeline gives the opportunity to develop the APEST callings and functions within a 5Q framework but it also means that APEST training can be tailored to suit the particular purposes and context of an organization. This means the training can be personalized but not individualistic i.e., training with the intention of bringing the organization to maturity, not just investing in an individual.

Do this for all the APEST profiles. Below is an example of what this could look like at Level Two and Level Three leadership (as referred to in Figure 9.6).

Leadership Development (Level Two)
Growth in self-awareness and competency:

- **Apostle:** Mobilizing people toward action and pioneering new missional frontiers
- **Prophet:** Helping everyone hear and know truth, and creating a depth and integrity of culture
- **Evangelist:** Encouraging and equipping people to share, and speaking/ sharing the gospel
- **Shepherd:** Loving others into fullness of life, and demonstrating the love of God to those who don't know him
- **Teacher:** Creating depth and maturity in the word of God, and creating access points to truth and for truth to be expressed to those that don't know God

Leadership Focus (Level Three)
Intentionality of the leaders' resources (time, money and effort) to primarily be invested in:

- **Apostle:** Impact (design, momentum, new ground broken)
- **Prophet:** Faithfulness (in action, of people and culture)
- **Evangelist:** Communication (offering of invitation and engagement of people
- **Shepherd:** Inclusion (depth of care and engaging with freedom)
- **Teacher:** Learning (systematic and thorough engagement with truth)

Once this is complete, you will not only have conceptualized a pretty potent agenda for discipleship, but you will have developed a pipeline for leadership development as well (see Figure 9.7 overleaf).

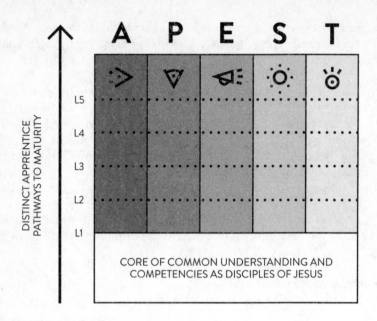

Figure 9.7 Competency-Based Training System

APEST Training Environments

As we begin to engage with 5Q not only personally but as a leader, we need to consider how we will enable those within our sphere of influence, and the organization itself, to embark on the journey of change. As a whole organization engages with APEST thinking (in terms of both functions and callings), we need to inform people well and train leaders effectively.

When training leaders within an organization there are three primary environments to consider:

- **Classroom**: creating teaching environments where input around APEST occurs for each individual calling and function, as well as general APEST overview. A disciple can then hear and learn the information about APEST and individual calling and functions. This is an essential part of the learning and training process (the classic "program" model employed by most churches) but is ineffective if it is the only part of the process, as in so many cases.

- **Apprenticeship**: creating relational training processes so that leaders who are more mature in their fivefold callings and functions are encouraging, empowering and equipping those with the same calling and function (e.g., an apostle training another apostle). Mature leaders can also apprentice those with a different APEST "base" or calling (e.g., an apostle training a teacher to grow in apostolic mindset and behavior). This apprenticeship and attentiveness process grows confidence, character and competency.

- **Immersion:** creating experiences where disciples are able to experience an environment where one of the functions is overtly expressed and the leading beat in setting culture and practice. In this experience, they can interpret the "feel" of a predominantly prophetic environment, for example. Immersion is also valuable to experience environments where there is a healthy fivefold balance so that some of the 5Q symphony and synergy can be experienced first-hand. This immersion process creates space for intuitive and experiential learning.

Utilizing the classroom (teaching program), apprenticeship (training process) and immersion (experiential learning) are all vital for a fruitful engagement for your leaders. Each of these three can provide experience, equipping, and empowering around 5Q.

APEST Culture

As an organization starts the 5Q journey and begins to perceive the symphony of 5Q, it can then engage with the component parts. Every organization is made up of culture and structure. We often make the mistake of attending to the structure and ignoring the culture. The stages outlined below will help identify the starting point for your community's APEST culture as it engages with 5Q.

Calling is about playing our part personally as we engage with the fivefold, and function is about partnership and purpose amongst and alongside others to edify the body and extend the kingdom. So 5Q understanding helps us mature and move forward together.

Below are the different levels to assess the *understanding, engagement, expression* and *multiplication* of APEST. The levels grow toward a process of maturity. A healthy culture expressing APEST culture well will have all five layers present.

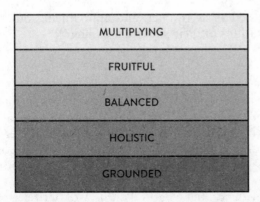

Figure 9.8 APEST Culture Building Blocks

- **Grounded**: are all five *understood?*
  - o Biblical truth and principles engaged and understood within the organization
  - o Healthy APEST examples present in the organization
- **Holistic**: are all five *present?*
  - o Pursuing intentionally; not accidental or reactionary; diversity and a healthy spread of APEST across the organization
  - o Each fivefold celebrated for their identity and contribution to the organization
- **Balanced**: are all five *working together?*
  - o All APEST functions coming together to serve, equip, partner and build up the Body and extend the Kingdom and so working in partnership for the good of the organization
  - o The culture of the organization is a healthy reflection of the strengths and participation of each of the APEST functions
  - o No competing, disjointed or individualistic perspectives or agendas
- **Fruitful**: are all five *accessing synergy and leveraging strengths?*
  - o Leaders bringing maturity to the culture of the organization by investing, partnering and serving fruitfully alongside other APEST functions
  - o Leaders engaging, training and releasing other leaders within other APEST gifting/functions as well as their own
- **Multiplying**: are all five *recreating* themselves?
  - o Conscious competence—leaders being self-aware about how they have grown in their fivefold ministry and intentionally training others in order to pass on wisdom and experience and grow maturity
  - o Each APEST is training and apprenticing others and releasing generations of their particular calling.

Conclusion

We can conclude this chapter by affirming that the main emphasis of biblical teaching is not on knowledge about God but rather about gaining knowledge of God; it's not about speculative reflection on the nature of deity but rather about imitation of, and obedience to, God. The Word of God tells us that if you do not do it, you do not believe it, do not yet understand it, and have not heard it (Matthew 7:26; James 1:23). This must never simply be understood as mechanical obedience, but a natural outflow of our relationship with God through Jesus our Lord. Obedience and imitation leads to an ever-increasing *approximation* of God's actions in our lives that can be summed up in the term *discipleship*. We follow Jesus as his apprentices and so become more Christlike:

> As Jesus' disciple, I am his apprentice in kingdom living. I am learning from him how to lead my life in the Kingdom of the Heavens as he would lead my life if he were I.[18]

We need to remember that, individually and collectively, we were originally given APEST by Jesus so that we might mature and somehow attain to his fullness. It is therefore not good enough for us to simply agree that the fivefold is good theology; we need to commit ourselves to its logic and allow it to shape the Body.

Chapter 10

To Get From Here to There

By Rich Robinson[1]

The journey of a thousand miles begins with one step.

—Lao Tzu

Ideas do not succeed in history by virtue of their truth but by virtue of their relationships to specific social processes.

—Peter Berger

Alice: Which way should I go?
Cat: That depends on where you are going.
Alice: I don't know.
Cat: Then it doesn't matter which way you go.

—Lewis Carroll, *Alice in Wonderland*

I'm sat at the kitchen table with my youngest and his math homework. Which has quickly become *my* math homework.

"What is 3×5, Dad?"

What do I do in this moment? It would be so easy to just blurt out "15." But to get to that answer, there are a number of processes that need to be followed. In that moment, when I know there is a whole long list of other things to do, my flesh wants to just give him the answer. The faint whisper of the Holy Spirit tells me "this is a learning opportunity," but the easier option of quick fix and comfort is extremely appealing.

I have a choice: a short-term win or a medium-term process. I could give the answer, and my son would pick up *one piece of information* from me, or I can show him my workings out and he can *learn a process* that he can apply for himself.

Giving the answer is always easier than teaching the process. And being given the answer is always easier than learning the process ourselves, whatever age or stage we are.

As I've read through this book, Alan has taken me, and hopefully you too, on a process. He could have just given us "the answer," but we've journeyed through his theological process and logic so that we too can fully comprehend 5Q and all that it can mean for us both personally and for the Body of Christ.

We live in a quick-fix, silver-bullet, "I want it yesterday" world. Just like my son and the math conundrum, giving (or receiving) "the answer" is a tempting option. We are looking for the package, the program or the manual to make it work—and fast! As Alan said in the preface, our craving for easy answers has hardened our eyes and predisposed us to merely repeating what we already know. So, please continue to keep your eyes soft as you look ahead, so that you don't simply satisfy the craving with another lethal dose of quick fix solutions. As Alan said, Jesus is the silver bullet, and in my experience (and I'm sure yours too) there are no short-cuts when it comes to Jesus.

In such a fast-paced world, it doesn't come naturally, or easily, to stop—to ponder, digest, process or practice. We want to run before we can walk. I've worked with many churches and organizations over the years, many of whom have tried to embrace new paradigms and principles. Those who have gone on to see lasting, significant and fruitful change are the ones who have chosen to be counter-cultural by actually taking the time to systematically reflect on where they currently are, and where they want to go, as they follow in the way of Jesus. They are the organizations who have been courageous enough to unlearn, and then relearn a new theological paradigm and live into a new praxis, setting the course and continuing faithfully and prayerfully toward that new direction.

I often say to leaders that we can change our structures in four to eight *months*, but it takes four to eight *years* to change our culture.

And it starts with us.

Both of those realities are usually met with a mixed response! So don't look for an easy answer. Don't just share on social media that you've read the book and then put it, and its revelation, back on the shelf. Discover and explore this for yourself. Embrace symphony. Not only, "what does this mean for the organization?" but also, "what does this mean for me?" How will you, and the organization you're part of, change as a result of this book?

Early in the book, Alan presented the challenge:

> If you are willing, relinquish the (false) security of hard eyes and adopt soft eyes. If you are able to sense something of the symphony of God's beautiful design along the way, will you have the courage to change? Are you willing to change? Will you pay the price to learn again?

And I present that same challenge again as we near the end of the book. The price for change is first and foremost repentance.

So I encourage you to engage fully, deeply and wholeheartedly with what you are about to read.

• Stop, Look, Listen

In the Christian sphere, repentance is a word that is bandied around frequently. But I also think it's something we're not very good at. We do guilt; we do shame; we do conviction. But we don't actually engage with a biblical understanding of repentance. In Mark 1:15 Jesus says, "The kingdom of God has come near. Repent and believe the good news!" Repentance is more than just turning away from sin. "Repent" can be better translated as "open your mind" or "expand your thinking." As Alan said in the preface, "we need to be willing to let go of obsolete ideas and open our eyes and our hearts to being willing to grow, mature, and get back on the road of discipleship and learn again."

In England, children are taught the Green Cross Code to help them cross roads safely. As we come to a road, we are told to **"Stop, Look** and **Listen."** Not only is it a mantra for crossing roads, it also has huge value when we come across new information or come into a new situation, or when we need to "unlearn" something. When I'm training leaders who are beginning to engage in a new missional context or leadership responsibility, I always teach them to Stop, Look and Listen. We all know the danger of putting our head down and trying to run across the road. There is also a danger that as we read this book our response is just that. We either put our head down to disengage with what stretches and challenges us or we try to push on ahead without due observation, reflection and process. And the danger is that we never cross the road or that there is a car coming whilst our head is down and we are halfway across.

Take a moment. Rather than rushing on, just Stop, Look and Listen.

• 5Q CHALLENGE •

Get out your journal. Scribble something on your iPhone or Tablet. Dig out your bible. Grab a notepad from the side. Reread a particular chapter. Go for a walk. Take some time to pray.

Do whatever you need to do to make sure you Stop, Look and Listen for God's truth.

- *What do you hear?*
- *How does God want to expand your thinking with new truth?*
- *Where have you settled for less or are stuck?*
- *How does what you hear lead you to know more of God or discover more of yourself or others?*

Repentance goes hand in hand with action. Once we've done Stop, Look and Listen, then we are also required to move from that place. We need to actually cross the road, or else the reflection is futile. There needs to be analysis and then action. "Believe the good news" from Mark 1:15 can again be translated as "stepping out upon this new truth." So how do you step out upon, and into, this new truth that you've been discovering as you've read this book?

Our aim over this chapter is to look at some of the ways that you can unlearn and then relearn—ways that you can Stop, Look and Listen, and then move toward analysis and action on a personal and leadership level.

Blooms taxonomy talks of six stages of learning: *knowledge* and *understanding*; moving to *application* and *analysis*; and finally, *evaluation* and *creation*.[2] So our hope is that your journey is firstly one of understanding, then of application, and finally to innovation and multiplication in the context you are called to live and lead. This is the journey that we need to go on as disciples, and this is our 5Q journey together.

• The Journey of a Thousand Miles

The 5Q journey isn't for the faint-hearted. It takes us into unchartered territory. It will stretch us in ways we couldn't anticipate, and in ways we wouldn't necessarily invite. But it will also reward us in ways we can't currently imagine.

Lao Tzu famously said, "the journey of a thousand miles begins with one step." Now you've read the book and caught a glimpse of the destination, let's look together at a few potential ways for us to start the journey.

Be Like a Child

As we move into the new terrain, I want you to think of this discovery and learning process like a child in the playground, not as a student in the classroom. As a child explores the playground, they are learning how to balance, understand spatial awareness, what they physically can and cannot do, how well they can do something, what they can jump to … and what they can't. They are learning the implications of their decisions and constantly applying the learning they are making in real time.

For a child, the playground is a three-dimensional, interactive learning environment. The learning comes through experience and experimentation, through listening to adults offer wisdom (or even adult "example"—let's be honest, we've all been down the slide or tried the monkey bars on occasion under the guise of "helping out the kids") and applying what they know. Knowledge is worked out, tested, internalized and then applied practically.

Dr Dave Aldred OBE, a UK sports coach who coaches and trains numerous elite sportspeople including major winners and world cup winners, has this to say about learning: "If I had to give a high-concept appraisal of my coaching philosophy, it would be 'To rekindle youthful learning and create a "no limits" mindset.'"[3]

So, I encourage you to approach learning, challenges and information with childlike faith.

In the classroom, we merely explore something from a mental or cerebral stance, and our ability to retain information or communicate it verbally is tested through the passing (or failing) of an exam behind a desk. Don't misunderstand me—information is vital, but it needs to be engaged and learnt deeply, interactively and personally. We all know how many exams we crammed for, wrote the paper or passed the exam and then two days later realized that we couldn't remember anything we'd learnt.

"Soft eyes, grasshopper." Throughout the book, Alan has reminded us to keep our eyes soft. Children have the gift of soft eyes. Their eyes haven't been hardened through experience, maturity or disappointment. We see a cloud; they see a unicorn. We see a room; they see a playground. We see a puddle to avoid; they see an opportunity for fun.

Don't just cram for the 5Q exam where you share the edited highlights and headlines with people in a sermon, story or 140 characters. Instead, explore the world as a playground and grow and learn with a 5Q mindset, awareness and toolkit.

Be a Padawan

Alan has talked about us reading as Padawans. Earlier in the book, Alan described Jesus as the exemplary model in all of the fivefold callings and functions. We need to learn from his ways. But we also need an Obi-Wan Kenobi, a Gandalf or Yoda—those who guide our path as we live out our great adventure. The apostle Paul understood this need. As well as an intellectual/theological factor to learning, Paul knew that there is an experiential and a *relational* element to learning. Paul speaks to a Greco-Roman context, referencing the parent-child dynamic in 1 Corinthians 4:15–17, rather than the rabbi-disciple dynamic of earlier writing in Scripture.[4] Young children being trained in reading, writing and arithmetic would have had a guardian, who would have passed on the information. But the parent, the role model, would have helped the child translate this into the real world. Though it was common in Paul's day to be taught the information and then to observe someone else as an apprentice, it is sadly a deficit in western culture, where the model of apprenticeship has been replaced by knowledge and information in classroom-based learning. Apprenticeship and attentiveness to our guide is vital for us as a Padawan.

Jesus lived out this same principle. God didn't send down a divine handbook for us to attempt to work out; he sent his Son for us to engage with and follow.

Jesus finishes the Beatitudes, probably the greatest information download and instructional manual for life, with a story of a wise and a foolish builder (Matthew 7:24–27). If you grew up in church, then you will have drawn, heard and crafted this story to death, I am sure! The story is well-known, but the positioning at the end of the Beatitudes is what I would like to draw on here. There is one of the two who *hears and puts into practice*. The other hears but chooses to do things his own way. Jesus is challenging his listeners to put into practice all they have just heard in the Beatitudes, so that it becomes a solid foundation for their life.

But Jesus doesn't just share the instructions and leave. He doesn't just leave the IKEA manual, saying, "Good luck assembling the wardrobe." *He lives the instruction manual out* with a small group of Padawans. Yes, Jesus is right in the midst of the assembly line with the annoying black plastic screws and complicated shelf construction.

In both Paul and Jesus we can see skeletal principles. Jesus operated in a rabbi-disciple model and Paul operated in a parent-child model—same skeleton with a different contextualized skin appropriate to the culture. Both are radically different from our teacher-student, current classroom mentality. We are instructed as students by a professional, in a set timetable, for a set amount of time in a certain subject, or subjects. And we have transposed our secular cultural methods of learning into our church culture. We may attend a course or conference, take a class, read a book, or study online in our attempt to learn more about the ways of Jesus. All those things can be useful but they are invariably a functional, informational transfer. We need to recapture the attentiveness the disciples would have had to their rabbi: waiting, watching, listening, following, and being attentive to any of the rabbi's words or actions as a learning experience.

Be a Long-Distance Runner

I would love to naturally swing a golf club and hit the middle every time; I'd love to look in the fridge and always make the right healthy decision of what enters my mouth; I'd love to be able to sit across the room from someone and intuitively know the right way to serve them.

But I know that good practice and good decisions don't happen by accident. We become what we repeatedly do, and it will take effort and intentionality. To see the transformation we desire to see, we will have to go on a journey of **Discipline > Habit > Lifestyle**:

- **Discipline** is *intentionally* doing the thing we want to do. As we learn something new and take it on intentionally it can feel heavy, formulaic or forced, like the first time we wear a new pair of shoes, or like the process of learning to drive.

- **Habit** means that we are *usually* doing the right thing. As we embrace discipline we move, over time, into habit. The thing we want to do (a behavior, action or learning) slowly becomes a default pattern that we live out and bounce back to if we have an off-day or a bump. It becomes the "usual" for us. It begins to settle and feel more "normal" and regular—like breaking in those new shoes or a new jacket.

- **Lifestyle** occurs when we are *naturally* doing the right thing—an unconscious reality that is part of who we are and what we do. We become unconsciously competent. Just think about the times you've turned the car off at your destination and thought, "I wonder how I got here." We function on autopilot, doing the right things without even thinking about it.

Here's an example of how this could play out with 5Q. You might have read this book and as you've Stopped, Looked and Listened, you've realized that the church or organization you lead has an evangelistic deficit. In response to this, some of the *discipline* stages may involve intentionally inviting people to make a commitment to Christ at the end of every service. It may be that you and your staff team are encouraged and challenged to have one evangelistic conversation a week. It may be taking time as a staff team for an hour a week, to serve in the community and engage with non-Christians, or to take one evening a week to connect with a Person of Peace in your neighborhood or relational network. It may even be to read through together the content pertaining to the evangelist calling and function laid out in this book.

This will cost something in terms of energy and time. It will bring a level of vulnerability, and at points will feel formulaic or clunky, but these are intentional, disciplined first steps toward it becoming a natural part of life for you as a leader and a natural part of your community.

So, over time, as you embrace the discipline of a regular engagement and overlapping of life with non-Christians, it will become more *usual* for you and your community to be aware of opportunities to share the gospel. It will become more normal for your staff to have engaged in evangelistic conversations and to start to regularly have natural interactions with non-Christians. A sense of expectation and faith will grow around evangelism and you will hopefully see one or two first fruits. Even when a pastoral crisis hits or a new ministry opportunity presents, it won't swamp evangelism, because it has begun to be rooted in the rhythms and disciplines of individual and church life.

You will also find that whereas most people have taken this up as a discipline, the evangelists in your community will really begin to step forward, rise up, take a lead, and encourage others because it's *already natural* for them. The latent potential in the Body of Christ is being released.

Eventually this becomes *lifestyle*. It becomes a normal and natural part of your life as a leader, and in the life of your church community. It becomes ingrained in culture and practice and begins to affect world view and decision-making (e.g., how money, time and effort is allocated). Latent potential becomes a fruitful reality.

We love things to happen naturally, but the reality is that most things actually don't come naturally, particularly when we're trying to shift centuries of theological paradigms and their resulting practice. Paul talks about the need for self-discipline in order to run the race "in such a way as to get the prize" (1 Corinthians 9: 24–27). As we seek to live in greater maturity and wholeness both personally and for those we are called to lead, I would encourage you to take on some of these 5Q truths as intentional activities and efforts, soaked in prayer and marinated in grace.

Be an Explorer

An explorer needs a **map**, a **guide**, a **destination** and a **compass**.

- The **map** gives us the information, guidance, picture and insight we need for the journey. It's an image and overview of the terrain that we need to cover. *From the pages of this book, what has given you greater clarity or visibility of the terrain to cover?*

- A **guide** is someone that has walked the journey before, who has been this way before. Who knows the 5Q paths and territory you are starting to explore for yourself? *Who could walk alongside and share their APEST knowledge, experience and wisdom with you as you set out?*

- The **destination** is a picture that compels us to step into the adventure. It is our North Star, our focus and fuel. It's a picture of a future reality that we live toward. *How has the vision for your life come into greater technicolor and compelled you to move ahead?*

- A **compass** is for setting direction and locating us as we journey. We have the Holy Spirit who not only sets the direction of travel but also the pace of our journey. *Where has the Holy Spirit brought revelation or repentance in revealing depth of truth or next steps to move forward?*

Be an Architect

As we think of 5Q with all its depth and truth, there are so many levels to engage on. The danger is that we can be overwhelmed. Engaging with 5Q is a lifelong project, and we need to think about our foundations before we think about peripheral, short-term or superficial changes.

Construction started on the Notre Dame Cathedral in 1163 and finished in 1345, nearly 200 years later (and numerous architects and workmen later). The first architect and builders who put the plans together and who started the foundations never saw the completed cathedral. They set the foundations without any of the buzz and celebration of the finished article. It's a sobering thought, and echoes the journey of our heroes of the faith we read about who "did not receive the things promised" (Hebrews 11:13). As a parent, I can identify with this, knowing that the decisions I make now have far-reaching future consequences not only for me but for those in my care.

As we look at blueprints for ourselves and our organizations to grow in depth and breadth, I would point you back to Alan's marks of the church from chapter eight. We see the five marks of the church defined by APEST as follows.

- Missional impact (A)
- Covenant faithfulness (P)
- Gospel proclamation (E)
- Reconciled community (S)
- Deep wisdom (T)

As you seek to build a foundation and develop "the house" of your life and organization, I would encourage you to intentionally engage with all five marks and seek to grow in understanding and application for them all. Alongside this, make a focus on your particular APEST calling and function. Seek out the master builders who can help develop your competencies or deepen your character.

Think about how you will set good foundations and frameworks for the long haul. The decisions you make today shape not only tomorrow but the journey ahead.

Conclusion

To conclude this chapter, I will leave you with three reminders and encouragements to help you on your 5Q journey.

Firstly, *don't be overwhelmed*, or worse, paralysed by the distance to travel. There is a long way to go, a lot of ground to cover. And it won't all be fixed and done by next week. But, as we said at the beginning of the chapter, it starts with a single step. Commit to starting the journey: one or two small and sustainable next steps.

Secondly, *don't go alone*. We need to journey with others. Who is your Yoda or Gandalf? Who are your travelling companions? Identify them. And then choose to pray, laugh, discuss, reflect, cheer on and step out together.

And thirdly, *stay in touch*. Alan and I would love the opportunity to journey with you further. We are producing resources, writing and training processes for a deeper engagement with 5Q. This will be called the 5Qcollective and will be part of 100Movements. You can find more and get involved through www.5Qcentral.com. If you are interested in hearing more, then do be in touch—we'd love to go on the adventure with you.

Conclusion

We shall not cease from exploration
And the end of all our exploring
Will be to arrive where we started
And know the place for the first time.

—T. S. Eliot, *Little Gidding*

No great improvements in the lot of mankind are possible, until a great change takes place in the fundamental constitution of their modes of thought.

—J. S. Mill

Reason cannot contemplate the phenomenon as it were from the outside and the inside at the same time. To want to see the stained glass window from the inside is already to believe.

—Hans Urs von Balthasar

When writers finish a book that has taken years, perhaps even a lifetime, to articulate, they can experience all kinds of complex emotions. All I can say is that in working on this book I have constantly felt the wonders of discovery;

I felt like some watcher of the skies
When a new planet swims into his ken[1]

I can honestly say that at many times I felt similarly to when I was writing and researching for *The Forgotten Ways.* In articulating the vision of that book, I often felt then that I was somehow peering over God's shoulder into the mysteries of the church as apostolic movement. I might well be deceived about this, but I feel the significance of this material in my very bones.

Throughout this writing, I have tried to cultivate understanding, to stir the imagination, provide practical wisdom, offer some tools, and to call leaders to a courageous response that equals the many challenges of our times. In the hope of stirring leaders to apply the vast potentials latent in

5Q, I have tried to give the reader something of a panoramic vision of the possibilities of *ecclesia* and discipleship organized around the elegant genius of what I have come to call 5Q. But in alerting you to this phenomenon, I am not pointing to some fancy new idea derived from best thinking in organization or leadership studies—as useful as these are—rather, I have tried to recover something that is already there, a potential latent in the very being and structure of the church, like a light switch, waiting to be activated.

This renewed theological vision of the ministry of God's people has encompassed elements that reach back into the primordial structures of creation; are centered in the redemptive work of the Messiah; and lean forward toward the eschatological horizon when our Lord Jesus Christ shall fill everything in every way (Ephesians 1:11–23; Colossians 1:1–23). The church is caught up in that grand drama as the mission of God works its way up the corridors of history. More importantly, I hope to have reconnected your sense of ministry and purpose with that of Jesus himself. In many ways you are his agent, commissioned to extend both the logic and impact of Jesus' work in the world.

Following the assumption that all our greatest truths are remembered ones, I have sought to connect the contemporary church with its most primary forms. I have encouraged the reader to begin the journey with soft eyes. My reasoning for doing so is because I believe that:

> The best way to escape the comfortable familiarity of an inherited picture of reality is to try to return to something more original, more immediate: to retreat from one's habitual interpretations of one's experiences of the world and back to those experiences themselves, as unencumbered as possible by preconceptions and prejudices.[2]

Soft eyes, grasshopper!

Like the good detective you are, with soft eyes you have searched for the appropriate clues and patterns. I believe that if you, the reader, have gotten to this point of the book, then you, like me, will have experienced a renewed sense of God's marvelous design and purpose for the discipling, worshipping, learning, missioning community that is the church. My appeal to you is that you now seek to apply what you have learned, for the times demand it.

Last words to Martin Buber, one of my favorite teachers and prophets, who, writing of the massive crisis facing the Jewish people in mid-twentieth-century Europe, called for the youth of that generation to seek God, discern the times, and respond:

> This generation must be made receptive for the Unforeseen which upsets all logical arrangements. Their ears and hearts must be open to the voice of the mystery which speaks in those utterances. We should not do all this with the purpose of preparing them to repeat the teachings and perform prescribed rites, but so that they may acquire the power to make the original choice, that—listening to

the voice with that power—they may hear the message it has for their hour and their work; that they may learn to trust the voice, and through this trust, come to faith, to a faith of their own.[3]

You, like them, must now make the decisive choice.
God guide and bless you in it.

Appendix 1

The Cessation of Cessationism

Cessationists believe that the fivefold, or more specifically the apostolic and the prophetic, has ceased with the coming of the canon of Scripture and the emergence of the Papacy and the priestly hierarchy that accompanied it.

To be clear, cessationists do not believe that all the APEST functions have been abrogated; only the apostolic, prophetic, and evangelistic.[1] But the brunt of their censure falls primarily on the first two, and mostly on the apostolic. So I will address these but with the view to keeping the integral nature of APEST intact. As I have said, in Ephesians 4, APEST comes as one cohesive unit or not at all.

As far as I can tell, there are some themes or motifs that seem to weave their way through the rationale used to eliminate the apostolic (and the prophetic) functions from the church's ministry. Almost all of these themes seem to have coalesced around the concerns of the post-apostolic and the Christendom period relying on anachronistic concepts of ecclesial authority and power that are alien to the New Testament itself. In other words the logic is not derived from the New Testament itself but deduced from later assumptions about ordination, canon, and ecclesial power. One gets a sense that cessationism is more a preference for a certain *type* of church and faith; one significantly less charismatic, more standardized, more static and controllable. In other words, I discern strong psycho-sociopolitical motivation hidden in the overt teaching.

The first theme, and one largely associated with various forms of fundamentalism, is that the primary role of the Apostles was simply to write the Bible.[2] And having written the New Testament, such thinking goes, they serenely passed the apostolic baton (now in the manageable form of the New Testament canon) over to the now-ascendant shepherds and teachers to study and interpret it in the ongoing life of the church. But this is quite clearly wrong. How can we know this? Well, we know that only five or six of the original twelve wrote canonical material. What about the other Apostles? Were they abject failures in their apostolic role? What function did they serve?

The second motif, a slight variation of the "write the Bible" canonical cessationism described above, maintains that once apostolic letters had been captured in the canon of the New Testament, and could be further extracted and condensed into the form of apostolic formulations or doctrine, the church no longer had any need for the ongoing functions or vocations of apostles and prophets. The Platonic assumptions driving this approach believe that logical truths can somehow simply be abstracted from personal truthfulness, the concept can be extracted from the percept, the essential can be extracted from the practical, the idea from its living expression. In this view, living obedience is excluded and concepts become our fate.

In other words, this triumph of the essential over the *function* suggests that once the church had codified what it considered to be apostolic doctrine, it no longer needed active apostolic persons and functions. But this too is clearly wrong. We can say with confidence that whatever the roles of the original Apostles were, they went far beyond just creating Scripture or writing doctrine, as important as these are. Apostles, then and now, have an ongoing purpose in maintaining vision, developing missional capacity, encouraging church planting, doing the necessary translocal networking that keeps movements together, and importantly in maintaining a deep sense of abiding purpose in the life of the church, among others. As central and important as doctrine is, it was never meant to replace the dynamic living function of the apostles in Jesus' church.[3] Besides, if this logic of cessationism were applied consistently, then all functions would have ceased with the coming of the canon of the New Testament, not just the apostolic—they are given as a whole after all.[4]

The third theme weaving its way into cessationism asserts that the unique primacy of the twelve Apostles, their prime role, it is claimed, is to be witnesses to Jesus and the Resurrection. They have an irreplaceable symbolic significance in the founding of the church. But because they are exceptional and unrepeatable, all apostolic ministry effectively died with them.

But this too doesn't make any real sense. For one, while it is clear that the original twelve Apostles did have some unique, irreplaceable, roles to play in the establishment of the original church (Revelation 21:14), this does not mean there are no other, ongoing, *apostolic functions* in the continuing life of the church and in other apostles—because there most certainly are others listed as apostles in the New Testament ... and at least one of them was a woman (Junia)!

Furthermore, a strict limitation of apostleship to "the Twelve" cannot account for Judas Iscariot's (one of the original) betrayal removal from the Twelve and his replacement by Matthias (Acts 1:15–26). And what about the fact that Paul himself was never part of the original twelve and yet plays such an absolutely foundational role in the early church? Are we talking about a "Thirteen" now? And what again of the other people called apostles? So you can see, cessationist appeals to the uniqueness of the original twelve needs a bit to make it stick as a coherent doctrine. It dies the death of a thousand qualifications.

Another aspect assigned to the primary function of the Twelve was that they were there to witness to Jesus' resurrection, that in constituting the new church, the original twelve give living and irreplaceable testimony to the Resurrection. Good and well, I think this is true, but in itself is not unique and does not exclude other witnesses. Ask yourself, how many other people also witnessed the resurrected Jesus? The answer? Five hundred! (1 Corinthians 15:3–8) plus Paul, plus the women in Jesus' band, etc. So even that is hardly unique.

So once again, recognizing some unique and irreplaceable aspects we can also affirm at the same time that there are things that were bequeathed by the original Apostles to history as the inheritance of the church—church planting, translocal networking, pioneering, and regional leadership are case in point. The issue is to discern the degree to which all subsequent apostolic functions and callings reflect the foundational functions of the original twelve *without* superseding their unique role in the history of the church. In *The Permanent Revolution*, we call this extracting the "little a" from the "big A." But just as we ought to do this in relation to the apostolic functions, so must we extract the "little apest" from "big APEST," all five functions that are based primarily on Jesus.[5]

Cessationists therefore can never explain *from the Bible itself* why God's various gifts and callings were so obviously present throughout the New Testament church and yet so glaringly absent in our own. Neither can cessationists account for the enduring presence of outstanding examples of all the various apostolic and prophetic callings evident in God's people in every age of the church—Patrick, Francis, Thérèse of Lisieux, John Wesley, Catherine Booth, Martin Luther King Jr., are just some who come to mind.

And the great tragedy in all this is that by arbitrarily excluding the apostolic (and to lesser degrees, the prophetic and evangelistic) functions from the fivefold, the early church fathers also thereby excluded those very functions, without which the church can never fully mature! A clear case of shooting ourselves in the foot—or worse. All this is bad enough, but then they bequeathed the reduction of the ministry to their ecclesial descendants … the Western church.

Truthfully, I strongly suspect that the prime motivation for all this limiting of apostleship to the original twelve was a sham ideology developed on the pretext of consolidating power in an increasingly bureaucratic hierarchy in order to bring the church under the more controllable, and increasingly administrative, episcopal jurisdiction of the bishops.[6] The logic of cessationism is profoundly anachronistic and procrustean—involving a tendency to retrofit facts and evidence onto the New Testament in order to resolve apparent categorical tensions in current thinking and behavior. It's dishonest and somewhat violent with the evidence. I just don't think the arguments hold up exegetically, theologically, historically, or from an organizational viewpoint. I am astounded by how many people have simply assumed that it is correct for so long.

Thankfully in the last few decades, many scholars and leaders have come to recognize that cessationism was at best an anachronistic reading of Scripture, at worst a flagrant manipulation of the clear teachings of the New Testament. There is *nothing* in the Scripture itself that suggests that three of the five APEST ministries would be done away with, leaving us with only two expressions of ministry. Rather the church is to conform to the original design that was given by our resurrected Lord—through his ascension no less. So for instance, if you were able to ask Paul (or the others for that matter) if he had ever conceived of a Christianity deprived of apostles specifically and APEST generally? I am *absolutely sure* that his answer would be something as follows; "What? Never! What am I? Chopped liver? The history of the church (Acts) is APEST writ large … isn't it? Besides, I thought I made it absolutely clear in my letter to Ephesians that these are *given* (aorist-indicative) as the victory-gifts of the ascending Lord to his Body as an integral unit of Christ's ministry.[7] A Christianity without apostles would be an un-missional Christianity and therefore untrue to itself. Why would I contradict my clear teaching and the church's standard practice throughout?"

It is no use appealing to church tradition by saying that the church fathers (particularly Clement of Alexandria) abandoned the fivefold ministry and opted for a hierarchical episcopate model, and therefore the fivefold ministry has been superseded and is now obsolete.[8] The best take on Clement is that he did what he thought was necessary in his day to secure the church against dissolution. At worst, Clement's decision was just plain wrong, profoundly unbiblical, and utterly disastrous in that it introduced a fatal flaw into the subsequent ministry of the church. We are still suffering that fatal decision today.

For those who feel somehow that Western ecclesial tradition is sacrosanct and the teaching and practices of the Fathers permanently binding, remember that church tradition is neither infallible nor ultimately authoritative. They too, like us, were subject to all the vulnerabilities, prejudices, and fears of their age. Besides, just imagine if we had to follow every dictate and tradition handed down to us. The burden would be intolerable, the task impossible, and the resultant church would be thoroughly mutant.

The good news is that as followers of Jesus we are not constrained to slavishly follow Clement's (or any other church leader's) bad decision here! We can, and indeed must, repent. Certainly, Clement does not annul Paul! Scripture trumps church tradition *every time!* This is true for all who would simply rely on traditional formulations to negotiate the complexities of their own time and context. In going further back to the underlying patterns of ministry and leadership in our *original and originating* sources (the Scriptures) I want to point out how Jesus has designed us to be a world-transforming agency.

Our consistent failure to live up to this high calling can sometimes be traced to choices made along the way which were subsequently written into the codes of the church. We need to pay renewed attention to the Word, to the very logic of the gospel, and ultimately to the Founder-Leader of the church. In the spirit of *semper reformanda*, we must reorient our thinking, repent where necessary, and chart a more biblical course.

Appendix 2

A Game of Thrones?
Charismatic or
Missional Approaches?

Related to cessationism, but a separate issue, is the perception of the fivefold as primarily a hierarchical leadership paradigm. Many non-cessationist individuals and organizations have embraced the fivefold through this lens. The most influential current model of this is found in the so-called New Apostolic Reformation (NAR) movement started by C. Peter Wagner and others.[1]

Aside from the contemporary NAR, it seems that when the fivefold ministry actually has been taken seriously in the last hundred years or so, examples have come largely, but not exclusively, from within the Pentecostal-Charismatic (P-C) tradition. And so I am going to focus here on the standard P-C expression, but in doing so I hope to indirectly address all those who see APEST in the light of a distinctively hierarchical, top-down, "charismatic" understanding of leadership and power. I do this because I believe this interpretation of the purpose of the fivefold is unfounded biblically and more often than not damages the church when it is applied. This fundamental misunderstanding of *ecclesia* in this view threatens to undermine the adoption of an idea that has strategic significance to the mission of the whole church in our time.

I come from the Pentecostal tradition and remain profoundly grateful for the heritage it has handed down to me—including something of a confidence in the ongoing validity of the fivefold. So consider me something of an insider here. However, I have come to see that charismatics generally interpret the fivefold texts in terms of two overriding preoccupations; namely that of the authority (*exousia*) and power (*dynamis*) of the individual believer and the corporate church. While I think that seeking power and authority is completely correct in relation to the empowerment of the church by the Holy Spirit, I believe these are category errors when applied to the Ephesians 4:11 vocations/functions.

Anyone in the P-C stream will be all too aware that when someone is called an apostle or a prophet it is generally attached to the idea that the individual is infused with an almost magical aura of spirit-power. Certainly, they seem to convey an idea of patriarchal power and priestly authority. In these situations, followers tend to be overawed and uncritically follow those who all too readily dominate and exploit them. This holy celebrity phenomenon is by no means limited to P-C streams (witness the rash of abusive leadership in macho new-Reformed and other evangelical circles) but it does seem to characterize an aspect of P-C history in relation to the fivefold.

To be sure, all Christians are to seek the empowerment of the Holy Spirit in all aspects of our lives; moreover, all the charismatic gifts articulated in 1 Corinthians 12–14 and elsewhere are given precisely to this end. But it is a fundamental mistake to interpret Ephesians 4:11 in terms of charismatic power and authority.[2] As I show throughout this book, APEST is to be understood as being directly derived from Jesus himself and is therefore a living index of his activity in the Body. The emphasis here falls on Jesus and not on the work of the Holy Spirit as such.[3] While this might seem a small point at first, keep your eyes soft and you shall see how this changes the paradigm, and in fact unlocks the real power of the APEST codes. Whereas the "spirituals" of 1 Corinthians 12–14 are manifestations of the Spirit given to individuals to empower their particular ministry, Ephesians 4:11 (APEST) is the heritage of the Body of Christ and is prescriptive for the church as a whole.[4]

It's Primarily about Ministry of all, Secondarily about Leadership of Some

But where the power-authority interpretation of the fivefold really reveals its inherent dysfunction is when it is bound together with the penchant of churches to view their leaders as "God's anointed"—holy men and women who are seen as untouchable and not to be questioned, who manifest their leadership through a hierarchically structured "office," and who therefore express power in a somewhat authoritarian manner. These together create the cult of religious celebrity that has brought such dishonor to the Jesus movement—throughout history but also in the last few decades. The CEO form of leadership that this authorizes thus misappropriates the APEST typologies in an effort to bolster hierarchical religious authority. This almost always turns out to be disastrous, mainly because it inverts power and authority as it is understood through the person and work of Jesus.

It is not, then, the APEST function itself that is problematic, but rather the *concept of leadership* that so often shapes and informs the function. APEST is entirely biblical and legitimate; the top-down CEO concept that permeates

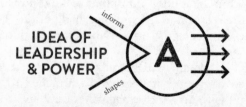

Figure A2.1 The CEO Form of Leadership

unbiblical understandings of leadership is not! We must derive our primary understandings of leadership, power, and authority from the humble, incarnational, cruciform, and self-emptying way of Jesus (Luke 22:24–26; Philippians 2:1–11) and not from secular understandings of power and leadership. Our Lord completely inverts "normal" understandings as to how power-authority are understood and exercised.

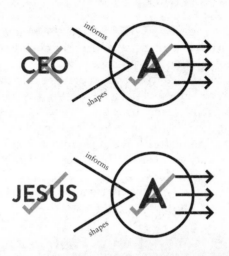

Figure A2.2 The CEO vs. Jesus Form of Leadership

All such co-option of the apostolic (and all APEST types for that matter) to worldly notions of power will have disastrous effects on the church, whose New Testament dynamic is based on the cruciform model of Jesus and is therefore meant to be radically non-hierarchical and polycentric.[5] Ephesians 4 understands ministry as given to the entire Body (v. 7), not just to leaders— leadership is not even mentioned in the text. Sadly, churches miss this point and approach Ephesians 4 as a leadership text, which inevitably seems to engender fractious political disputes, dysfunction and even church splits. As far as I can tell, just about every time the "power-understanding" of Ephesians 4 predominates, it inevitably leads to an ecclesial bus crash.[6]

Many have rejected APEST because it can so easily lend itself to the misuse of religious power. Witness that in most of the mainline Pentecostal denominations in North America, the fivefold has fallen into disrepute and has all but become a vestigial doctrine. Like an appendix, it is "there" but nobody quite knows what to do with it, and so they too have defaulted to the safer, domesticated reduction handed down to us from Clement.

How can the fivefold be activated without causing a big bust-up? Essentially the approach I take, and the one laid out in this and my other books, is that APEST is to be best understood as the proper expression of the ministry of Christ, through the Body of Christ, leading to the fullness of Christ. It is a non-negotiable part of the *nature of the ecclesia* itself. And importantly, it is absolutely essential for the effective mission and ministry of the church. Ephesians 4:1–16 is not a leadership text, but rather a *ministry text*. Paul is not writing to a limited group of "leaders" but to the whole assembled *ecclesia*, including the culturally marginalized women and slaves, as well as people of different races. He even *explicitly* states that *each member* of the whole Body is given an apportioned gift by Jesus himself (Ephesians 4:7).[7]

The whole Ephesians 4 passage is about the functionality of the whole Body of Christ. And this in turn is entirely consistent throughout New Testament ecclesiology that absolutely insists that *everyone is in the game.* Clearly the Bible has things to say to leaders—while the concept of leadership is not explicitly mentioned in Ephesians 4, it certainly is implied!—but in the case of the fivefold they must be extrapolated from what is given to all the members of the Body as agents of the King. Leadership is a calling to some given within a calling to all. We must not transpose the false dichotomy between clergy and laity on the New Testament, including of course this text.

Approaching the fivefold with this Christological understanding thus relieves us of the power dynamic that can so easily ruin communities and bring disrepute to our Lord.

Appendix 3

The Exiling of the APEs

By Alan Hirsch and Tim Catchim, 2012

> The basic trouble [with the modern church] is that the proposed cure has such a striking similarity to the disease.
>
> —Elton Trueblood

> In a revolutionary era ... you need to learn to think and act like a revolutionary. People in revolutions who don't act that way have a particular name: victims.
>
> —Joshua Ramo Cooper

We can all recall the almost ubiquitous stories about a renegade hero who, once famous and brilliant, has now found himself rejected, scorned, and cast aside—think Jack Bauer in the 24 series if you need an example. Mocked by his peers, alienated from all but a few friends, given to alcohol binges, and generally feeling very sorry for himself, the protagonist is all alone and given up as a loser. However, the plot soon reveals that the very organization and people that rejected him (usually the police, the special ops unit in the military, or in Bauer's case, CTU) realize that the fallen hero is the only person who can resolve a particular problem. Our hero, now freshly deputized, enters into the fray and ends up saving the day.

The reason why this theme is so prolific in the countless stories, poems, and movies is that it is mythic. And it is mythic because it points to some real, lived, experience in human affairs. There is a wisdom deeply embedded into our myths that tell us that many of the answers we need will come in the form of radical outliers, people who exist on the margins of what is considered conventional. The myth-become-real involves the profound recognition that these exiled heroes are in some real sense what we really needed to resolve the issues we currently face—that the answer *does not come from within* the existing state of affairs, but rather from outside the ingrained understandings of what is considered normal and conventional. As in the many movies we see, the outlier does bring the much-needed dissonance into the status quo, a dissonance which jolts the system out of complacency, initiates a learning journey, and results in the eventual resolution of the problem at hand.

Whilst de-emphasizing the silver-bullet bravado side of the myth, we think that this myth of the exiled hero is entirely applicable to the nature of our dilemma—the exiling of the APEs fits this narrative—and reflects our desperate need to re-embrace them in our own day. We need to re-embrace and reintegrate the ministries of the apostle, prophet, and the evangelist with those of the shepherd and teacher.

Monopoly, Anyone?

How did the shepherd-teacher model of leadership come to occupy such an exclusive place in the church's life? How could the other three vocations of apostle, prophet and evangelist drift so far from sight that they hardly even make it on the map, much less into our vocabulary and conversations about leadership? We believe that the answer to this question lies in the unique nature of the APEST itself and the outcomes when the system becomes dysfunctional. As we have seen, each ministry type produces a certain ministry impact that together produces a holistic result. But the opposite is also true: when each ministry is taken by itself, divorced from the other ministries, it produces a dysfunctional, aberrant, result in the people of God.

So, for instance, the Shepherd and Teacher (ST) will tend to design more stable environments where people can learn to relate and grow in their understanding of the faith. However, as the learning and maturing are to be lifelong activities, communities led *primarily* by these STs will lack urgency and will likely concentrate on issues relating to long-term sustainability. The net result will be to move inexorably toward a state of what living systems theorists call *equilibrium*.

The ST functions are ones that bring needed equilibrium into the system. And this is completely necessary for long-term sustainability—few can survive in chaos situations for too long. The problem, however, arises when the ST functions become disengaged from the full APEST system. The result is that much-needed balancing with disequilibrium-producing ministries is undone. When this happens, the dialectical pressure is removed and equilibrium becomes a settled state ... and when a living system is in perfect equilibrium it is effectively dead.

Jeffrey Goldstein in his insightful book *The Unshackled Organization* describes equilibrium as the state in which a system is at rest or not changing. At equilibrium, an organization seeks to stay the same, simply repeating its habitual patterns and in a sense over-relying on solutions that worked for it in the past. He notes that as a result "it is a condition of the lowest organization and complexity." And because of the addiction to the stable state and to past approaches, "the emergence of any new patterns of behavior in the system are experienced as opposition to the deeper, more dominant force of equilibrium."[1]

The truth is that organizations in this state are extremely difficult to change—even when their very survival is being threatened. This is because equilibrium, like any death, is experienced incrementally, as an encroachment, slowly creeping up on the unwitting subject. Humans are classic deniers of our own impending death ... the same is precisely true for all human organizations. In fact, in many ways institutions are Babel-like attempts to perpetuate life and thus deny death.

And should the organization and its leadership perchance rouse from its death slumbers, and become alert to the danger, in most cases it would probably be too late to do anything about it. Is this not the sad pattern involved in almost every closure of a local church or the decline of entire denominations? The real problem here is assuming that the dying organization (along with the incumbent leadership that led it to that condition in the first place) were actually willing to pay the price for change, by the time it made that decision it would likely lack the internal resources (both theological and ministerial) to do anything about it. All the generative resources needed would have been already invalidated and/or ejected from the organization long before. Therefore, such organizations lack the theological architecture, a deep-seated sense of apostolic urgency, or the leadership capacity to solve their own problems. If desired, these would have to be "imported" from outside.

And just so that we are not being misunderstood here, we want to assert again that it's not that the ST variation of leadership intends to produce such stifling equilibrium. We fully believe that the vast majority of Christian leaders are sincere in their desire to serve God and his people in whatever way they can, and thankfully very few willfully intend to damage the church and its mission. What we *are* saying is that ST forms of ministry are simply not wired to produce *missional* movement—as community builders and wise philosophers, it's not what they were designed to produce in the first place. Rather STs provide the *integrative/operative* aspects of ministry, whereas the APEs furnish us with the more *generative/adaptive* forms.

This just underscores yet again that all ministries are intended by Jesus to be part of the broader, synergistic, interplay between various other ministry types. Each type contributes something that the others cannot. APEST represents an organic whole in which none are meant to operate independently of the other—we are called into a Body function where there is significant diversity of ministry form and expression.

All this highlights the need for the reinstatement of the permanent revolution originally intended in Ephesians 4. That it is permanent and inbuilt is highlighted in verses 7 and 11 where we learn that Jesus has placed, indeed permanently given (here expressed in two aorist indicatives of *didomi*), the intrinsic capacities to his people to keep them precisely from such a situation. Here is the algorithm of ecclesial maturity: the internal self-renewing system that we need to keep on the journey and to fulfill our tasks.

Back to the Dialectic: Toward Synthesis

Living systems approaches rightly note that all living systems resist change and tend toward equilibrium. The status quo is called that for good reason, and it has a long history of, and an inbuilt capacity to, resist change. In other words, resistance to change is entrenched into the system caught in status quo. This means that when trying to stimulate change and activate mission, church leaders will need to be very prepared for some conflict. Churches that are used to equilibrium will resist being moved out of the somewhat predictable, safe routine they have settled into overtime.

Furthermore, we need to recognize that the very equilibrium itself is produced and maintained by the incumbent leadership that created that condition in the first place! Leaders are part of the system, one way or another. And we must recognize that it is not easy for anyone to acknowledge culpability because it means taking responsibility for failure to grow and advance the cause. Pride, ego, paradigm blindness, and vested interests are not easily exposed. But we *can* trust the Holy Spirit, that he desires his church to grow, and we can trust that the deepest instincts of every Christian will resonate with the missional calling of God's people. These can, and must, be awakened. And when they are, we can be sure it is a work of God's grace. However, if leaders and/or members of any organization are not willing to re-engage the missional Spirit and go where he leads us—and it will inevitably mean change—then it is highly doubtful whether the much-needed adaptation can take place.

And so, organizational dynamics, spiritual warfare, and plain human nature conspire to play their part in perpetuating the monopoly of the more maintenance-driven forms of organization and leadership. As the collective representation of human concerns, organizations almost inevitably develop an uncanny capacity to actively resist change. Haven't we all heard that age-old bureaucratic refrain, "we just don't do things like that around here!" The sad truth is that unless the necessary precautions are taken, over time all organizations tend to become more important than their founding mission. When this happens, they will actively enforce conformity, codify behavior, and actively weed out dissent. In other words, they tend to equilibrium and resist disequilibrium.

It is because of this that innovators are seen as rebels, dissenters, and upstarts. They are almost always marginalized because their very existence and nature imply that things are not as they should, or could, be. In other words, the very act of innovation involves an implied critique. Any suggestion that there might be more to ministry than shepherding and teaching can invite the full range of responses, ranging from being accused of being "unbiblical," to suggesting that those proposing a broadening of the categories are "cultish," or that the would-be apostles and prophets are simply power-hungry people who are trying to lord it over the flock.

And there is no doubt that there have been APE type people who do fit any or all of these descriptions. But demagoguery and powermongering are certainly not limited to the APE claimants. For instance, the Inquisition, surely the ugliest chapter in church history, was initiated and operated by STs no less—all in the name of religious conformity and ideological control! The truth is all humans are susceptible to misuse of power and to wrong motives, and history amply indicates that the priestly classes who have monopolized leadership roles in the church up to this point have had more than their share of abusive power. In fact, priestly types of abuse are possibly one of the worst because they violate people where they are most vulnerable (in their relation to God) and bear false witness to the Gospel. This is not about laying blame in either direction but is a call to a much-needed self-awareness on the part of those defending the status quo.

This dismembering of the Body of Christ has done violence to the ministry of Christ through his church. More specifically, it has meant that the more generative forms of ministry, representing as they do the impulses that naturally drive us toward missional engagement, spiritual renewal, cultural revitalization, and ecclesial innovation, have been negated in that process. In many ways, this process has taken something of the adventure of missionality out of the venture of church. Rather than audaciously engaging the significant challenges that we face, we have become known as being an overly defensive religion, conservatively defending our ground and trying to hold on to our diminishing status in Western society.

We do well to remember at this point that it is a key task of Christian leadership to lead the church into God's purposes and future—it's a Kingdom of God affair. This involves significant risk and requires that we overcome our impulses for safety and security and to burrow down in fear and defensiveness.[2] The Great Commission is hardly a call to safety and equilibrium! And we should also remind ourselves that Jesus never promised that the church would be "safe" but rather that he will be with us in our ordeal of witness (John 16:33; 2 Corinthians 1; Hebrews 11–12; 1 Peter, etc.). Surely we need to re-embrace the exiled ministries in order to creatively engage the challenges we face.

Appendix 4

A Threefold or Fivefold Pattern

Christians have over the centuries developed models by which they can somehow categorize the various disparate elements of Jesus' life and ministry. For instance, there is the classical teaching on Christology called the *Munus Triplex*, or the Threefold Offices of Christ. Originally developed by Eusebius, it is now largely associated with Calvin as well as the subsequent Reformed churches shaped by Calvin's theology. This model sees Christ's person and work as a fulfillment of the Old Testament offices of Prophet, Priest, and King. It is understood by its proponents to adequately represent all the critical aspects of the work of Christ, including Jesus as Lord, Savior, Mediator, Intercessor, Revealer, Redeemer, and so on.[1]

More recently there have been efforts to translate this "tri-perspectival" model of Christology into the life and ministry of the church.[2] So, following the Christocentric instinct of ministry, believers are also meant to find themselves somewhere in the threefold typology of ministry as prophets, priests, and kings.

I believe the *instincts* to base ministry directly in the exemplary life and model of Jesus are absolutely correct and must be affirmed. But I do not think Jesus' fulfillment of Old Testament "offices" makes an easy fit for Christian ministry. Apart from the fact that it is doubtful that it carries the full load in terms of the doctrine of Christ, it is awfully hard to make a case for believers in these offices (e.g., king?). And so while a tri-perspectival model of ministry certainly is an improvement from the narrow "bi-perspectival" reduction associated with the traditional Christendom orders of ministry (namely, pastor and teacher) I think it fails to have direct biblical support.

I believe that the best way for us to grasp the multiple dimensions of Jesus' ministry is to broaden the typology from the somewhat reductionist threefold characteristics to that of the perfect embodiment of Apostle, Prophet, Evangelist, Shepherd, and Teacher. These, I believe, provide a more nuanced and enhanced framework for both understanding Jesus' ministry and translating these into the life of the *ecclesia*. In other words, we best conform ourselves to his ministry when we understand and engage it in APEST terms. Paul himself locates the source of APEST ministry in Jesus Christ as the origin and giver of these gifts to the church. Fullness of Christ is expressed through APEST forms and practices. For instance look again at the Ephesians text with my emphases:

To each one of us grace has been *given as Christ apportioned it ...* So Christ himself *gave the apostles, the prophets, the evangelists, the pastors and teachers,* to equip his people for works of service, so that the body of Christ may be built up until we all reach unity in the faith and in the knowledge of the Son of God and become mature, attaining to the whole measure of the fullness of Christ.

Then we will no longer be like infants, tossed back and forth by the waves, and blown here and there by every wind of teaching and by the cunning and craftiness of people in their deceitful scheming. Instead, speaking the truth in love, *we will grow to become in every respect the mature body of him who is the head, that is, Christ. From him the whole body,* joined and held together by every supporting ligament, grows and builds itself up in love, as each part does its work.

The point of Ephesians is to show how the ministry of Christ is embedded into the Body of Christ and fulfilled through the ministry of the followers of Christ. It's all about being the fullness of Christ.

So much is at stake—this not merely impacts on our effectiveness; it is an issue of faithfulness to our calling.[3] Any diminishment of our engagement with the fivefold archetypes/dimensions of Jesus' own ministry will inevitably degrade our capacity—individually and communally—to reflect and embody Jesus in our lives.

Notes

Preface

1. *The Wire*, created by David Simon, Blown Deadline Productions HBO.

2. Living systems thinker Margaret Wheatley warns that "analysis narrows our field of awareness and actually prevents us from seeing the total system. We move deeper into the details and farther away from learning how to comprehend the system in its wholeness." Margaret J. Wheatley, *Leadership and the New Science: Discovering Order in a Chaotic World* (San Francisco; Berrett Koehler, 2006), 160.

3. Alvin Toffler, *Third Wave* (New York: Bantam, 1980), 4.

4. Daniel H. Pink, *A Whole New Mind: Why Right Brainers Will Rule the Future* (New York: Riverhead, 2005).

5. "That the Christian truth is symphonic is perhaps the most necessary truth which must be proclaimed and taken to heart today." In David L. Schindler (Ed.) *Hans Urs von Balthasar: His Life and Work* (San Francisco: Ignatius Books, 1991), 180.

6. For the dialectics of renewal, see Alan Hirsch and Tim Catchim, *The Permanent Revolution: Apostolic Imagination and Practice for the 21st Century Church* (San Francisco: Jossey-Bass, 2014), 143–145.

7. Hans Urs von Balthasar, *The Glory of the Lord: A Theological Aesthetics, Vol. 1* (San Francisco: Ignatius Press, 2009), 474.

8. von Balthasar, a very gifted musician, notes that, "Everyone who has listened to Bach knows that, in the classical fugue, the rhythmical arrangement is oppositional: the first theme is slow and reposeful, the second runs along swiftly, and the third contains a rhythmical hammering; and every hearer knows that this varied thematic construction is determined by the rationale of the fugue's total architecture." Ibid., 500. By knowing the whole we make sense of the various elements of the total symphony.

9. von Balthasar, ibid., 500.

10. Ernst Käsemann in an address given to the theological faculty of the University of Marburg-Lahn, November 25, 1981. http://apprenticeinstitute.org/spiritual-formation-unlearning/

11. "To look at something as though we had never seen it before requires great courage ... An artist should never be a prisoner of himself, prisoner of style, prisoner of reputation, prisoner of success, etc. The artist must summon all his energy, his sincerity, and the greatest modesty in order to shatter the old clichés that come so easily to hand while working." https://goo.gl/FqczSs

12. "It is repentance that allows us to be forgiven for our infertility and intransigence, to recalibrate, and so start again. The gift of repentance allows us to seek new solutions for the way we can reconceive of and restructure our life in God and in accordance with his eternal purposes in the gospel. This is sheer grace, and we should embrace it wholeheartedly in our common life as much as in our personal one. And it should certainly be a living aspect of what it means to be a believing church full of faith." Hirsch and Catchim, *The Permanent Revolution*, xxix.

13. "As uncomfortable as critical appraisals of the church tend to make us feel, we do well to remind ourselves at this point that despite the towering effect that institutions have on us, they have to be seen for what they truly are: mere products of human activity. As human

constructs, institutions cannot adequately reflect back to us our own intrinsic worth. Jesus' own rejection by the religious and political establishment of his day bears witness to the tendency of institutions to develop their own metrics and categories for what should and should not be valued or deemed essential. It is in Jesus himself that we can find the higher authority—one that transcends the towering effect of the institutions—with which to speak the corrective word into our context." Hirsch and Catchim *The Permanent Revolution*, xxii–xxiii.

Introduction

1. Another, more recent illustration derived from the politics of empire, involves the more recent British Empire itself. At its peak the British, a relatively small island nation, created a global empire that ruled half the earth—an incredible feat indeed! It required real vision and capacity to pull that off in a world of sailboats and muskets! In fact, the colonizers engineered a worldwide system so robust that it's still with us today. The problem is that in this postcolonial era, the imperial system is still cranking out people that are perfectly suited to a system that no longer exists.

2. Damian Thompson, "2067: The End of British Christianity," *The Spectator*, 13 June 2015, http://bit.ly/1JjE7Ve. While the subtitle does acknowledge that culture and society seldom travel along linear lines of progression or regression ("Projections aren't predictions ..."), nonetheless the overall trend is not good (" ... there's no denying that churches are in deep trouble"). This ought to cause some alarm among church leaders in that context. Even more shocking perhaps are the official statistics of the Church of Scotland, the largest denomination in Scotland. By its own measures, at the current rate of decline the Church of Scotland will cease to function by 2037! (The official statistics maintained by Rev. Colin Brough, used with permission.)

3. The Nones is the name researchers have given to the growing number of people who now claim to have "no religion." The Dones on the other hand are people who are disillusioned with church. Though they were committed to the church for years—often as lay leaders— they no longer attend. Whether because they're dissatisfied with the structure, social message, or politics of the institutional church, they've decided they are better off without organized religion. See "'Nones on the Rise'", Pew Research Center, October 9, 2012 on this topic http:// www.pewforum.org/2012/10/09/ nones-on-the-rise/. Also see Joshua Packard, "'Meet the 'Dones,'" *Leadership Journal*, Summer 2015, http:// www.christianitytoday.com/le/2015/ summer-2015/ meet-dones.html

4. In such a situation, it is incumbent on us to return to our primary sources (the founding story, theology, ideas, and approaches) to reflect critically on our inherited paradigms and to thoroughly audit the rationality, methods, and practices of the church as we have it. The Protestant Reformation might be thought of as largely a thoroughgoing audit on the church's doctrines of salvation, but except for the so-called radical reformation, it left the ecclesiological paradigm of Christendom completely intact, assuming its essential correctness. And so the inherited church-state relationship remained largely untouched by the Reformation. Christendom is thus deeply embedded in our theological imagination; shapes our core assumptions about our place and purpose in the world; skews the foundational theology by which we must negotiate our way; and continues to form our practices through religious tradition and liturgy. It has significantly hardened our eyes. For a more thorough analysis of the original, nature, and outcomes of Christendom, see chapter two of the new edition of *The Forgotten Ways : Reactivating Apostolic Movements 2nd Ed.* (Grand Rapids: Brazos, 2016).

5. This renewal process is inherently theological, a matter of softening our eyes to once again gain perspective from the big picture, and to make good use of the evidence we rediscover. Reengaging APEST, in this respect, is first and foremost a theological issue: It is about our (re) alignment with the definitive teachings on ministry, leadership, and the church in the Bible.

For a comprehensive account of the nature and dynamics of apostolic movements, see my book *The Forgotten Ways: Reactivating Apostolic Movements* 2nd Ed.

6. Quoted in Phillip Yancey, *What's So Amazing About Grace* (Grand Rapids: Zondervan EPub Format, 1997), 13.

7. *The Everlasting Man.* E-book on https://goo.gl/JseV

8. Robert M. Pirsig, *Zen and the Art of Motorcycle Maintenance: an Inquiry into Values* (New York: HarperTorch, Kindle Edition, 2009-04-10), 94.

9. R. E. Quinn, *Change the World* (San Francisco: Jossey-Bass, 2000), 61.

10. See Hirsch and Catchim, *The Permanent Revolution* and the associated group study called *The Permanent Revolution Playbook: APEST for the People* (Denver: Missio, 2014); and Hirsch, *The Forgotten Ways: Reactivating Apostolic Movements* 2nd Ed. In the last few years a few books have been released that have developed the church's thinking in regards to APEST and apostolic in particular: JR Woodward, *Creating a Missional Culture: Equipping the Church for the Sake of the World* (Downers Grove, IL: IVP, 2012), Neil Cole, *Primal Fire: Reigniting the Church with the Five Gifts of Jesus* (Carol Stream, IL: Tyndale Momentum, 2014), and Sam Metcalf, *Beyond the Local Church: How Apostolic Movements Can Change the World* (Downers Grove, IL: IVP, 2015).

11. Alan Hirsch and Jessica Cruickshank, *Activating 5Q: A User's Guide to Understanding and Applying 5Q in Your Church or Organization* (Atlanta: 100M Publications, 2017).

12. Essentially, Christology comprises the biblical teaching of and about Jesus the Messiah. For instance, when I say that Christology must inform all aspects of the church's life and work, it means that Jesus must be first and foremost in our life and self-definition as church and disciple. The adjectival form simply means that the element being described must be referenced primarily by our understanding and experience of Jesus the Messiah.

13. In our considerable research for *The Permanent Revolution*, we could find fewer than 50 books on the topic at all! Most of these were coming out of the more immoderate aspects of the charismatic movement, in particular the controversial New Apostolic Revolution. There are some (very few!) post-graduate theses that explore the topic, but on the whole there is a deafening silence. When you consider the amount of books and theses on completely marginal topics of biblical grammar or church history, this amounts to an indictment against our scholarship and integrity.

14. Please read appendices "The Cessation of Cessationism" as well as "The Exiling of the APEs" at the back of this book. Also refer to the appendix in Hirsch and Catchim, *The Permanent Revolution*, as well.

Chapter 1

1. Again, I strongly encourage readers to acquaint themselves with APEST thinking by at least reading the first section of *The Permanent Revolution*. What follows here is the briefest of summaries of what I believe to be a thoroughly paradigmatic piece of Scripture.

2. Eugene H. Peterson, *Practice Resurrection: A Conversation on Growing Up in Christ* (Grand Rapids: Eerdmans, 2010), 14–15.

3. Markus Barth, *Ephesians: Translation and Commentary on Chapters 4–6*, Vol. 2, The Anchor Bible (New York: Doubleday, 1974).

4. This long-term philological massacre is an indictment against our theology and our love of truth. "Take it or leave it, but you cannot cherry-pick the [APEST gifting] you want and the ones you don't ... the grammar and the theology simply do not allow that." Hirsch and Catchim, *The Permanent Revolution*, 20.

5. Gk. teleon... "perfect", (a) complete in all its parts, (b) full grown, of full age, (c) especially of the completeness of Christian character" J. Strong, *A Concise Dictionary of the Words*

in the Greek Testament and The Hebrew Bible 1 (Bellingham: Logos Bible Software, 2009)

6. Gk. *pleroma,* "sum total, fullness, even (super) abundance." Ibid.

7. "In this way the Church develops from the stage of 'children, tossed to and fro and carried about with every wind of doctrine' and grows into 'the stature of the fullness of Christ' by the mutual interpenetration of the charismatic functions and insights of all the individual members (Eph 4:13 ff)." von Balthasar, *Prayer* (San Francisco: Ignatius Press, 1986), 214.

8. Adapted from Hirsch & Catchim, *The Permanent Revolution,* 16.

9. The richest understanding of the text becomes available when the metaphorical and the literal are brought together without denying either kind of truth. This is a real presence, but here it is appropriately applied to the church and not the sacraments of the church—we are the Body of Christ.

10. According to Paul, a fully functioning fivefold ministry is actually the Christ-given defense mechanism against heresy and false doctrine (see comments on *katartitzo* in this book). There is something about APEST as a whole that moves the church past theological narrowness and anchors it in a more integrated understanding of its central message and core doctrines (Eph 4: 14–15). Ironically enough, it is the very diversity contained within APEST that aids the church in attaining to the "unity of the faith."

11. Taken from an email communication with Tim Catchim. Used with permission.

12. Peterson, *Practice Resurrection,* 47.

13. "καταρτίζω" katartizō, "to make, prepare, restore, establish, mend, repair, make whole or perfect, of setting bones, mending nets." C. Spicq and J. D. Ernest, *Theological Lexicon of the New Testament 2* (Peabody, MA: Hendrickson, 1994), 271. *Strong's Concordance* says that "*katartismós* ... describes how (enables) the individual parts to work together in correct order (used only in Eph 4:12)... complete furnishing, perfecting." See J. Strong, *A Concise Dictionary of the Words in the Greek Testament and The Hebrew Bible* 1 (Bellingham: Logos Bible Software, 2009), 40.

14. If the reader wishes to critically evaluate this claim, then I refer you to the latest edition of this book. See Hirsch, *The Forgotten Ways: Reactivating Apostolic Movements 2nd Ed.* In this fully updated version of the 2006 book, I am more convinced of the necessity of the fivefold than ever! And as far as I can tell, there are very few of our leading missiologists (e.g., Darrell Guder, Dave Fitch, Martin Robinson, Michael Frost, et.al.) who would disagree.

15. In the same way that the last few decades has seen a rise in what has been called missional—or if one prefers the Greek, *apostolic*—hermeneutics, so too perhaps one can extend hermeneutics to include all the APEST categories. In other words, it could be a more systematic hermeneutical grid through which to understand revelation of God in Scripture.

16. The writings of Walter Brueggemann and Abraham Herschel are cases in point.

Chapter 2

1. In many ways, my book *The Forgotten Ways* is about identifying the system that is comprised of six meta-ideas—they are called mDNA in that book—that, if taken seriously, prime the entire system for movement.

2. I am indebted however to Andrew Dowsett for suggesting the concept of APEST in the created orders which led me down this path. See his, "'... as each part is working properly ...' Recovering the five-fold ministry of the local church." Unpublished dissertation, St. John's College Nottingham, 2009, 8–9, 15–16. The document is available online at http://bit.ly/plPNdT. Used with permission.

3. But one of the clearest expressions of recurring messianic patterns is evidenced in an American presidential election: The various campaigns draw deeply from the American archetype of "the good Sheriff," the messianic savior who rides into a town dominated by

outlaws, who cleans up the town, and sets all things aright so the good folks can get on with their lives. Just about every campaign is driven on this ideal type. False messiahs also draw upon the messianic archetype as history all too often shows. Hitler is of course an extreme case in point; the führer image is profoundly messianic in its appeal. Movies, as well as the presidential campaigns, have a perennial appeal precisely because they draw upon an ancient archetype of leadership that is prevalent throughout human history. And the messianic is simply one of many enduring archetypes of leadership in culture—as we shall soon explore.

4. To put this into the context of the model I am proposing in this book, I had got the second part (the Christology and ecclesiological aspects of APEST) right, but I was profoundly underdone in the first part of the equation—the truly *foundational* God/archetypes aspects. APEST is thus not some marginal aspect of New Testament doctrine as so many have treated it, but a meta-idea that is actually a key to the living system of culture and the church.

5. What was genuinely new and revelatory to me (and I believe new in broader theological discourse) was trying to understand the dynamics of how it was that Jesus redeemed and re-established the fallen archetypes. This question led me to the rediscovery of a crucial aspect of Paul's theology developed by the early church father, Irenaeus. Irenaeus is the theologian who developed a full-blown theory of recapitulation to explain the work of Jesus in redeeming the world: Following Paul's seminal teaching here, Irenaeus elaborated on the redemptive pattern whereby Jesus, the second Adam/Man, recapitulates (relives and through his very life all that was broken by the Fall. The fivefold archetypes, along with all of the created order, suffered from the Fall and therefore required reconstituting. Through his incarnation, perfect human life, and atoning death, Jesus re-deemed, re-presented, re-established, re-calibrated, and re-purposed APEST in the life of his people. I will explain the importance of recapitulation theory more fully in chapter five, but needless to say that for me at least, it meant seeing Jesus not as the archetypal originator of APEST, as I had previously understood him to be, but rather as the redeemer and perfector of the APEST archetypes already pre-existing in creation. Look at all the "re" words in the paragraph. It is this "re" aspect of Jesus' human life, teachings, and death that implies something needed to be "re-ed"—restored and redeemed and repurposed. See my book with Mike Frost, *ReJesus: A Wild Messiah for a Missional Church* (Baker: Grand Rapids, 2012) for a thorough exploration of the centrality and significance of Jesus in the life of his people.

6. "Although creative individuals are often thought of as working in isolation, much of our intelligence and creativity results from interaction and collaboration with other individuals, with their tools and with their artifacts [Csikszentmihalyi, 1996]. In many traditional approaches, human cognition has been seen as existing solely "inside" a person's head, and studies on cognition have often disregarded the physical and social surroundings in which cognition takes place. Distributed intelligence [Fischer, 2005; Hollan et al., 2001; Salomon, 1993] provides an effective theoretical framework for understanding what humans can achieve and how artifacts, tools, and sociotechnical environments can be designed and evaluated to empower human beings and to change tasks." G. Fischer, "Creativity and Distributed Intelligence" NSF Workshop Report Creativity Support Tools, http://www.cs.umd.edu/hcil/CST/report.html.

7. An interpretive lens is a disciplined means of looking at something, of gaining perspective, through a controlling set of ideas or framework. For instance, feminism is a lens by which one can view society and history—reality looks a whole lot different from that view than from the male perspective. We are just looking at the same reality differently. When we say something is Freudian, we are looking at some aspect of human behavior through Freud's model of the psyche. The same of course is true for any ideology e.g., Marxist or postmodern, schools of art, or whatever. Applied to the church, Calvinism is a different lens of viewing theology than is Catholicism. Baptist perspectives differ from Anglican, etc. We use interpretive lenses all the time.

8. Luther subsequently developed more fully the doctrine of justification as portrayed in Galatians and Romans and he asserted that this was the very axis of biblical revelation.

He then continued by projecting this axis back into the Old Testament. In other words, he articulated the system that still defines how we see the gospel today.

9. For Jewish ethical monotheism, the interpretive key is the confession of the oneness of God and the requirement to unify all of life under him, concentrated in the Shema of Deuteronomy 6:4–9. Everything is passed through that grid in order to be legitimized. So much so that Jesus (the quintessential Jew) completely regards the Shema as the key to understanding revelation (Mark 12:28–34). For Pentecostals and Charismatics, the key is found in an interpretation of the teaching of the baptism of the Spirit in Acts 2 by which the work of the Holy Spirit is reconceived and reappropriated in a whole new light.

10. For instance, seminal theologian Robert Webber sees Christ as the all-important key, experienced as a form of conversion, which in turn opens us up to understand the God at work in the world and in our lives. He testifies, "In the Christian faith the key to the puzzle is the work of Jesus Christ. Once we have a solid grasp of the meaning of his work, the rest of the faith falls together around it. When I discovered the universal and cosmic nature of Christ, I was given the key to a Christian way of viewing the whole world, a key that unlocked the door to a rich storehouse of spiritual treasures." In Scot McKnight, *A Community Called Atonement* (Kindle Edition, Abingdon Press, 2007), Kindle Locations 150–154.

11. Karl Barth, *Church Dogmatics: The Doctrine of the Word of God,* I, Part 2, (Edinburgh: T & T Clark, 1963), 696.

12. *The Matrix,* film, directed by The Wachowski Brothers. USA: Warner Bros. pictures, 1999.

Chapter 3

1. 1 Corinthians 12–14.

2. See *Spiritual Gifts:* A Report of the Commission on Theology and Church Relations of The Lutheran Church—Missouri Synod September 1994, http://www.lcms.org/Document.fdo-c?src=lcm&id=413. This section has drawn heavily from the excellent summary of creational gifts.

3. "God has not only provided the orders of creation, he has also placed upon them his divine blessing. The divine blessing is still what God does throughout all creation. God remains hidden behind all acts of blessing, not just religious ones." To be sure, the non-believers "often serve as instruments of God unwittingly and unwillingly, but God continues to carry out his work even through non-Christian parents, employers, and government leaders." Ibid., 36.

4. The doctrine of *vestigia Dei,* developed by Augustine and later by Thomas Aquinas, teaches that the world having been made by God bears within it "traces of the Creator," and that these vestiges exist in all reality and are available to us through scientific investigation and reasoned reflection. Aidan Nichols, *Redeeming Beauty: Soundings in Sacral Aesthetics* (Hampshire: Ashgate, 2007), 81–2.

5. Bonaventure, the Medieval theologian makes a case for this "analogy of being" when he says that, "All created things of the sensible world lead the mind of the contemplator and wise man to eternal God ... They are the shades, the resonances, the pictures of that efficient, exemplifying, and ordering art; they are the tracks, simulacra, and spectacles; they are divinely given signs set before us for the purpose of seeing God. They are exemplifications set before our still unrefined and sense-oriented minds, so that by the sensible things which they see they might be transferred to the intelligible which they cannot see, as if by signs to the signified" (*Itinerarium mentis ad Deum,* 2.11). Quoted in Matthew Milliner "Who's afraid of the Analogia Entis," http://www.millinerd. com/2006/12/whos-afraid-of-analogia-entis.html

6. The fact that God blesses all human beings and continues to work through what the Reformers called the "orders of creation" (Luther) or "common grace" (Calvin) means that we can acknowledge that all human beings have distinctive skills, gifts, and capacities. The

variety and combination of all these creaturely gifts are what partly distinguish one person from another. They make each of us unique and unrepeatable, so much so that no two people can ever share identical narratives, personalities, narratives, interests, skills, or abilities. To a large extent these differences are what determine our unique identity, what we do, and where we carry out our lives.

7. As part of the shared experience of a race or culture, many archetypes are ways we try to make sense of our world and include common themes like love, religion, death, birth, life, struggle, survival, etc. According to *Cummings Study Guides,* archetypes are "(1) Original model or models for persons appearing later in history or characters appearing later in literature; (2) the original model or models for places, things, or ideas appearing later in history or literature; (3) a primordial object, substance, or cycle of nature that always symbolizes or represents the same positive or negative qualities" http://bit.ly/1GHj38T

8. In psychology archetypes are often located below the conscious level (Freud and especially Jung) and in the collective unconscious (the collective memory of the race) and appear in dreams, art, symbol, story. Sociologists and philosophers that have developed the idea are Jürgen Habermas, Cornelius Castoriadis, Jacques Lacan, James K.A. Smith, Pierre Bourdieu (habitus), and Charles Taylor.

9. Clotaire Rapaille, *The Culture Code: An Ingenious Way to Understand Why People Around the World Live and Buy as They Do* (New York: Broadway, 2007).

10. For instance, considered archetypally, rivers represent the passage of time or life; sunlight represents happiness, a new beginning, glory, truth, or even God; the color red represents passion, anger, blood, or war; the color green represents new life, a new beginning, or hope; winter represents death, dormancy, or atrophy, etc. The mythical Hercules provided us with an original model of a strong man. Consequently, exceptionally strong men who appear later in history or literature are said to be archetypically Herculean. See ibid. Also, see "archetype" on http://bit.ly/1GHj38T

11. See for instance "5 Archetypes of Organizational Culture," Jeff McNeill, http://bit.ly/1J-5TkJ9, and "Which Persona Are You?", Good & Co, http:// bit.ly/1J5T9gP

12. *Arche means* beginning or root cause. Variants on the term include ideas as diverse as to begin, to rule; ruler, prince, ruler, leader, or being old, ancient. "In Greek philosophy it means (a) beginning, start, (b) starting point, original beginning, (c) the first cause, (d) power, authority, rule. The vb. archo commonly means (a) to be the first, to begin in the sense that one is the first, the one who does something before others, (b) to begin by doing something in contrast to what one does later, (c) as leader to be first, to rule."... "The NT use of the word-group, implies, as does secular Gk., a certain priority, both of time and of standing and prestige. In other words, the NT uses the concepts in much the same way as secular Gk. We find them used especially to denote a first point in time and to indicate an area of authority." H. Bietenhard, "Beginning, Origin, Rule, Ruler, Originator," in *The New International Dictionary of the New Testament*, Vol. 1, ed. Colin Brown (Grand Rapids, Zondervan, 1975), 164–68. Walter Wink, who has done the most extensive work on the powers, notes that "Archon (always, without exception in the LXX, Josephus, and the New Testament) refers to an incumbent-in-office. Arche can indicate the office itself, or an incumbent, or the structure of power (government, kingdom, realm, dominion). Exousia denotes the legitimations and sanctions by which power is maintained; it generally tends to be abstract. Dynamis overlaps with exousia in the area of sanctions; it refers to the power or force by which rule is maintained." Walter Wink, *Naming the Powers: The Language of Power in the New Testament* (Minneapolis: Fortress Press, 1984), Kindle Locations 171–175.

13. See also Rom 8:38-39; 1 Cor 2:8; 1 Cor 15:24–26; Eph 1:20; Eph 2:1–2; Eph 3:10; Eph 6:12; Col 2:15.

14. Hans Urs von *Balthasar The Glory of the Lord: A Theological Aesthetics Vol. 1* (San Francisco: Ignatius Press, Kindle Edition, 2009-06-01), Kindle Location 5965-5968.

15. Of course the same principle is at work in the anti-hero—the person who embodies the dark archetypes.

16. Quoted in Rollo May, *The Cry for Myth* (New York: W. W. Norton, 1991), Kindle locations 711–713. His section on heroes and their mythic role in society is excellent. He also highlights that the lack of real contemporary heroism is a huge problem in current Western culture, which has foolishly traded fake celebrity for real heroes.

Chapter 4

1. Chris Parish, *Being British: Our Once and Future Selves* (Arlesford: Chronos Books, 2016),

2. Ibid., 203.

3. Phenomenologically speaking, while the terms used to describe these various types of APEST aptitudes/intelligences might well differ from those used in the Bible and in the church, the phenomena themselves can be patently observed outside the church.

4. All the standard theological dictionaries (e.g., Kittel's TDNT, NIDNTT, Anchor Bible Dictionary, etc.) of the Bible track the origin and development of words. Look up the individual APEST terms if you are interested in the source of words.

5. Adapted from http://mozcom/blog/the-power-of-archetypes-in-marketing

6. The four Types in turn have 12 sub-types that form the matrix of the entire system. They are the categories of;

   • The *Artisans* comprising the subcategories of the Promoter (ESTP), the Crafter (ISTP), the Performer (ESFP) and the Composer (ISFP);

   • The *Guardians* in turn comprising the Supervisor (ESTJ), the Inspector (ISTJ), the Provider (ESFJ), the Protector (ISFJ);

   • The *Idealists* comprising the subcategories of the Teacher (ENFJ), Counselor (INFJ), Champion (ENFP), and Healer (INFP);

   • The *Rationals* comprising Field Marshal (ENTJ), Mastermind (INTJ), Inventor (ENTP), and Architect (INTP).

   See the foundational book on MBTI by David Keirsey, *Please Understand Me II: Temperament, Character, Intelligence* (Del Mar: Prometheus-Nemesis Books, 1998).

7. See http://www.5voices.com In a conversation with me, Steve said the following: "Five Voices wasn't an attempt to directly translate the Fivefold into secular language; it was more an attempt to drive the 16 MPTI types into 5 Descriptors that everyone could understand and use immediately without an expert. The Voice order being the most important, everyone speaks all 5 Voices but some are more natural and easier to access than others."

8. Erica Ariel Fox, *Winning from Within: A Breakthrough Method for Leading, Living, and Lasting Change* (New York: Harper Collins, 2013).

9. See http://www.tapestrymag.com/personas/

10. See chapter two of *The Permanent Revolution* for a detailed exploration of APEST intelligence.

11. Just to be sure of what we are referring to here, when I use the language of domains, I am simply using standard theological language to refer to those extra-ecclesial dimensions of life that form the various structures of society. In fact these too are part of the orders of creation that are disciplined, sanctified and redeemed by the kingdom work of Jesus.

12. I need to reiterate that while I believe that the kingdom of God does call us to relate to, and work redemptively, in and among all the various domains of society, I do not personally adhere to the theocratic domination theology of the so-called New Apostolic Reformation along with the associated Seven Mountains movement. They rightly use the language of APEST but in my opinion generally have a hierarchical notion of leadership that runs clean

contrary to the model that Jesus set for us to follow—that of the servant leader (Matthew 20:25–27; Philippians 2:1– 11). Don't let the similarities of the language—which ironically is also used in Reformed theology—obscure the importance of the topic for the broader missional conversation of which I am very much a part. See a review of this movement by my friend and researcher Brad Sargent "Examining 'The Seven Mountains' Movement" 2009, http://bit.ly/1HjQrTl

13. At the very least, while I believe Paul is talking about the ministry of all believers (Ephesians 4:7, "to each one of us") leadership is implied in Paul's articulation of ministry.

14. John David Lee, "An Interpretative Phenomenological Analysis of Five-fold Apostolic Leadership in Conjunction with Executive Leadership Theory and Practice," (PhD thesis, University of Charleston, November 2013), 63.

15. Alan Hirsch and Michael Frost, *The Shaping of Things to Come: Innovation and Mission for the 21st-Century Church,* 2nd ed. (Grand Rapids: Baker, 2013), 215. The first edition came out in 2003.

16. Lee, "Interpretative Phenomenological Analysis," 73.

17. Ibid., 73–74.

18. Walt Pilcher, *The Five-Fold Effect: Unlocking Power Leadership for Amazing Results in Your Organization* (Nashville: Westbow Press, 2013), 52–53.

19. The following information is presented, and elaborated on, in chapter seven of *The Five-Fold Effect.*

20. http://fivecapitals.net/

21. https://giantworldwide.com/

22. http://plf.org/

23. Momentum http://goo.gl/1D7W5b Anyi http://goo.gl/X6eN25 and The Center for the Working Poor http://goo.gl/MRdTQY Except for the Center for the Working Poor, these organizations are secular agencies.

24. Paul Engler and Mark Engler, *This Is an Uprising: How Nonviolent Revolt Is Shaping the Twenty-First Century* (New York: Nation Books, 2016).

25. Though marred through the Fall, the *imago Dei* still abides and has in fact been restored through the work of the Second Adam on our behalf.

26. e.g., Jn 10:30.

27. Chapters five and six will make the case that Jesus, far from being detached from 5Q, is in fact the perfect embodiment/recapitulation of the APEST archetypes/ identities/ purposes.

28. While the great Karl Barth, reacting to nineteenth-century theological liberalism and Immanentalism, taught a radical discontinuity between creation and the being of God—that God was wholly other than his creation and that creation gave us no analogy to the fully transcendent Other—the vast majority of theologians believe that creation does in some sense reflect God.

29. I agree with Wolfhart Pannenberg that creation is not just something God did a long time ago, but something God does all the time. In fact creation is not really just about origins. It is more about seeing the whole cosmos, throughout time, as dependent on God. Wolfhart Pannenberg, *An Introduction to Systematic Theology, Vol. 2* (Edinburgh: T & T Clark, 2004), chap. 7.

30. R.R. Reno, *Genesis: Brazos Theological Commentary on the Bible* (Grand Rapids, Brazos, 2010), comment on Gen.1:10 http://ref.ly/o/brazos01ge/136569?length=463 .

31. C. S. Lewis, *Miracles* (New York: HarperOne, 1996), 220f. Neither Lewis nor Pannenberg thinks that God is Mother Nature or Gaea. They don't identify God with natural processes. But God, who is above and beyond nature, is also behind nature.

Chapter 5

1. Incidentally storytelling itself as an expression of the evangelistic archetype, always highlights the narrative structure of the Jesus story of redemption. In fact Brueggemann's classic study on evangelism shows that the Gospel and its proclamation involves multilayered storytelling. W. Brueggemann *Biblical Perspectives on Evangelism: Living in a Three-Storied Universe* (Nashville: Abingdon, 1993).

2. See Michael Frost and Alan Hirsch, *The Faith of Leap: Embracing a Theology of Risk, Adventure, and Courage* (Grand Rapids: Baker, 2011), 104–112 for a detailed analysis of the relation of Jesus to the Hero's Journey. See especially the table on 109 where we track this through the Gospels.

3. Joseph Campbell. *The Hero with a Thousand Faces.* (Princeton: Princeton University Press, Novato, New World Library, 2008), 23.

4. The twelve stages of *the hero's journey* monomyth following the summary by Christopher Vogler (originally compiled in 1985 as a Disney studio memo): 1. The Ordinary World. 2. The Call to Adventure, 3. Refusal of the Call, 4. Meeting with the Mentor, 5. Crossing the Threshold to the "special world," 6. Tests, Allies and Enemies, 7. Approach to the Innermost Cave, 8. The Ordeal, 9. Reward, 10. The Road Back, 11. The Resurrection, 12. Return with the Elixir, "The Hero's Journey," https://en.wikipedia.org/wiki/Hero%27s_journey.

5. von Balthasar, *The Glory of the Lord,* Vol. 1, 21.

6. C.S. Lewis quoted in Peter Schakel, *Imagination and the Arts in C.S. Lewis* (Columbia: University of Missouri Press, 2002), 65

7. "Now as myth transcends thought, Incarnation transcends myth. The heart of Christianity is a myth which is also a fact. The old myth of the Dying God, without ceasing to be myth comes down from the heaven of legend and imagination to the earth of history. It happens— at a particular date, in a particular place followed by definable historical consequences. We pass from a Balder or an Osiris, dying nobody knows when or where, to a historical Person crucified (it is all in order) under Pontius Pilate. By becoming fact it does not cease to be myth: that is the miracle." C.S. Lewis, *God in the Dock,* "Myth Became Fact" (1944), para. 11, 66–67 in Wayne Martindale and Jerry Root, *The Quotable Lewis* (Tyndale House Publishers: Kindle Edition, 2012-03-08) Kindle Locations 8573-8574.

8. Louis A. Markos, *A To Z With C. S. Lewis* (Kindle Edition, 2012-10-01). Kindle Locations 522–530.

9. Indeed, if the life, death, and resurrection of Christ had been a wholly foreign thing, with no glimpses or foreshadowing in the myths and legends of the world's peoples, then it would seem that Christ was an alien god, one whose plan of salvation bore no resemblance to our most ancient and persistent longings ... But if Christ is truly the myth that became fact— then the God of the Bible is not just the God of the Jews but of all the nations. Christians believe that the events of Good Friday and Easter Sunday fulfilled the messianic prophecies recorded in the Old Testament. What Lewis learned from Tolkien is that Christ fulfilled as well all the deepest yearnings of the pagan peoples" Ibid., Kindle Locations 522–530.

10. These verses are somewhat enigmatic, and as a result are usually put in some form of parenthesis so as to maintain the causal link between verses 7 and 11. But we can't afford to ignore the power of metaphor in these verses—something important is being implied in the descent (incarnation) and subsequent ascension of the victorious Messiah.

11. As we have already noted, the word for "given" in vv. 7,11 is an aorist indicative: It is the most constitutional verb form something that is given once-for-all. This is because Jesus' ascension is a once for all event. The gifts are given along with his ascension.

12. von Balthasar, *Prayer,* 297.

13. "According to Iraneus' famous recapitulation theory, Jesus traversed the same ground as Adam but in reverse. Through his obedience he overcame the powers that hold humankind in

thrall—sin, death, and the devil. To establish his theory, Irenaeus contended that Jesus experienced every phase of human development—infancy, childhood, youth, mature adulthood—sanctifying each by obedience." Glenn E. Hinson, "Irenaeus," in *Encyclopedia of Religion,* ed. Lindsay Jones, 2nd ed. (Detroit: Macmillan Reference USA, 2005), 7:4538-41.

14. Quoting Irenaeus, Southern Baptist theologian Gregg Allison notes that "when the Son of God was incarnate and made man, he recapitulated—or summed up—in himself the long line of the human race. In so doing he obtained salvation for us in a brief and complete way, so that what we had lost in Adam—that is, to be according to the image and likeness of God—we could recover in Jesus Christ." He then goes on to note: "Irenaeus' model focused on the events in the life of Jesus Christ as the recapitulation, or summation, of all the life events of fallen humanity. However, instead of these being lived out in disobedience to God, Christ lived them obediently. Therefore, he reversed the sinful direction in which people were headed, saved them, and provided them with a new orientation ... Thus, Christ's life repeated the course of human existence, with this important difference: the sinful course was reversed, and Christ's obedient life was exchanged for it." G. Allison, "A History of the Doctrine of the Atonement," *Southern Baptist Journal of Theology,* 11, n. 2 (Summer 2007), 4–5.

15. Stanley Hauerwas, *Matthew,* Brazos Theological Commentary on the Bible (Grand Rapids: Brazos, 2006), 155.

16. "Since man could not come to God, God has come to man, identifying himself with man in the most direct way. The eternal Logos and Son of God, the second person of the Trinity, has become true man, one of us; he has healed and restored our manhood by taking the whole of it into himself." Kallistos Ware, *The Orthodox Way* (New York: St. Vladimir's Seminary Press, 1979), 89.

17. Peter J. Leithart, "Recapitulation", 2005, https://www.firstthings.com/blogs/leithart/2005/11/recapitulation.

18. Kevin Vanhoozer, N.T. Wright, Craig Bartholomew, et.al., *Dictionary for the Theological Interpretation of the Bible* (Grand Rapids: Baker, 2005), 837. Hans Boersma, "Redemptive hospitality in Irenaeus: a model for ecumenicity in a violent world." *Pro Ecclesia* 11, n. 2 (Spring 2002), 207–26.

19. Note that GK *kephale* and Latin *caput* both means "head." The word literally means "to restore in the new head." This use of the term kephale (head) in different settings in the same book is unlikely to be a coincidental.

20. Let me be clear, I do not believe that APEST is the only aspect of fallen creation that is recapitulated in Jesus, but one that specifically relates to the description of the ascension gifting in Ephesians 4:9–11.

21. It is not hard to discern this interweaving of monotheistic worship and the process of recapitulation when Paul talks about the logic of the Resurrection, for instance, in the following passage: "For since death came through a man, the resurrection of the dead comes also through a man. For as in Adam all die, so in Christ all will be made alive [i.e., recapitulation]. But each in turn: Christ, the firstfruits; then, when he comes, those who belong to him. Then the end will come, when he hands over the kingdom to God the Father after he has destroyed all dominion, authority and power. For he must reign until he has put all his enemies under his feet ... When he has done this, then the Son himself will be made subject to him who put everything under him, so that God may be all in all" (1 Corinthians 15:21–28).

Chapter 6

1. D. Bonhoeffer, Ethics (Minneapolis: Fortress Press, 2009), 23.

2. Aidan Nichols, *Divine Fruitfulness: A Guide to Balthasar's Theology beyond the Trilogy* (Washington DC: The Catholic University of America Press, 2007), 284.

3. Charles Van Engen notes that "the Church is there because Jesus Christ lives in the midst of

the members of the community." *God's Missionary People: Rethinking the Purpose of the Local Church* (Grand Rapids: Baker Academic, 1991), 149.

4. It is worth engaging this in the more colloquial form in Eugene H. Peterson's *The Message*, which reads as follows: "God rescued us from dead-end alleys and dark dungeons. He's set us up in the kingdom of the Son he loves so much, the Son who got us out of the pit we were in, got rid of the sins we were doomed to keep repeating. We look at this Son and see the God who cannot be seen. We look at this Son and see God's original purpose in everything created. For everything, absolutely everything, above and below, visible and invisible, rank after rank after rank of angels—*everything* got started in him and finds its purpose in him. He was there before any of it came into existence and holds it all together right up to this moment. And when it comes to the church, he organizes and holds it together, like a head does a body. He was supreme in the beginning and—leading the resurrection parade—he is supreme in the end. From beginning to end he's there, towering far above everything, everyone. So spacious is he, so roomy, that everything of God finds its proper place in him without crowding. Not only that, but all the broken and dislocated pieces of the universe—people and things, animals and atoms—get properly fixed and fit together in vibrant harmonies, all because of his death, his blood that poured down from the cross."

5. We should always expect a correspondence between the Founder and his followers ... individually and collectively. If the movement fails to resemble, act, and sound like the Founder, then something must be deeply wrong. See *The Forgotten Ways* (2nd Ed.), ch.4 for an extended rationale about the absolute centrality of Jesus in the life of his people.

6. Hauerwas, *Matthew*, 231

7. George R. Beasley-Murray, *John: Word Biblical Commentary* Vol. 36 (New York: Thomas Nelson, 1999), 380.

8. These identities, or aspects of his person, are derived not just from their source in God (and as Son he mirrors the Father), or just in the recapitulation of creational archetypes, but are also prefiguratively expressed in various biblical archetypes throughout the Old Testament. Abraham, Moses, David, Elijah, Ruth, etc. are shadow types of APEST in the Old Testament. All these find their perfection in Jesus.

9. Hans Urs von Balthasar, "Theology and Aesthetic" trans. Andrée Emery, *Communio*, Vol. 08–01, 1981, 62–71; here, 65.

10. We have huge blind spots when it comes to thinking through the lens of the apostolic metaphor and as a primary ministry archetype. And as a result we fail to fully appreciate all the distinctive theology, along with the implied methodology, that is directly associated with the term. We have somehow managed to keep the Latin and drop the Greek! I continue to encounter devout Christians who are actually surprised to find out that the Latin term *"missio,"* from which we derive the English word "mission" and its derivatives, is actually a translation of the Greek word *"apostello"!* Why would we not be willing to use biblical words to accurately describe biblical phenomena associated with them? Imagine if we applied the same suppressive logic to other key words in Scripture? For instance; what if we censured the word-group related to the concept "righteousness"? We would as a result never be able to fully understand what is being referred to in the language if we cannot use the term in the way the Bible itself uses it. It would end up in a rather heretical bus crash. And yet this is precisely what we have done to the widely used, very biblical, word-metaphor "apostle."

11. See Lk 4:18–19, 4:43; Mk 9:37; Jn 3:34, 4:34, 5:23–24, 5:36–38, 6:29, 6:57, 7:29, 11:42, 12:45, 17:3, 20:21, 21—these are just a few! In fact, in the Old Testament there are over 200 references to sentness where God is the subject of the verb. In other words, it is God who commissions and it is God who sends in the Old Testament. In John, the Gospel that centers on the mission of Jesus, the language of sentness (*apostello* and *pempo*) is used in association with Jesus over 60 times! See the excellent article by my colleague Brad Brisco titled "Sending Language" on his website http://missionalchurchnetwork.com/missional-sending-language/.

12. A man's agent is like the man himself, not physically, but legally. As apostle or agent Jesus was sent with the full authority of the One who sent him. Jesus said that the one who received his own apostles whom he had sent received Jesus himself, and not only Jesus, the One who had sent him (Mt 10:40–42; Jn 13:20). An apostle must be sent by someone else, is sent on a particular mission with sufficient power to accomplish the mission. So while the NT apostles (and by implication the church) were apostled by Jesus, Jesus was *apostled* by God. It is in this context that Jesus could say both, "He who has seen me has seen the Father" (Jn 14:9), and without contradiction, "The Father is greater than I" (Jn 14:28). In character and authority, he could be seen as identical with the Father, but in all other ways the Father was greater.

13. The meaning of the term "apostle" comes from its root verb "send" (*apostello*). Its basic meaning is an agent or an ambassador, who, within the limits of his assignment, had the same authority as the One who sent him. The apostle was legally identical to his master. He had the power of attorney and "apostle" accurately describes the office Jesus held and his relationship to God.

14. But he said to them, "I must preach the good news of the kingdom of God to the other towns as well; for I was *sent* [apostello] for this purpose" (Lk 4:43 ESV).

15. For he whom God has *sent* [apostello] utters the words of God, for he gives the Spirit without measure" (Jn 3:34 ESV).

16. Whoever receives one such child in my name receives me, and whoever receives me, receives not me but him who sent [apostello] me (Mk 9:37 ESV).

17. Much of the theme of Messiah is contained in this aspect of Jesus' ministry. The Messiah is God's anointed King, prophesied in and through the Israel story, the One who ushers in the full reign of God, who brings salvation to the nations.

18. Walter Brueggemann, *Prophetic Imagination: Revised Edition* (Minneapolis: Fortress Press, 2001-06-26), 102. But he goes on to note that while clearly "Jesus cannot be understood simply as prophet, for that designation, like every other, is inadequate for the historical reality of Jesus. Nonetheless, among his other functions it is clear that Jesus functioned as a prophet.", 81). Note the recognition that there is more than one function in the ministry of Jesus. This at least opens us up to recognition that his ministry is multidimensional. And certainly there is more than a teacher in him as well. The fivefold makes a lot of sense.

19. H. Klassen, "Jesus the Evangelist" http://goo.gl/qwndwb

20. Jesus is not only the great Evangelist; he also sets the primary pattern for our evangelism. I suggest that the church cannot do any better than in approaching evangelism the way Jesus did. He had a brilliant way of opening the heart to respond to God's grace. He dealt very graciously with so-called sinners and opened salvation to all those who had been previously excluded. A few good books have tried to reset our understanding of evangelism in the way of Jesus, e.g., Jerram Bars, *Learning Evangelism from Jesus* (Wheaton: Crossway, 2009); Richard Phillips, *Jesus the Evangelist: Learning to Share the Gospel from the Book of John* (Lake Mary: Reformation Trust, 2007).

21. For instance, see Kenneth E. Bailey, *The Good Shepherd: The Thousand-Year Journey from Psalm 23 to the New Testament* (Downers Grove: IVP, 2014).

22. And while I absolutely believe that the pastoral ministry is one of Jesus' five archetypal ministries, it has tended to so dominate and organize our imagination in ways that have effectively obscured the reality of the other four APEST archetypes. In other words, it has tended to be a "controlling metaphor" and has crowded out the other, equally legitimate, ways of viewing ministry—Jesus' and ours. I believe therefore that in order to truly understand the ministry of shepherd in the church, we need to narrow it down to biblical proportion.

23. If it does seem novel to us, I believe this is largely because the language around some of these fivefold giftings (especially that around the apostolic) has become censured and politicized. I would argue that the fivefold patterning exemplified by Jesus actually expands our under-

standing of Christology in ways that get us beyond the somewhat reductionist traditional tri-perspectival approach (Prophet, Priest, King).

24. Take for instance one example of Paul's kerygma/gospel in Colossians 1:25–29: "By the commission God gave me to present to you the word of God in its fullness— the mystery that has been kept hidden for ages and generations, but is now disclosed to the Lord's people. To them God has chosen to make known among the Gentiles the glorious riches of this mystery, which is Christ in you, the hope of glory. He is the one we proclaim, admonishing and teaching everyone with all wisdom, so that we may present everyone fully mature in Christ. To this end I strenuously contend with all the energy Christ so powerfully works in me." These verses contain decidedly *apostolic* (commission, to make known among the Gentiles), *evangelistic* (him we proclaim), *prophetic* (disclosure of God's mystery, warning/admonishing), *didactic* (teaching with all wisdom), as well as *pastoral* (to present everyone mature in Christ) concerns in Paul, and by extension in Paul's gospel.

25. Eugene Peterson, himself a lover of the church, says, "Paul's metaphor of the church as members of Christ's body is not a mere metaphor. [Biblical] metaphors have teeth. They keep us grounded to what we see right before us. At the same time, they keep us connected to all the operations of the Trinity that we can't see." Eugene Peterson, *Practice Resurrection*, 28.

26. "But if the Church is the body and the bride of Christ, then her own disposition can be only an outflow and a reflection of Christ's and, in so far as she is Christ's continuance into the world and the means by which he unites and incorporates the world to himself." von Balthsar, *The Glory of the Lord: a Theological Aesthetics*, Vol. 1, Kindle Location 4152.

27. See J. A. Phillips, *The Form of Christ in the World: A Study of Bonhoeffer's Theology* (New York: Collins, 1967).

28. Theologians have long debated whether there is a real presence of Christ in the sacraments. I believe that the focus of these theologians in history is misguided insofar that attention is misdirected away from the presence of Jesus himself to his apparent presence within the sacraments. I would argue the church itself—as the Embodiment of Christ—is the true locus of the real presence of Christ, not its rituals and sacraments.

29. George Hunsinger, *Disruptive Grace: Studies in the Theology of Karl Barth* (Grand Rapids: Eerdmans, 2001), 264-5.

30. This reflects upon Augustine's doctrine of *totus Christus* where the whole Christ is understood to comprise of head and body.

31. W. Lock, *"Pleroma"* in *Dictionary of the Bible*, Vol. 5, ed. James Hastings et al. (New York: Scribner and Sons, 1911), 1–2. In the same article, Lock notes in Ephesians 1:23 that the fullness of Christ is related to "His full embodiment, that fullness which He supplies to the Church—emphasizing the thoroughness with which the *Church is the receptacle of His powers and represents Him on earth.*"

32. Frank Viola, *Jesus Now: Unveiling the Present-Day Ministry of Christ* (David C. Cook Kindle Edition), 164.

33. Michael Harper, *Let My People Grow: Ministry and Leadership in the Church* (Plainfield: Logos, 1977.) Himself an Anglican, Harper is here quoting from the Anglican-Roman Catholic Statement on Ministry and Ordination, 45-46.

34. Karl Barth, *Church Dogmatics The Doctrine of Reconciliation*, Vol. 4, Part 2: (Edinburgh: T&T Clark, 1958), 59-60.

35. Movement leaders Neil Cole and Mike Breen also base their understandings of APEST on the person and work of Christ and call us to follow in his way. See Neil Cole, *Primal Fire: Reigniting the Church with the Five Gifts of Jesus* (Carol Stream, IL: Tyndale Momentum: 2014) esp. chap. 2; and Mike Breen, *The Apostle's Notebook* (London: Kingsway, 2002).

36. W. Lock, *"Pleroma,"* 1–2.

37. Timothy Keller, *Center Church: Doing Balanced, Gospel-Centered Ministry in Your City* (Grand Rapids: Zondervan, 2013), 344ff.

38. Paul's teachings on the Body of Christ are entirely consistent with this well-studied phenomenon in organizational theory. See Hirsch and Catchim, *The Permanent Revolution*, 22–24.

39. The sociologist Max Weber famously taught that any organization renews and re legitimizes itself by regularly returning to its "founding charism" embodied in its originator.

40. And before some Calvinist or High-Church reader feels particularly self-righteous about the self-destructive decline of Methodism; subject your own system to a similar analysis. What did your church/denomination do to the 5Q latent in Christ's Body? Most of the other historic churches never even had much of a movement to begin with so there are no grounds for boasting.

41. One need only to peruse his *Evangelii Guadium* to sense the sheer missional brilliance of the man. I would put him as a very well rounded EPATS in terms of vocational profile. And I am not alone in this assessment. For what it is worth, my many colleagues in the Diocese of Pittsburgh agree with me. One such leader uses a military metaphor to describe the role of Francis in the contemporary church. He says that, "Francis is giving Catholic APEs air cover like they've never had before. The openness to APE functionality within Catholic structures has dramatically increased under Francis." See William Simon's article on "the Francis Effect," *The Francis Effect: The Lessons of Collaborative Leadership in the Catholic Church,* September 25, 2016 https://goo.gl/K4T5Ei

Chapter 7

1. See appendix three, "The Exiling of the APEs" at the end of this book.

2. This exiling of the APEs is disastrous because along with a person's sense of calling comes a corresponding understanding of our own particular, unrepeatable, role in God's purposes. Those who are called to be As, Ps, or Es have no validation of who they feel God has made them to be. When we get our sense of vocation out of sync with our actual roles in any organization, it becomes a mere job that is experienced as something of a burden. I can't tell you how many people I meet who feel misaligned with their actual roles in the church. For one, not all who go by the title pastor are gifted as pastor-shepherds. This confuses both the minister as well as the people around them, as well as being a cause of great frustration and disappointment, because the misaligned person is unlikely to rightly exemplify or embody the function in a way that has spiritual ambiance and impact.

3. I think knowing the shape and contours of one's calling is vitally important. I believe that our unique destinies are somehow bound up with us finding our vocational sweet spot. So much so that I have written extensively on this topic, and have developed a verified APEST test that helps believers get a vocational signature of their callings (www.apest.org.) We are told in Ephesians 4:1 that we are to "live a life worthy of the callings we have received." It's our life's purpose to integrate the calling of God into our individual lives—to live worthily. The idea of calling and commissioning always reminds me of the last scene in the movie *Saving Private Ryan,* where Captain John Miller, upon sacrificing his life to save Private Ryan, utters these dying words to him: "Earn this!" It is this challenge to live up to his calling that shapes the rest of James Ryan's life. Visit www.apest.org to complete your own personal profile.

4. When we fail to address the functional dimension of APEST we weaken the basis and context for the various callings. When we focus solely on function, we depersonalize ministry and make it a dry, somewhat organizational, affair. So that while the practices and the practitioner are inextricably bound together, they remain two aspects of the same phenomenon.

5. When it comes to issues of leadership and organization, when we use the fivefold typology rather than using generic leadership-portfolio language derived from management and social

studies, not only are we using the Bible's own primary terms and definitions to describe biblical ministry itself, we are structuring our understanding of leadership on the prototypical Christian leader—Jesus himself. And so church leaders are called, in all times and places, in formal ministry or not, to a way of leadership that reflects the character and manner of the ministry of Jesus Christ. It is because of this direct association of church ministry with Jesus that the five functions set the comprehensive agenda for all Jesus-shaped leadership.

6. And so this book will not primarily explore the nature of the callings of particular believers (as essential as these are) but rather the ministry of the church as a whole. I have come to see more clearly that all ministry is, in a real sense, our participation in Christ's ministry through his *ecclesia*. We need to understand what the church's ministry was intended to look like. And importantly, I am convinced that whatever the sense of personal calling we have, they originate in Jesus and come to us via the functions constitutionally given to the universal Body of Christ itself. I want to therefore emphasize the functions, but I want you to see the ways in which people in the community might embody the functions in their relative callings.

7. Darrell Guder, foreword to *The Permanent Revolution*, xv1. On topic, see the work by Dr. Guder's disciple, John G. Flett for a thorough exploration of the meaning of apostolicity in the church. *Apostolicity: The Ecumenical Question in World Christian Perspective* (Downers Grove: IVP, 2016).

8. It is worth quoting him in full here: "The Church is, by its nature and calling, in the first and last instance an apostolic body ... By 'apostolic body' we mean the Church is 'sent' into the world, has a specific 'mission': it has a message for the whole world that must be heralded. Although it may be considered as an unfounded pretension or felt as an unbearable arrogance, the fact is there. And without genuine understanding of this fact there can be no real understanding of the Christian Church. As an apostolic body the Church is commissioned to proclaim—by its *kerygma* of God's acts of salvation in Christ, by its *koinonia* as a new community, living by the bonds of peace and charity—the message of God's dealings with, and purpose for, the world and mankind. This message has to go out to all men, in all lands, in all situations and civilizations, in all conditions and spheres and circumstances of life, so witnessing to God's redemptive order in Jesus, by word and deed." H. Kraemer, *Religion and the Christian Faith* (Cambridge: James Clarke, 1956), 17–18.

9. Quoted in Charles E. Van Engen, *God's Missionary People: Rethinking the Purpose of the Local Church* (Grand Rapids: Baker Academic, 1991), 27.

10. See Hirsch and Catchim, *The Permanent Revolution*, 242–47, and Metcalf, *Beyond the Local Church*.

11. Charles E. Van Engen confirms apostolicity as a mark. "The gift that the Church is apostolic would itself be a task for applying the apostolic gospel, living in the apostolic way, and being sent as apostles to the world." From Van Engen, *God's Missionary People*, 109.

12. See Neil Cole, *Church 3.0*, (San Fancisco: Jossey Bass, 2010) 58–60, 85 for exploration of what it means to plant the Gospel.

13. Although not exclusively so; I believe that entrepreneurialism is a skill, a talent for initiative, that can inform all of the APEST types but is likely to be expressed mainly by evangelists and apostles.

14. Hirsch and Catchim, *The Permanent Revolution.*, p. xxxviii.

15. The prophets really are the keepers of the religion we know as ethical monotheism—an encounter with the One God was experienced as both radical embrace and a challenge to holiness. Every summons is a sending.

16. Woodward, *Creating a Missional Culture.*

17. D.A. Bosch, *Transforming Mission* (Maryknoll: Orbis Books, 2011), 420.

18. These descriptions of the evangelist are drawn largely from Hirsch and Catchim, *The Permanent Revolution*, 35-36.

19. M. Gladwell, *Tipping Point: How Little Things Can Make a Big Difference* (New York: Little, Brown, 2002), 38

20. Ibid.

21. The full quote is worth reading. "I am suggesting that the only answer, the only hermeneutic of the gospel, is a congregation of men and women who believe it and live by it. I am, of course, not denying the importance of the many activities by which we seek to challenge public life with the gospel– evangelistic campaigns, distribution of Bibles and Christian literature, conferences, and even books such as this one. But I am saying that these are all secondary, and that they have power to accomplish their purpose only as they are rooted in and lead back to a believing community." Lesslie Newbigin, *The Gospel in a Pluralist Society* (Grand Rapids, MI: Eerdmans, 1989), 227; cf. Darren Cronshaw and Steve Taylor, "The Pluralist Society: Rereading Newbigin for Missional Churches Today," *Pacifica* 27:2 (June 2014), 206–228.

22. This description is drawn largely from Hirsch and Catchim, *The Permanent Revolution,* 43–44.

23. This description is drawn largely from Hirsch and Catchim, *The Permanent Revolution,* 45–46.

24. Bob Hyatt and J. R. Briggs, *Eldership and the Mission of God: Equipping Teams for Faithful Church Leadership* (Downers Grove: IVP, 2014), 116-17.

25. I am deeply grateful for my colleague Jessie Cruickshank for helping me to see the problems of the church in terms of the metaphor of arrested development and precocious learning. See for instance the article "The Child with Poor Social Relations – The Precocious or Immature Child" on https://goo.gl/sg9S2b or the more complex theoretical work of Catherine Ayoub, et.al., called "Cognitive and emotional differences in young maltreated children: A translational application of dynamic skill theory" in *Development and Psychopathology* 18 ~2006, 679–706.

26. A comment by Jessie Cruickshank in a conversation. Used with permission.

Chapter 8

1. David Foster Wallace's 2005 commencement address at Kenyon College, *The Economist* Sept. 19, 2008, https://www.1843magazine.com/story/david-foster-wallace-in-his-own-words

2. This will also serve as a rationale for the 5Q Systems Test described toward the end of this chapter. This multidimensional test can be accessed at www.5Qcentral.com

3. Seth Godin, "Measuring without measuring," June 1, 2013, https://goo.gl/Xasd6

4. A phrase used by my colleague and friend Bill Couchenour. But the idea of a metric is well established as a principle of leadership. For instance, organizational consultants Kouzes and Posner suggest that in order to create a culture that embodies core values then "you need to constantly reinforce the behavior you want repeated. Keep score and measure performance to determine consistency with values. Tangibly and intangibly recognize performance that's consistent with espoused values. Simply measuring performance often improves it. But rewards and recognition will reinforce values as well. The important message to keep in mind is that what you choose to reinforce is what people will choose to value." J.M. Kouzes and B.P. Posner, *The Leadership Challenge: The Fourth Edition* (San Francisco: Wiley, 2007), 331.

5. The marks are "the signs of the presence of Christ in the Church." Robert Slesinski, "On the Catholicity of the Church," *Faith and Reason,* Winter 1984, 314. One Reformed commentator says that "the marks of the church are used to answer a question about the legitimacy of religious assemblies in their *collective* capacity." http://www.swrb.com/newslett/ actualNLs/4_shipwr.htm

6. So why bother defining stuff at all? Good definitions are really valuable assets. They allow us

to assess situations better, have more meaningful conversations and make better decisions. In contrast, imprecise definitions make it really difficult to even agree on what is being spoken about. The conversations end up circling around, going nowhere. Using the wrong word can cause needless arguments; using a less specific word can cause confusion, and many other effects.

7. And yet I agree with seminal missional theologian Darrell Guder when he says that "the Nicene marks of the church need to be interpreted in the reverse order—apostolic, catholic, holy, and one—so that apostolicity defines every aspect of the life and action of the church. Only when apostolicity functions in that way can God's mission be served obediently." Darrell Guder, foreword to Hirsch and Catchim, *The Permanent Revolution*, xvi. See also the new book on the apostolic mark of the church by John Flett, *Apostolicity: The Ecumenical Question in World Christian Perspective* (Downers Grove: IVP, 2016).

8. The irony is that the mark of church discipline actually gets us closest to an observable mark in that it is meant to be the indicator of community. But in the traditional formulation it is actually a community defined by exclusion from community (e.g., when the church disciplines people by excommunicating them)! In chapter six of *The Faith of Leap,* Michael Frost and I lay out what we see as four marks of the church there ... namely worship, mission, community, discipleship. In suggesting now that APEST more adequately identifies the church, I am not annulling the significance of these at all. In fact, I believe they are more adequately covered in the APEST marks.

9. Look at. Jn 13:1–17, 34, 8:31; Mk 12:28–31; Mt 28:16–20, etc. These are expected to be visible signs of Jesus' presence. And given the reduction of Jesus' church to the receiving of sacraments and the hearing of preaching, the marks are not only uninspiring, they bolster the authority of the religion institution. There is no explicit mention of God, nor even an implied recognition of the preeminence of Jesus in his church! But, how can we possibly define the church without any reference to the primacy of Jesus Christ? As my friend Neil Cole says, "If you can define church without Jesus then you can do church without Jesus." It is a point well worth pondering.

10. George R. Hunsberger, *The Church Between Gospel & Culture* (Grand Rapids, MI., Eerdmans, 1996), 337.

11. Tom Northup says, "All organizations are perfectly designed to get the results they are now getting. If we want different results, we must change the way we do things." *Five Hidden Mistakes that CEOs Make* (New York; Solutions Press, 2008). This is in turn a reflection on an axiom known as Conway's Law; that the organizational bias of any organization is in a real sense a reflection of the consciousness of the people who designed it in the first place.

12. More recently, reformed Baptist pastor Mark Dever proposed nine marks of a church. These do reintroduce the gospel and the vital functions of evangelism and discipleship. But they lack anything close to apostolic and prophetic functions. His list is as follows: expositional preaching, biblical theology, biblical understanding of the gospel, biblical understanding of conversion, biblical understanding of evangelism, biblical understanding of member-ship, biblical church discipline, promotion of Christian discipleship and growth, biblical understanding of church leadership. Mark Dever, *Nine Marks of a Healthy Church,* 3rd ed. (Wheaton: Crossway, 2013

13. The full quote is worth reading for its emphasis on the utter centrality of Jesus: Balthasar writes: "The fact that Christ is this center—and not, for instance, merely the beginning, the initiator of an historical form which then develops autonomously—is rooted in the particular character of the Christian religion and in its difference from all other religions. Judaism has no such center: neither Abraham, nor Moses, nor one of the Prophets, is the figure around which everything else is ordered. Christ, by contrast, is the form because he is the content. This holds absolutely, for he is the only Son of the Father, and whatever he establishes and institutes has its meaning only through him, is dependent only on him and is kept vital only by him. If for a single moment we were to look away from him and attempt to consider and

understand the Church as an autonomous form, the Church would not have the slightest plausibility. It would be plausible neither as a religious institution (for its sacraments and the service belonging to them are 'bearable' only as modes by which the living Lord is present) not as an historical power for order and culture ... The plausibility of Christianity stands and falls with Christ's, something which has in essence always been acknowledged. For even the doctrine of the *notae Ecclesiae* [marks of the church] has never seriously been intended to be taken in isolation from Christology: *the notae are the properties which are exacted by Christ's promises and which can be discovered in history as the fulfilment of Christ and as proofs of his living power* [italics mine]." von Balthasar *The Glory of the Lord*, Vol. 1, Kindle Location 7537. Remarkably, von Balthasar here is actually denying that the sacraments and worship are viable marks in that they themselves are actually founded on the active presence of Jesus! In other words, they are derivative and that all too often worship and sacraments actually serve to obscure that to which they are dependent. Protestants take note!

14. Markus Barth, *Ephesians 4–6*, 434.

15. Interestingly, the Dutch Reformed Church eventually renounced this as heresy and repented publically for its racist sins. See the Belhar Confession (http://bit.ly/1A0ixkH), which profoundly corrected the prophetic imbalance. Listen to just a few of the lines in the confession.

"We believe ...

• that God has revealed himself as the One who wishes to bring about justice and true peace among people;

• that God, in a world full of injustice and enmity, is in a special way the God of the destitute, the poor and the wronged;

• that God calls the church to follow him in this, for God brings justice to the oppressed and gives bread to the hungry;

• that God frees the prisoner and restores sight to the blind;

• that God supports the downtrodden, protects the stranger, helps orphans and widows and blocks the path of the ungodly;

• that for God pure and undefiled religion is to visit the orphans and the widows in their suffering;

• that God wishes to teach the church to do what is good and to seek the right (Deut 32:4; Lk 2:14; Jh 14:27; Eph 2:14; Isa 1:16–17; Js 1:27; Js 5:1-6; Lk 1:46–55; Lk 6:20–26; Lk 7:22; Lk16:19–31; Ps 146; Lk 4:16–19; Rom 6:13–18; Amos 5);

• that the church must therefore stand by people in any form of suffering and need, which implies, among other things, that the church must witness against and strive against any form of injustice, so that justice may roll down like waters, and righteousness like an ever- flowing stream;

• that the church as the possession of God must stand where the Lord stands, namely against injustice and with the wronged; that in following Christ the church must witness against all the powerful and privileged who selfishly seek their own interests and thus control and harm others."

16. David K. Hurst does a thorough study of the shifts in purposes and leadership as movements move to stability and then to institutionalism. He uses the overriding metaphor of shifting from *hunters* to *herders*.

• Mission becomes Strategy
• Roles become Tasks
• Teams become Structure
• Networks become Organization
• Recognition becomes Compensation

It's as if he lists the from the generative APE functions to that of the more operational ST functions. It's the loss of the whole that shifts the functions. See his *Crisis & Renewal: Meeting the Challenge of Organizational Change* (Boston: Harvard Business Review, 2002) 41–46

Chapter 9

1. Henry Beston *The Outermost House* (New York: Holt, 2003), 23–25.

2. This metaphor is adapted from Frank Viola, "Rethinking the Fivefold Ministry" http://frankviola.org/2010/10/27/rethinking-the-five-fold-ministry/

3. See Ettiene Wenger, "Introduction to communities of practice: A brief overview of the concept and its uses," http://goo.gl/JAPdHA; or explore more deeply in E. Wenger, *Communities of Practice: Learning, Meaning, and Identity* (Cambridge: Cambridge University Press, 1998).

4. Alan Hirsch, *The Forgotten Ways,* 120–125.

5. Michael Polanyi is the philosopher par excellence who has helped us see the educative aspects of our actions. See also James K. A. Smith, *Desiring the Kingdom: Worship, Worldview, and Cultural Formation* (Grand Rapids, Baker Academic, 2009).

6. In the West, the classroom dominates and we have lost the art of apprenticeship done in an appropriate context. The word "learner" is usually associated with a classroom and "apprentice" with a job.

7. Alan Hirsch & Tim Catchim, *The Permanent Revolution Playbook: APEST for the People of God* (Denver: Mission Publishing, 2015).

8. As noted in the introduction, many denominations, including The Evangelical Covenant Order of Presbyterians (ECO), Four Square Church USA, the Churches of Christ in Australia, and The Mennonite Church USA, have embraced the fivefold typology and are applying it across the system.

9. Charles Duhigg, *The Power of Habit: Why We Do What We Do in Life and Business* (New York: Random House, 2012). My colleague Rich Robinson says that for a practice to become embedded into the fabric of life we need to be intentional by choosing to be disciplined. The regular application of discipline in turn becomes a habit and begins to feel like normal practice. Normality eventually becomes natural behavior that in turn is experienced as lifestyle.

10. For a good example of how APEST is being embedded into local church networks see Ben Kat's podcast series on becoming a better pastor in your neighborhood available here https://goo.gl/7G1WWe

11. E.g., James Davidson Hunter, *To Change the World: The Irony, Tragedy, and Possibility of Christianity in the Late Modern World* (Oxford: Oxford University Press, 2010) and Andy Crouch, *Culture Making* (Downers Grove, IL: IVP Books).

12. The only tool that is not original with us is the "Base and Phase" tool made popular by the good folks of 3DM. See below. For deeper training in the use of these tools, go to www.5Qcentral.com

13. Alan Hirsch and Jessica Cruickshank, *Activating 5Q: A User's Guide to Understanding and Applying 5Q in Your Church or Organization* (Atlanta: 100M Publications, 2017). Get this direct from www.5Qcentral.com or from other online retail outlets.

14. e.g., *White hat.* Think of white paper. It is neutral and carries information. White hat thinking asks what information we have, what information is missing, what information we would like to have, and how we can get that information. E. de Bono, *Serious Creativity: Using the Power of Lateral Thinking to Create New Ideas* (New York: HarperBusiness, 1993). This tool was originally used in *The Shaping of Things to Come,* 244–5.

15. See Mike Breen with Paddy Mallon, *Knowing Your Role in Life* (3DM Publishing, 2006) and Mike Breen and Steve Cockram, *Building a Discipling Culture,* 2nd ed. (3DM

Publishing, 2014), chap. 10. This description is taken largely from Alan Hirsch and Tim Catchim, *The Permanent Revolution Playbook*, which itself is a fantastic group learning tool.

16. While the functions test does this, it does a whole lot more by seeking to get a perspective regarding levels of awareness of the function (what are the blind spots) and the competency of the organization in each of the functions (levels one to five).

17. Learners ought to *demonstrate* mastery or competency before they move to the next level of competency. For example, people learning to drive manual transmission might first have to demonstrate their mastery of "the rules of the road"—safety, defensive driving, parallel parking, etc. Then, they may focus on two independent competencies: using the clutch, braking with the right foot, and shifting up and down through the gears. Once the learners have demonstrated they are comfortable with those skills, the next required skills might be finding first gear, from full stop to a slow roll, followed by sudden stops, shifting up, and downshifting.

18. Dallas Willard, "How Does a Disciple Live?" http://www.dwillard.org/articles/artview.asp?artID=103

Chapter 10

1. Rich Robinson will be working alongside me leading 5Qcollective and also leads Catalyse Change (www.catalysechange.org) which coaches and trains leaders.

2. http://www.teachthought.com/critical-thinking/blooms-taxonomy/249-blooms-taxonomy-verbs-for-critical-thinking/

3. Dr Dave Alred MBE, *The Pressure Principle* (Penguin Life, 2016), 7.

4. In the Jewish context "rabbi-disciple" made sense because there were cultural landmarks and norms that meant they understood what a rabbi was. If you know what a rabbi is then you can understand what a disciple is. There is a context to the relationship and the learning process.

    As the gospel spread to a Greco-Roman context Paul took the principle, or skeleton, of rabbi- disciple and reskinned it, putting flesh on it as parent-child. This was a model Paul's audience understood as many had lived through teaching from the guardian (from a pedagogue), then training and apprenticeship (from a parent) and then, finally, the responsibility to live as an adult as part of an extended family. The word "disciple" disappears from the text mid-way through Acts and isn't seen past this point. The cultural context changed and so the language did too.

Conclusion

1. John Keats, "On First Looking into Chapman's Homer," http://goo.gl/1ZAFgG

2. David Bentley Hart, *The Experience of God* (Boston: Yale University Press, 2013), 314.

3. Martin Buber, *Israel and the World: Essays in a Time of Crisis* (New York: Shocken, 1976), 163.

Appendix 1

1. This alone exposes the violence they do to the grammar of Ephesians as described in chapter one. Also see appendix three, "The Exiling of the APEs."

2. I have adapted this section from mine and Tim's book, *The Permanent Revolution*, 98–99.

3. As for the displacing of function by form, this is an example of that old "gnostic trap" that has haunted Western theology all along. The assumption of religious gnosticism is that logical truths could simply be abstracted from personal truthfulness and the personal could be disposed of. The personal and functional is a mere husk of the essential. It was in

these conditions that apostolic doctrine was used to displace apostolic function. It was also this kind of thinking that resulted in the disastrous substitution of active discipleship and obedience with mere intellectual confession of creedal belief. In my opinion, we have seldom recovered from this dangerous subversion of discipleship.

4. And so following its own intrinsic logic of extraction, why does cessationism not apply the same extraction technique to the pastoral and teaching function? Why stop in abstracting apostolic doctrine? Why not do the same with the pastoral and teaching functions for instance—why not also replace these functions with doctrine?

5. Hirsch and Catchim, *The Permanent Revolution,* 98–100. For far too long we have managed to submit the apostolic and prophetic functions to a different set of criteria than the other functions. However, it is increasingly clear that the criteria applied are purely arbitrary, are likely sociopolitical in motivation, and cannot be derived from Scripture itself.

6. See the appendix in *The Permanent Revolution* for a more substantial exploration of the sociopolitical process by which the apostolic was coded out of the ministry of the church. Also see the appendix in this book titled, "The Exiling of the APEs".

7. I believe that an inductive, unforced, non-tendentious reading of the New Testament cannot come to any conclusion other than that Paul explicitly teaches on the validity of APEST in the New Testament church. In fact such a radical exclusion of APE especially could not have ever been conceived by any of the New Testament writers themselves.

    Interestingly, most cessationists quote Ephesians 2:20 saying that the apostles and prophets mentioned there are now the Bible. This is their interpretation of the text but it is by no means a settled one. Not only is this clearly anachronistic—Paul didn't have what we later called the canonical New Testament when he wrote Ephesians—but it puts Paul at odds with what he very clearly states in 4:1–16! How can he mean one thing in the one text and something completely different in the other? In the same book!

8. This argument in fact formed the basis of Gregory Metzger's critique of *The Permanent Revolution,* http://www.booksandculture.com/articles/2012/julaug/apostolic-movement.html. The problem is that Metzger does not (cannot?) argue against our position from Scripture; the basis of his rejection remains the "post-apostolic" Fathers, Luther, Calvin, and tradition. See our reply to Metzger here, http://www.booksandculture.com/articles/2012/sepoct/letters-so12.html?paging=off

Appendix 2

1. See the book by non-cessationist Pentecostal scholars R. Douglas Gievett and Holly Pivec, A New *Apostolic Reformation?: A Biblical Response to a Worldwide Movement.* (Wooster; Weaver Book Company: 2014) for a critical appraisal of the NAR.

2. In Ephesians 4 it is Jesus who is portrayed as the Giver of APEST. This really is a game changer. Secondly, APEST is framed in terms of the essential functions and purposes of the Body as well as the identity-calling-vocation of believers. APEST therefore defines our callings in the church and to the world. The charismatic gifts never do; rather they are given to perform certain functions. They always remain the possession of the Holy Spirit ... they are rightly called manifestations of the Spirit, not manifestations of God's people. A friend of mine says that APEST is therefore like an umbrella under which the gifts of the Holy Spirit "fit" and make sense. Without APEST we did not understand our particular "package" of spiritual gifts. I sense that my spiritual gifts are a function or in service of my APEST calling.

3. I want to strongly assert the absolute priority of Jesus in the ministry of his people, to affirm in the strongest possible terms the *Christological,* not the *pneumatological,* basis of APEST ministry as it is taught in Ephesians 4. I trust that it is clear that this is not meant to be an argument for cessation of these necessary and empowering charismatic gifts in the church. It's just that I think that the essential basis lies in the person and work of Jesus and not in what charismatic gifts we have been given. This changes the equation of ministry from the

standard charismatic definitions to the issue of authentic Jesus ministry through the agency of his Body. This is a significant change to traditional neo-charismatic placements of the Ephesians 4 typology.

4. This shift in focus will allow Pentecostals to re-embrace the heritage of fivefold practice without the seemingly inevitable church splits and conflict that have plagued their expression in Pentecostal-Charismatic circles. It will also open the conversation to the historic denominations in a way that sidesteps the controversies that have plagued the whole charismatic issue to date.

5. A useful term used in JR Woodward's articulation of APEST in his book *Creating a Missional Culture.*

6. In fact, I would venture to suggest that this suggested category error and subsequent misplacement of the APEST discussion by many Pentecostal and neo-charismatic movements has tended to historically lead to disunity, power-plays, and immaturity! They have generally been applied to bolstering a hierarchical notion of power rather than seeing them in terms of vocation and role in the Body of Christ. Witness the very mixed impact of the New Apostolic Reformation in contemporary P-C circles. But research into the history of every major Pentecostal denomination in North America will show that most of their schisms have come from an inappropriate use of power and authority expressed through the fivefold ministry. This is not because APEST is wrong—they all sense its rightness—it is because they have an inappropriate understanding of power and authority in relation to what they call the "offices."

7. We can therefore say that in the New Testament, the ministry of the Body of Christ is radically demo-cratic (lit. people-power) in terms of Kingdom agency given to *all* of God's people, and polycentric where power and function are distributed throughout all Christians.

Appendix 3

1. *The Unshackled Organization* by Jeffrey Goldstein (New York: The Productivity Press, 1994),14

2. In *The Faith of Leap,* Michael Frost and I explore the role of adventure, courage, and risk in the church, mission, discipleship, and leadership. See Frost and Hirsch, *The Faith of Leap.*

Appendix 4

1. The minus triplex is a reasonably good way to understand the nature and impact of Jesus' ministry. But because the phrase is never used in this formula in the Bible itself, it needs to be acknowledged that it remains something of an arbitrary, deductive, model anachronistically used to help understand something of the person and work of Christ.

   Furthermore, while it is very useful (if imperfect) as a model to frame Christology, attempts have been made to reconstruct a notion of Christian ministry in relation to this. But it is when trying to correlate this with the ministry of believers where the model becomes somewhat forced. For instance, it is hard to make a case for the ministry of the kingship of all believers. In practice, this can become nightmarish, as European Christendom (the theocratic society that arose from blending of church and state) amply demonstrates. While I am certain that we are called to be agents of the kingdom of God, believers are simply never called kings as far as I am aware.

   At the very least, the tripartite view of ministry is a definite advance of the restrictive pastor- teacher monopolization of the "orders of ministry." However, in my opinion it is inadequate as a full typology of the ministry of the God's people, and it lacks the kind of nuance we need for full missional functionality—the ministries of apostle and evangelist particularly. In fact, it cannot even fully describe all the dimensions of Jesus' own ministry, let alone that of the New Testament *ecclesia.*

In order to make it fit Reformed templates of theology, there have to be so many qualifications in how we believers are called to be expressions of prophets, priests, and kings. For instance, how exactly are believers to be kings? Clearly not in the way that Jesus was! The same is true for priesthood, and so on. And so begins a death by a thousand qualifications. I believe that the connection between the ministry of Jesus and that of his people is enhanced and best correlated through an APEST typology—a *fivefold* offices of Christ model. Furthermore, an APEST classification allows more nuanced understanding of Christ's impact (five constructs rather than three) than the threefold office.

2. More famously Tim Keller, *Center Church*, and Drew Goodmanson and David Fairchild, Triperspectival Leadership, June 4, 2008 https://goo.gl/oui235

3. As already stated—but definitely worth repeating—we can say that in a very real, irrevocable, and fundamental sense, the *ecclesia* exists to extend the experience, logic, and impact of Jesus' ministry in the world. The church is the primary agency of the kingdom of God, the principal arena through which God is blessing and redeeming the world. It is through the deliberate choices, actions, and activities (ministry) of all his people that Jesus chooses to extend his kingdom in the world. Ministry is the part that we get to participate in extending God's reign in Christ—nothing less than the kingdom agency of the worshipping community is at stake here. It is precisely because of this that getting it right is an issue of such significance. And this is also why getting it wrong has such a devastating effect of the nature and effectiveness of the mission.

FINISHED 5Q AND WANT
TO KNOW SOME NEXT STEPS?

• CONNECT IN THE FOLLOWING WAYS •

TESTS (www.5Qtests.com)

The **diagnostic test** provides a straightforward assessment of current APEST capacities. The **5Q systems test** provides a more in-depth analysis that measures organizational awareness in relation to APEST.

RESOURCES

5Q **modules** which will cover each of the key topics within 5Q and explore personal practices, leadership development and culture change. 5Q **tools** to develop APEST leadership development, balanced culture and mature churches and organizations.

TRAINING

Short-term (14 weeks) **coaching cohorts** and longer-term (14 months) **training cohorts** on 5Q leadership, culture and practice for individual leaders or leadership teams.

BOOK

Alan has written, along with Jessie Cruickshank, *Activating 5Q: A User's Guide to Understanding and Applying 5Q in Your Church or Organization.* This is an accessible summary of many of the ideas of 5Q and provides guidelines about the method and interpretation of the 5Q Systems Tests.

For more info on the tests, training opportunities, resources, blogs and all things 5Q, **visit www.5Qcentral.com**